John Wesley Hanson

A Cloud of Witnesses

John Wesley Hanson

A Cloud of Witnesses

ISBN/EAN: 9783337345679

Printed in Europe, USA, Canada, Australia, Japan

Cover: Foto ©Lupo / pixelio.de

More available books at **www.hansebooks.com**

A
CLOUD OF WITNESSES

CONTAINING

Selections from the Writings of Poets and Other Literary and Celebrated Persons, Expressive of the Universal Triumph of Good Over Evil.

By J. W. HANSON, A. M., D. D.

One far-off divine event,
To which the whole creation moves.
TENNYSON.

Out of the Strong came forth Sweetness.
BIBLE.

CHICAGO:
THE STAR AND COVENANT OFFICE.
1880.

Preface.

Poets and philosophers, writers and thinkers, those who have weighed the problem of human destiny, whatever may have been their educational bias, or religious proclivities, have often risen to a more or less distinct conception of the thought that evil is transient and good eternal, and that the Author of man will ultimately perfect his chief work. The deliverance of the whole human family from sin and sorrow, its final holiness and happiness, has been the thought of multitudes, even when the prevailing doctrines around them were wholly hostile; and, in and out of Christendom, the great thought has scarcely ever been without witnesses among men. It was distinctly revealed by Jesus, in his Gospel, and forms the burthen of prophet and apostle, bard and seer, from Genesis to Revelation, and it has also brightened the pages of literature in every age of the world, since man possessed a literature.

Twenty-five years ago the compiler of this volume published a little work entitled "Witnesses to the Truth, containing Passages from Distinguished Authors, developing the great Truth of Universal Salvation." The subsequent quarter-century has added immensely to the testimony that men of genius have given in attestation to the sublimest fact in human history that has ever come to human knowledge, and the further reading of the compiler has enabled him to adduce authors whose words were then unknown to him, some of whom are among the best who have ever written.

Such men as COLERIDGE, SOUTHEY, THOMPSON, and TENNYSON are in accord with DAVID, JOHN, PAUL, and that OTHER, who "spake as never man spake."

The Compiler will be under obligations to any reader of these pages who shall direct him to authors not named in this volume, and their testimony will be added in subsequent editions.

CHICAGO, NOVEMBER, 1880.

INDEX.

Adamantius Origen, 8.
Adams Sarah F., 110, 111.
Addison Joseph, 42.
Aiken Dr. J., 12.
Akenside Mark, 15, 66.
Alexandrinus Clem., 7, 24.
Alger W. R., 20, 314.
Americana Encyc., 266.
Ames C. G., 287.
Andersen, H. C., 174.
Anonymous, 130, 177, 208, 247, 256, 280, 292, 307, 308, 314, 319.
Aquinas Thomas, 29.
Aratus, 22.
Argyll Bishop, 9, 132, 267.
Arnold Edwin, 293.
Arnold Matthew, 261.
Aspland Robert, 12, 79.
Augustine, 15.
Bacon Lord F., 23, 31.
Baillie Joanna, 85.
Bailey P. J., 236.
Balantine, 11.
Ballou Hosea, 93.
Barbauld Anna L., 73.
Barbauld Rochemont, 12.
Barnard Lady Anne, 72.
Barrow Isaac, 9.
Bartol C. A., 223.
Barton Bernard, 120.
Basil the Great, 8.
Baumstark C. E., 191.
Baxter, 48.
Beard J. R., 204.
Beatty James, 70.
Beecher Dr. E., 8.
Beecher H. W., 222.
Behmer, 12.
Belsham Thos., 12, 78.
Benecker, 111.
Bennett S. F., 305.
Blackie J. S., 203.
Bleek, 11.
Bloomfield Mrs., 286.
Bohler Peter, 54.
Bonnet Charles, 66.
Bostwick H. L., 310.
Bowring John, 143.
Bremer Frederika, 160.
Bronte Sisters, 240.
Brooke Stopford A., 258.

Brooke Henry, 66.
Brooks H. C., 66.
Broughton Thos., 12.
Brown Baldwin, 13.
Brown John M. D., 284.
Browne Sir Thos., 34.
Browne James, 12.
Browne J. Ross, 223.
Browning E. B., 199.
Browning Robt., 221.
Bryant, W. C., 145.
Buchanan Robt., 311.
Bulwer E. L., 169.
Bulwer R. L., 297.
Burnet Thos., 9, 12, 36.
Burns R., 29, 80, 84, 128, 168.
Butler Bishop, 51.
Butler Wm. Archer, 302.
Buzurgi, 21.
Byron Lady, 111, 136.
Byron Lord, 15, 111, 134.
Caird Principal, 318.
Calvin, 15, 112.
Campbell, A. G., 260.
Campbell, J. MacLeod, 217, 268, 304.
Campbell, Thos., 112.
Carlyle Thos., 139.
Carpenter L., 12, 117, 207.
Carpenter Mary, 207.
Cary Sisters,
Celsus, 24.
Chalmers Thos., 131.
Channing W. E., 116, 173.
Chapin E. H., 213.
Chauncey Chas., 12.
Chatfield Paul, 102.
Chatham Lord, 66
Charles Elis. Arundel, 279.
Cheyne, 14.
Child Lydia M., 165.
Chrysostum, 15.
Clarke Adam, 13.
Clarke George, 12.
Clarke J. F., 86, 142.
Clarke J. G., 239.
Clarke McDonald, 155.
Clarke Richard, 9, 45.
Clarke Samuel, 12.
Clarkson, 111.
Cleaveland, E. H. J., 288.

Cleanthes, 22.
Clemens Alex., 7, 24.
Clephane E. C., 303.
Clodd Edward, 206.
Clough Arthur H., 249.
Cobbe F. P., 207, 255, 262.
Cockburn Alison R., 72.
Cogan Thos., 12.
Colenso Bishop, 233.
Coleridge Hartley, 150.
Coleridge S. T., 15, 37, 87, 90, 111.
Coquerel Athenase, 104
Cornwall Barry, 274.
Cowper Wm., 67.
Crabbe, 79, 80.
Craik Dinah M., 276.
Credner, 11.
Crombie Alex., 12.
Cromwell Oliver, 14, 35.
Cudworth Ralph, 9, 38.
Cunningham A., 81, 128.
Dante, 124.
D'Aranda Peter, 9.
Davidson Dr., 13.
Dawson George, 234.
Defoe Daniel, 41.
De Joinville, 37.
Delitzsch Franz, 227.
Denk, 11.
De Quincey Thomas, 125.
De Stael Madame, 69.
Dick Thos., 95.
Dickens Chas., 214, 221.
Didymus the Blind, 8.
Dies Irae, 28.
Diodorus of Tarsus, 8.
Doddridge Philip, 53, 166.
Dodwell Henry, 9.
Doederlein, 10.
Donne John, 52.
Dove, 12.
Duchee Dr. 12.
Duganne A. J. H., 264.
Duncombe Wm., 50.
Earburg, 14.
Eberhard, 11.
Edinburgh Review, 138.
Edinburgh Scotsman, 139.
Edwards Jona, 13, 15, 216
Emerson R. W., 168.
Encyc. Americana, 266.

Epictetus, 23.
Epicurus, 25.
Erigena J. S., 28.
Erskine Lord, 9.
Erskine Thos., 13, 131, 217, 267, 304.
Espy Professor, 127.
Estlin J. P., 13, 75.
Euripides, 168, 314.
Eusebius, 25.
Ewing Bishop, 9, 168, 276.
Faber F. W., 93, 104.
Farrar Canon, 51, 160, 168, 252, 267, 285, 295.
Ferguson Fergus, 224.
Fenwick, 12.
Field Wm., 76.
Figuier Louis, 250.
Foster John, 43, 90.
Fox W. J., 12.
Franklin Benj., 58.
Frederic the Great, 65.
Froude J. A., 245.
Fry Mrs., 173.
Gainsborough Thos., 67.
Gay Rev. Mr., 48.
Giradin E., 178.
Goethe J. W., 77, 84.
Gould S. Baring, 269.
Greeley Horace, 145, 213.
Greene Gen. Nath'l, 14.
Greg W. R., 255.
Gregory Nyssen, 8, 26.
Gregory Thaum., 8.
Griffith Thos., 270.
Griswold H. T., 313.
Grotius Hugo, 9.
Gurney, 100.
Guthrie Thos., 167.
Halsey ——, 71.
Hamilton Sir Wm., 130.
Hanna Dr., 131.
Harte Bret, 301.
Hartley D., 11, 45, 48, 56.
Harwood Edward, 12.
Hase Karl, 156.
Harris T. L., 265.
Haven Gilbert, 221.
Hawthorne N., 171.
Hay John, 309.
Hemans F. D., 144.
Hetzer, 11.
Hey John, 12.
Higginson T. W., 264.
Hinton James, 288.
Hobbes Thos., 33.
Hogg James, 96.
Holland J. G., 252.

Holmes O. W., 195.
Hood Thos., 152.
Hopkins Dr., 216.
Hoppe J. P., 231.
Howitt Mary, 171.
Howitt Wm., 171.
Humboldt Alex. V., 87.
Hume, 72.
Hunt L., 15, 35, 73, 121.
Hunt Rev. John, 34.
Hurd Bishop, 12.
Hutchinson, 12.
Ingelow Jean, 293.
Ingersoll R. J., 306.
Irving Washington, 120.
James Henry, 279.
Jenyns Soame, 54.
Jerome, 8.
Johnson Samuel, 56, 62.
Jortin Dr., 14.
Judd Sylvester, 223.
Kant Immanuel, 67.
Kennedy Dr., 134.
King Wm., 48.
Kingsley Chas., 252.
Kipps Dr., 14.
Kling C. H., 165.
Lactantius, 25.
La Fontaine, 40.
Laighton Albert, 292.
Lamb Chas., 15, 105, 111.
Lambert Brooke, 285.
La Mennais Abbe, 118.
Landor W. S., 110.
Lange J. P., 162.
Larcom Lucy, 270.
Latham T., 176.
Lavater J. K., 73.
Lavoisier, 251.
Law Edmund, 9.
Lawrence G. W., 96.
Law Wm., 48.
Le Clerc, 14.
Leggett Wm., 167.
Leibnitz, 111, 245.
Leicester Francis, 12.
Leonard C. H., 200.
Lessing, 228.
Letsone, 14.
Lincoln Abraham, 202.
Lindsay Lord, 72.
Lipsius Dr. R. A., 248.
Littleton Lord, 9.
Lockhart J. G., 151.
Longfellow H. W., 182.
Lowell J. R., 246.
Luther Martin, 11, 30.
Lytton Bulwer Robt., 297.

Macdonald G., 218, 271.
Mackay Chas., 218.
Mackenzie, 72.
Mackintosh Sir J., 86.
McLeod Donald, 217.
MacLeod N., 217, 304.
Macrina, 8.
Mann Horace, 149.
Martineau Harriet, 166.
Martineau James, 173.
Marvin L. C., 189, 202.
Massey Gerald, 289.
Marryatt Frederic, 143.
Marshall Christopher, 76.
Matthews, 12.
Maurice J. F. D., 9, 181, 199, 218, 268.
Maximus Confessor the, 26
Mayhew Jona, 13.
Mayo S. C. E., 253.
Miles J. E., 96.
Mill J. S., 175.
Miller Joaquin, 317.
Milman Dean, 9, 140.
Milnes R. M., 203.
Milton John, 35, 86, 105.
Montgomery J., 94.
Moore Geo., 211.
Moore Thos., 15, 112.
More Hannah, 121.
More Henry, 9.
Mosheim, 24.
Morris Wm., 298.
Motley, 27.
Mueller, 11.
Muloch D. (Craik), 276.
Munroe J. B., 300.
Murphy J. J., 287.
Murray J., 14.
Neander, 11, 26, 139.
Neckar James, 69.
Newman Thos., 12.
Newton Bishop, 55.
Newton Sir I., 41, 113.
Nichol J. P., 172.
Nightingale Florence, 317.
Nitzech, 11.
Norton Caroline E. S., 192.
Oaksmith Appleton, 316.
Oberlin J. F., 71.
Olshaussen Herman, 11.
Olympiodorous, 26.
Oracles Sibylline, 7.
Origen Adamantius, 8, 23, 25, 36, 113, 244.
Orr Rev. John, 299.
Ossoli M. F., 210.
Owen Robert Dale, 40.

Paley, 113.
Parker Theo., 207.
Parr Samuel, 76.
Parr Thos., 12.
Parsons Theophilus, 152.
Pearson, 38.
Percival J. G., 149.
Petersen, 11.
Petitpierre F. O., 70.
Picus John, 9.
Pierpont John, 126.
Pindar, 22.
Pistorius H. A., 11.
Plato, 22.
Plumptre Prof., 51, 254.
Plutarch, 23.
Pollok Robt., 155.
Pope Alex., 49, 66.
Price, 111.
Priestley Dr., 56, 59, 69, 111.
Procter A. A., 274.
Pullman R. H., 306.
Pusey E. B., 160.
Pythagoras, 22.
Quarles Francis, 34.
Radbod Prince, 27.
Ramsay Chevalier, 46.
Raynold, 9.
Reade Chas., 235.
Reville Rev. A., 305.
Relley Thos., 12.
Richardson Samuel, 50.
Ritter, 27.
Robertson F. W., 268.
Robinson Anthony, 111.
Robinson C., 90, 93, 100, 104, 110, 111, 136.
Rogers Samuel, 86.
Ross Alex., 267.
Rothe, 9.
Rousseau J. J., 64.
Rush Benj., 59, 74.
Ruskin John, 248.
Russell W. H., 255.
Rust Bishop, 12.
Rust Geo., 265.
Salomon, 9.
Sand Geo., 169.
Sawyer Caroline M., 225.
Saxe J. G., 240.
Say Thos., 59.
Schaff Dr., 24.
Scheffer Leopold, 261.
Schelling F. W. J., 109.
Schenkel Daniel, 225.
Schiller Johann von, 84.
Schleiermacher, 11, 24, 100, 229.

Scholten J. H., 215.
Schweizer Alexander, 228.
Scott Julia H., 316.
Scott Sir W., 72.
Scudder Eliza, 286.
Seebach, 11.
Selden John, 33.
Shakspere Rev. Wm.
Shakspere, Wm., 31.
Shelley P. B., 140.
Sherwood M. M., 106.
Shippen Dr. Wm., 59.
Shrigley J. Rev., 128.
Short Chas., 282.
Sibylline Oracles, 7, 28.
Siegvolk Paul, 76.
Simon J. F. S., 234.
Simpson John, 69.
Smith Alexander, 291.
Smith E. O., 178.
Smith Gerritt, 151
Smith G. Vance, 232.
Smith Horace, 115.
Smith James, 115.
Smith Seba, 315.
Smith T. Southwood, 80, 114, 133, 134.
Socrates, 21.
Sonner, 11.
Southey Robt., 48, 87, 88, 97, 100, 111.
Spectator The, 285.
Stanley Dean, 131.
Steinbart, 11.
Stephen Sir J., 136.
Sterling John, 179.
Stilling Jung, 70.
Stonehouse Geo., 64.
Stowe H. B., 215.
Strahan Alex., 217.
Street J. C., 175.
Sumner Chas., 212, 266.
Swedenborg E., 168.
Swift Dean, 66.
Symonds, 142.
Tauler Johann, 9, 30.
Taylor, 88.
Taylor Bayard, 276.
Taylor Dr. John, 62.
Taylor Jeremy, 37.
Taylor John, 12, 62.
Taylor J. S., 210.
Tennyson Al'd, 181, 197.
Tertullian, 8, 15.
Thackeray W. M., 214.
Thaumaturgus Greg'y, 8.
Tholuck, 11.
Thomas A. C. Rev., 35, 95, 123, 171, 190.

Thom Rev. Dr., 109.
Thompson J. R., 193.
Thompson James, 52, 174.
Tillotson John, 9, 40, 113.
Tipple S. A., 281.
Titus, of Bostra, 8.
Townsbend C. H., 157.
Trench Archdeacon, 183.
Tupper M. F., 212.
Turner Sharon, 315.
Tyler Rev. John, 12.
Ullman, 11.
Vail J. C., 235.
Vandyke, 67.
Vane Sir Harry, 36.
Van Oosterzee J. J., 244.
Varnum Gen., 14.
Walker Geo., 14.
Wallace Dr., 255.
Wallace John, 266.
Wallace W. L., 308.
Warburton Acton, 245.
Warburton Bishop, 12.
Washington Geo., 14.
Watts Isaac, 43, 288.
Wesley Chas., 61.
Wesley John, 13, 48, 54, 87, 88, 98, 111, 288.
Whewell Wm., 148.
Whichcote Benj., 9.
Whiston Wm. 12, 41.
Whitefield G., 58, 88, 98.
White Jeremy, 35.
Whitman Walt, 249.
Whitney A. D. T., 268.
Whittier J. G., 30, 184.
Wilkins N. C., 301.
Williams David, 12.
Williams H. M., 104, 111.
Williamson, I. D., 120.
Wilson John, 126.
Wilde —, 280.
Willis N. P., 178.
Winchester E., 59, 74.
Winans Ross, 194.
Winthrop Theo., 290.
Wistar Dr. Caspar, 59
Wistanley, 14.
Woehlner, 11.
Wolpan Bishop, 27.
Wordsworth W., 92, 111
Wotton Sir Henry, 32.
Wright Frances, 40.
Wright Richard, 12.
Young Edward, 25, 44.
Young John, 128.
Zend-Avesta, 19.
Zinzendorf, 54.
Zoroaster, 19.

A Cloud of Witnesses.

INTRODUCTION.

The sublime idea of the deliverance of mankind from evil has illumined the pages of literature in every generation since, and long before, it was first fully developed by Jesus Christ, the destined agent of its accomplishment. It is believed that traces of it can be found in all the religious literature of the world. From the birth of Christ to the present hour it has never been wholly extinct in Christendom, though owing to the baleful influence of Heathenism, the shrines of Christianity were, during the darkest centuries of the Christian era, lurid with the fires of endless sin and wrath. Some of the proudest names in the annals of the church were identified with the doctrine, and advocated it unopposed. The Sibylline Oracles (A. D. 150) contain it; Clemens Alexandrinus (A. D. 190-217), the most eminent of the earlier Christian fathers, proclaimed it; and there is not extant a word of contemporaneous opposition to the sentiment. The first announcement of the dogma of endless torment, by a Christian, is not older than A. D. 200, when Tertullian avowed it, but even he does not condemn the doctrine of universal restoration. The ripest scholar, the keenest intellect, the ablest polemic, and one of the holiest of Christian saints, Origen Adamantius (A. D. 185-253), was distinguished for his constant advocacy of the doctrine. He was followed by Gregory Thaumaturgus (A. D. 240); Titus of Bostra (A. D. 360); Basil the Great (A. D. 370); Gregory Nyssen (A. D. 370); Didymus the Blind, Jerome, Diodorus of Tarsus, Macrina, sister of Gregory of Nyssa and of Basil the Great, and many others (A. D. 370-390). It was not until A. D. 394 that the first condemnatory word is known to have been written, and at some periods at least, during the first four centuries after Christ, it was the prevalent doctrine of the church. Dr. Edward Beecher shows, in his "History of Future Retribution," that at about the time of Origen, out of the six theological schools in Christendom, four taught universal salvation as the faith of the Christian church. Its written declaration in Christendom antedates the annunciation of the cruel sentiment since so rife.

When Heathenism and Christianity had begotten their hybrid daughter, Catholicism, endless evil became an essential of self-styled orthodoxy, and, accordingly, in the sixth century, the doctrine of universal salvation was pronounced a damnable heresy. This condemnation was repeated by the Councils which assembled A. D. 649, 680, 787, and 869, proving that though not popular, the faith was still in existence. A few of those who denied the popish error, were John Scotus Erigena, the greatest scholar and genius of the ninth century; Raynold, Abbot of St. Martin (A. D. 1190); Salomon, Bishop of Bassorah (A. D. 1222); the German Stadlings (A. D. 1231-4); Tauler (A. D. 1290-1361); many of the Lollards (A. D. 1315); people in Canterbury, England (A. D. 1368); Men of Understanding in Flanders (A. D. 1400-12); John Picus, Earl of Mirandola (A. D. 1480-94); Peter D'Aranda (A. D. 1490-8); Hugo Grotius (A. D. 1645); Dr. Isaac Barrow (A. D. 1677); Benjamin Whichcote (A. D. 1683); Ralph Cudworth (A. D. 1688); Archbishop Tillotson, etc. Besides these, and many other distinguished names, may be mentioned Richard Clarke, Bishop Edmund Law, Dr. Henry More, Dr. Thomas Burnett, Henry Dodwell, Bishop Newton, Rothe, and more recently Prof. F. D. Maurice, Dean Milman, Lord Littleton, Thomas Erskine, Dr. Ewing, and others. Never has the sublime fact that sin will finally end been lost sight of, though it was nearly extinct during the gloomiest periods of the world's history. In the dark ages, when truth and learning were eclipsed, and error and ignorance reigned, its opposite bore almost exclusive sway, and the persecution, and barbarism, and frightful multitude of horrors which then swarmed throughout the world, were natural consequences. The condition of the church during those perilous times, compared with its triumphal career during the first four centuries, when Pagan and Jewish errors were routed by the good news of the Gospel, gives us notable proof of the power of the truth that "God is in Christ reconciling the world unto himself" to win souls from darkness unto light. With comparatively few exceptions, but those generally brilliant ones, the church entered the gloom of the great night of the dark ages, led by the all-engrossing falsehood that God would hate and curse forever those who should not serve him on earth.

Could the past open its inexorable doors, could the forms of the sainted martyrs pass before us, thousands who have entered heaven through baptismal fires, from the cross and the scaffold, and by the dark doors of dungeons and gloomy cells, would be seen to have gone with the assurance of a universal heaven, and many of them should we hear say that they had "labored, and suffered reproach," and perished at last, "because they trusted in the living God as the Savior of all men, especially of those that believe."

With the dawn of the Reformation, this central orb in the Gospel system began to shed its light into the hearts of men, and it has promoted intelligence and human progress, in the exact ratio of its reception. So true is this, that we may say,—given the prevalence of this truth, in any age, the enlightenment of the human mind in that age may be gauged. The great German theologian, Dœderlein, has said:—

"The more profoundly learned any one was in Christian antiquity, so much more did he cherish and defend the hope that the suffering of the wicked would at some time come to an end." And the eminent and learned German, Dr. Herman Olshausen, says:—"Universalism is, without doubt, deeply rooted in noble minds; it is an expression of the longing for perfected harmony in the universe."

The entire body, almost, of German divines, has always denied endless punishment. Even Luther said, "How it may be with those who in the New Testament are condemned, I say nothing *certain*,—I leave it undecided." And before the doctrine had prevailed much among the English, Germany had produced the Universalist writings of Sonner, Denk, Hetzer, Petersen, Woelner, Seebach, Eberhard, and Steinbart. In 1850 there were 1,600 Universalists out of the 1,800 Protestant clergymen in Germany, and among them were Neander, Balantine, Credner, Nitzech, Julius Mueller, Tholuck, Ullmann, Bleek, the great Schleiermacher, and others. Hermann Andrew Pistorius (A. D. 1790), translated Hartley's celebrated work. Universalism has for a century been evangelical in Germany.

The Episcopal church has always been quickened by its divine spirit. Previous to 1562 the creed consisted of forty-two articles, one of which condemned universal salvation; now it has but thirty-nine, the one condemning our faith having been eliminated. When we see to what an extent the

Truth has prevailed in that church, the reason of the omission will be evident. Besides the eminent men of letters hereafter quoted, the following have either rejected the dogma of an endless hell, or embraced Universalism:—Dr. John Hey, Divinity Professor at Cambridge, Eng.; Bishop Warburton, Bishop Hurd, Rev. Thomas Broughton, Relley, Hutchinson, Dove, Matthews, Behmen, Dr. John Taylor, James Brown, D. D., Rev. Francis Leicester, Bishop Rust, Rev. John Tyler, Norwich, Conn.; Rev. Thomas Newman (A. D. 1750); Edward Harwood, D. D. (A. D. 1794); Rev. David Williams (A. D. 1780); Charles Chauncey (A. D. 1787); George Clarke (A. D. 1789); Richard Wright (A. D. 1800); Dr. Thomas Cogan (A. D. 1813); Dr. Thomas Parr (A. D. 1825); Alexander Crombie (A. D. 1829); Dr. Duchee, Philadelphia; William Whiston, and Dr. Samuel Clarke. It would be difficult to match these names with an equal number as able, in the Episcopal church. How many more have held our faith in secret, can never be known. "The time will come," says Dr. Thomas Burnet, "when this doctrine, which is now whispered in the ear, may be proclaimed upon the house-tops; but that time is not yet."

The English Unitarians have been nearly unanimous in declaring the temporal duration of punishment. Eminent as defenders of the "faith everywhere spoken against" may be mentioned Thomas Belsham, Lant Carpenter, Aspland, W. J. Fox, Fenwick, Rochemont Barbauld, husband of Anna Lætitia; Dr. Aiken, her brother; Dr. Estlin, and Theophilus Lindsey. The American Unitarians are nearly unanimous in accepting the doctrine.

Even the Congregationalists are frequently found straying from the savage creed of Edwards. Dr. Jonathan Mayhew did this, and Rev. Dr. Davidson, President of the Congregational College in Lancashire, seceded from the Evangelical Alliance, and gave the following, among other reasons:—"It is not difficult to foretell the reception which the clause relating to the everlasting punishment of the wicked will meet with among a number of thinking men in this country. I know men, of whose Christianity there can be, in my opinion, no doubt, who hesitate about receiving the doctrine of punishment literally eternal. I believe, too, there are many highly intelligent Christians all over England, both ministers and laymen, who are either averse to the doctrine, or have not at least sufficiently studied it, so as to be prepared to subscribe it." Baldwin Brown, of England, has spoken to the same purport.

The Methodist creed contains among its many points of belief no word in favor of endless misery. Dr. Adam Clarke and John Wesley have said much that might be construed into a belief in universal salvation, when the finer instincts of their moral natures spoke. Had they listened to them, they would have been wiser. Indeed, the great error of theologians has been that they have listened too much to tradition, and have given too little heed to the moral instincts, which rarely err. What they have said when the old creed was forgotten, tells us where all men would be if they could but listen to that sacred oracle which God has stationed in every soul.

Other great names besides those in the body of this book, have found rest in this hope. Dr. Jortin, the distinguished scholar; Jeremy White, the chaplain of Oliver Cromwell; Coquerel, the patriot and Christian; Siegvolk, Cheyne, Chevalier Ramsay, Petersen, LeClerc, Letsone, Geo. Walker, Dr. Kipps, Robert Robinson, Richard Coffin, Earbury, Wistanley, and thousands of less distinguished, though ardent defenders of the great truth, have rejoiced to follow it through good and evil report.

At the time when John Murray began to evangelize the Western continent, he found many ready to receive the good seed. Generals Greene, Varnum, and others of the Revolutionary heroes accepted it, and when the hated heretic was appointed chaplain of the Rhode Island regiment, though all the chaplains united in a petition for his removal, and though the religious people of the time abhorred the doctrines he professed, yet George Washington confirmed Mr. Murray in his office, and retained him as chaplain at his own headquarters. It is not supposable that he would have done this, had he not sympathized with the generous views of the apostle of our faith.

Every sect has frequently transcended its creed—thousands in all communions have gone beyond the narrow limits of all forms of partialism, and have openly advocated punishment for the good of the punished, the triumph of truth and goodness, and heaven at last for all, while infinitely more have nourished the glorious hope in secret, as fire shut up in the bones.

The foregoing names are chiefly of men distinguished as theologians or patriots. But the principal object of this volume is to develop the progress of this great idea in literature. It runs like a thread of gold through belles lettres. The best of our literature is embroidered with it, and, in proportion as authors have won exalted positions they have illustrated the spirit of our faith.

And surely it becomes us to listen attentively to what the gifted ones of our race have said and sung. The words of Byron, Moore, Akenside, Hunt, Coleridge and Lamb, are entitled to as much consideration as those of any Christian Father. With intellects as large, and hearts infinitely larger, and thus better developed men, are not their words as weighty as those of Augustine, Tertullian, or Chrysostom? We often adduce concessions from theologians, and think we have gained something worth our while, if they speak in behalf of our faith. But what did the morose Edwards, inspired by Calvin and Augustine, understand of the prophetic aspirations and longings of the human soul? A gloomy theology had silenced the heart's voices. Theologians can expound Calvin's Institutes, or explain the points of Augustinism;

but for the feelings of the human soul, and for a knowledge of its intuitions, we should go to those who have cultivated the gentler affections, and who, although they care not to prove a dogma, logically, can speak prophetically from the depth of the spirit. The heart and intellect of the poet and child of genius will speak more truly, and their voices are entitled to more attention, than those of narrow sectarians, who have relinquished to party what was meant for mankind. The former have at least given free and full scope to the aspirations and longings of the soul, which the latter have rarely done, and, though sometimes the former have been classed with scoffers, it may have been not because of their disregard of God and religion, but because they have hated the foul deformities christened as such. Shelley was no infidel—he hated the demon the church called God, and the blasphemy it styled religion. Byron would have been a better man, had he fully seen the glorious truth occasionally and partially revealed to his soul. Infidelity would have been a phenomenon of rare occurrence, had Christian truth been fully presented, instead of those gross perversions at which every intellect revolts, and which every good heart loathes, and that in proportion to their faithful presentation.

Volumes of eloquent poetry and prose might be given from our own denominational writers, expressing the great truth in language of surpassing beauty but the scope of this book does not include such. It contains the language of those literary men and women whose words have passed under the eye of the compiler—a portion only, without doubt, of those who have enrolled themselves as witnesses to the truth of "the restitution of all things, spoken by the mouths of all God's holy prophets since the world began."

An immense number of authors has been named to us, while this volume was in preparation, the spirit and tendency of whose writings are hostile to ancient error, and in harmony with the more generous faith of universal salvation, but we have been obliged to omit such. The very best of modern literature might be compiled into volumes, entirely in harmony with the truth. The spirit of our faith is the soul of modern literature. The literary men of the present generation utter an almost unanimous voice in announcing the end of evil, and the universal triumph of good, and the children of genius, for the past three centuries, have generally accorded in sentiment with the children of a higher inspiration.

The subject is presented from different points of view, by modern writers, and there is every indication that the time is not far distant when the Christian church, however orthodox or heterodox on other points, will be a unit in regarding God as a Universal Father, mankind as a Universal Brotherhood, and heaven as the Universal Home of the common family, and when the pen and tongue of genius will universally declare the

> "One far-off divine event,
> To which the whole creation moves."

With these preliminary observations we proceed to present to the reader such quotations as we have found in literature, regretting that while we have named most of the authors known to us, who have announced the great fact, our limited space compels us to omit all but brief extracts from each.

THE WITNESSES.

We make our first extract from one of the most ancient of the
"Bibles old
That from the heart of Nature rolled."

The Zend-Avesta.
(Date Unknown.)

Zoroaster is probably the author of this Bible of the Parsees, which commands that

Every believer shall say every morning as he fastens his girdle, "Douzakh (hell) will be destroyed at the resurrection, and Ormuzd (the Lord of good) shall reign over all forever."

The Pythagoreans said—is it a passage from the Zend-Avesta?—

The One from which all things flow, and to which all things ultimately tend, is Good.

The Zoroastrian doctrine is unmistakably that of universal deliverance. Says their holy book:

I am wholly without doubt in the coming of the resurrection of the later body, in an invariable recompense of good deeds and their reward, and of bad deeds and their punishment, as well as in the continuance of Paradise, in the annihilation of hell and Ahriman and the Devas; that the god

Ormuzd will at last be victorious, and Ahriman will perish, together with the Devas and the offshoots of darkness.—*Khordah-Avesta, Patet Erani 1st—Spegel, Vol. III, p. 163.*

In the same (Naumetaisne 7th):

Praise to the Overseer, the Lord who rewards those who accomplish good deeds according to his own wish, purifies at last the obedient, and at last purifies even the wicked out of hell.

The Pythagoreans style this "the most holy verse" in the Veda:

Let us adore the supremacy of that divine Sun in the Bhargas, or Godhead, who illuminates all, who recreates all, from whom all have proceeded, to whom all must return.

Alger, in his "Future Life," paraphrases the teachings of the Persian Bible concerning the wicked:

Those who have not, in the intermediate state, fully expiated their sins, will in the sight of the whole creation, be remanded to the pit of punishment. But the author of evil shall not exult over them forever. Their prison-house will soon be thrown open. The pangs of three terrible days and nights, equal to the agonies of 9,000 years, will purify all, even the worst of the demons. The anguished cry of the damned, as they writhe in the lurid caldron of torture, rising to heaven, will find pity in the soul of Ormuzd, and he will release them from their sufferings. A blazing star, the comet Gurtzscher, will fall upon the earth. In the heat of its conflagration, great and small mountains will melt, and flow together as liquid metal. Through this glowing flood all mankind must pass. To the righteous it will prove as a pleasant bath, of the temperature of milk; but on the wicked the flame will inflict terrific pain. Ahriman will run up and down Chinevad in the perplexities of anguish and despair. The earth-wide stream of fire, flaming on, will cleanse every spot and everything. Even the loathsome realm of darkness and torment shall be burnished and made a part of the all-inclusive Paradise. Ahriman himself, reclaimed to virtue, replenished with primal light, abjuring the memories of his envious ways, and furling thenceforth the sable standard of his rebellion, shall become a ministering spirit of the Most High, and together with Ormuzd, chant the praises of Time-Without-Bounds. All darkness, falsehood, suffering, shall flee utterly away, and the whole universe be filled by the illumination of good spirits, blessed with fruitions of eternal delight. In regard to the fate of man,

> Such are the parables Zartusht addressed
> To Iran's faith in the ancient Zend-Avest.

Buzurgi.

This Persian poet sings:

What is the soul? The seminal principle from the loins of
    Destiny.
This world is the womb: the body its enveloping membrane:
The bitterness of dissolution, Dame Fortune's pangs of child-
    birth.
What is death? To be born again, an angel of eternity.

Socrates.—B. C. 470–399.

This great sage said:

No one knows but death is the greatest of all goods to man.—*Apol. 17.* It is impossible that they think correctly, who think death an evil.—*Ibid. 31.*

Plato.—B. C. 429–328.

For the natural or accidental evils of others, no one gets angry, or admonishes, or teaches, or punishes them, but we pity those afflicted with such misfortunes. * * For if, O Socrates, you will consider what is the design of punishing the wicked, this of itself will show you that men think virtue something that may be acquired; for no one punishes the wicked looking to the past only, simply for the wrong he has done,—that is, no one does this thing who does not act like a wild beast, desiring only revenge without thought—hence he who seeks to punish with reason, does not punish for the sake of the past wrong deed, * * but for the sake of the future, that neither the man himself who is punished may do wrong again, nor any other who has seen him chastised. And he who entertains this thought, must believe that virtue may be taught, and he punishes for the purpose of deterring from wickedness.—*Protag., Sec. 38.* God, the parent and author of this system, beholding the world placed in this calamitous situation, and resolving that it should not be entirely destroyed by the disorder into which it was thrown, again seizes the helm, and carefully guides it, that he may unite its loosened, and, as it were, incongruous materials, and restoring them to their original order, may finally adorn and improve them.

Cleanthes.—B. C. 330–240.

Four of the ancient poets expressed the thought of the divine paternity:—Aratus, "We are also his (Jove's) offspring;" Cleanthes, "Are thy (Jove's) offspring;" Pindar, "God and men are of the same race;" Pythagoras, "The descent of man is divine."

The hymn of Cleanthes is acknowledged by scholars to be the sublimest religious hymn outside the Bible, to be found in all antiquity. We extract a single passage:

> Harmony from discord thou dost bring;
> That which is fateful thou dost render fair;
> Evil and good dost so coördinate,
> That everlasting reason shall bear sway.

Plutarch.—A. D. 49–120.

Surely, I had rather a great deal men should say there was no such man at all as Plutarch, than that they should say that there was one Plutarch that would eat his children as soon as they were born.

Quoted by Lord Bacon in his "Essay of Superstition."

Epictetus.—A. D. 60–120.

This celebrated Stoic said:

> You do not go to a place of pain: you return to the source from which you came,—to a delightful re-union with your primitive elements; there is no Acheron, no Tartarus, no Cocytus, no Phlegethon!

Origen.—A. D. 180–254.

The greatest of all the so-called Christian fathers was so much of a Universalist that he insisted on the salvation of Lucifer himself, of whom he says:

He once could fall before he was bound by the power of love, though placed among the cherubim. But after the love of God is shed abroad in the hearts of all, it is sure to be true, even of him, that love shall never fail.

His writings abound in statements of universal redemption. Dr. Schaff (orthodox) styles him the "Schleiermacher of the Greek church," and Mosheim affirms that he "possessed every excellence that can adorn the Christian character." Celsus, the Heathen philosopher, accused the Christian's God of being merciless in threatening to burn the world with fire. Origen replied:

The sacred Scripture does indeed call our God a consuming fire (Deut. iv: 24), and says that rivers of fire go before his face (Dan. vii: 10). As therefore God is a consuming fire, what is it that is to be consumed by him? We say it is wickedness, and whatever proceeds from it, such as is figuratively called hay, wood, and stubble. These are what God in the character of fire consumes. He shall come also as a refiner's fire, to purify rational nature from the alloy of wickedness, and from other impure nature which has adulterated, if I may so say, the intellectual gold and silver. Rivers of fire are, likewise, said to go before the face of God, for the purpose of consuming whatever of evil is admixed with the soul.—*Contra Celsum, Lib. IV, Cap. xiii.*

Clemens Alexandrinus.—A. D. 190.

How is he a Savior and Lord, unless he is the Savior and Lord of all? He is certainly the Savior of those who have believed, and of those who have not believed he is the Lord, until, by being brought to confess him, they shall receive the proper and well adapted blessing for themselves.—*Stromat. Lib. VII, Cap. ii, p. 833.*

The Lord is the propitiation, not only for our sins, that is, of the faithful, but also for the whole world (I. John ii: 2); therefore he indeed saves all, but converts some by punishments, and others by gaining their free will; so that he has the high honor, that unto him every knee should bow, of things in heaven, on earth and under the earth; that is, angels, men, and the souls of those who died before his advent.—*Fragmenta Adumbrat in Epist. I. Johan., p. 1009.*

Lactantius.—A. D. 260–325.

In "The Anger of God" he makes Epicurus urge the strongest arguments against the eternity of evil, which Lactantius answers in a way to give the impression that he knew and meant them to be inadequate. Like Young in "Night Thoughts," he pretended to defend for the purpose of assailing with greater force.

Eusebius.—A. D. 270–338.

The father of ecclesiastical history was a Universalist. He published a defense of Origen in six books. In "De Eccl. Theol.," he says:

If the subjection of the Son to the Father means union with him, then the subjection of all to the Son means union with him. * * * As the Apostle, when he said all shall be subjected to the Son did not mean union of essence, but obedience flowing from free-will, together with the honor and glory which all give him as the Savior and King of all, in the same way his subjection to the Father means nothing else than the glory and honor and veneration and exultation and voluntary subjection which he is to give to God the Father, when he has made all worthy of his paternal Godhead.

Olympiodorus.—A. D. 550.

Do not suppose that the soul is punished for endless æons, (*apeirou aiōnas*) in Tartarus. Very properly, the soul is not punished to gratify the revenge of the divinity, but for the sake of healing. But we say that the soul is punished for an aiōnion period, (*aiōnios*) calling its life, and its allotted period of punishment, its æon.

Maximus the Confessor—A. D. 580–662.

Neander says:

The fundamental ideas of Maximus seem to lead to the doctrine of a final universal restoration, which is, in fact, intimately connected also with the system of Gregory of Nyssa, to which he most closely adhered. Yet he was too much fettered by the church system of doctrine, distinctly to express any theory of this sort.—*Neander's History of the Christian Religion, etc., Torrey's Translation, Vol. III, p. 175.*

In a note Neander mentions the doctrine of Maximus, that

The reunion of all rational essences with God is the final end of the divine economy, and that God will finally be glorified by the extinction of all evil.

Ritter, the historian of philosophy, confirms this statement:

The doctrine of Maximus, concerning the union of all things with God, leads him by consequence to the doctrine also of the restoration of all fallen souls. * * * * The Word of God is to become all in all, and to save all: at the end of the world, there shall be a universal renewal of the human race. Stated by Ritter, "Geschichte der Christliche Philosophie," 2ter Theil, sec. 550-551.

Prince Radbod the Frisian.—A. D. 692.

The Pagan Radbod had already immersed one of his royal legs in the baptismal font—according to Motley, Vol. I, p. 20, "Dutch Republic"—when he paused, and turning to Bishop Wolpan, he said:—"Where are my dead forefathers at present?" "In hell, with all other unbelievers," said the bishop. "Mighty well," replied the sturdy Pagan, "then will I rather feast with my ancestors in Woden, than dwell with your little starveling band of Christians in heaven." With a spirit more Christian than his so-called Christian conquerors the Frisian chief refused a rite that would separate him forever from his kindred, and he died a Pagan, but a better Christian than he would have been to accept salvation on such selfish terms.

John Scotus Erigena.—A. D. 875

The punishment of eternity, he said, is the absence of bliss:

In igne æterno nihil aliud esse pœnam quam beatæ felicitatis absentiam. Evil, being negative, as is punishment, neither can be eternal.

All things shall ultimately return to God. The final apokatastasis he dwells upon continually.

Dies Iræ.

The great judgment hymn of the Middle Ages, Dies Iræ, virtually indorses Universalism by ranking the author of the Sibylline Oracles with David. The hymn says:

> Dies Iræ, dies illa,
> Solvet sæclum in favilla,
> Teste David cum Sibylla.

The day of wrath, that dreadful day, shall crumble earth to ashes, as David and the Sibyl testify. The Sibylline Oracles declare that the holy cannot be happy in heaven until the lost are redeemed, therefore the redeemed petition God, and he delivers the wicked from the devouring fire, and from eternal (*aiōnion*) gnashing of teeth.

St. Thomas Aquinas.—A. D. 1224–1274.

His "Prayer for the Devil" conclusively shows that he sympathized with the idea of the deliverance from evil of evil spirits. His hope harmonizes with the amiable wish of Burns, "Oh, wad ye tak' a thocht and men."

"Oh God," he said, "it cannot be
Thy morning star with endless moan
Should lift his fading orb to thee
And thou be happy on thy throne.
It were not kind, nay, Father, nay,
It were not just, Oh God, I say,
Pray for the devil, Jesus, pray!

"How can thy kingdom ever come,
While thy fair angels howl below?
All holy voices would be dumb,
All loving eyes would fill with woe,
To think the lordliest peer of heaven,
The starry leader of the Seven,
Could never, never be forgiven!

"Pray for the devil, Jesus, pray!
O Word that made thine angels speak,
Lord, let thy pitying tears have way,
Dear God, not man alone is weak!
What is created still must fall,
And fairest still we frailest call,
Will not Christ's love avail for all?

"Pray for the devil, Jesus, pray!
Oh Father think upon thy child;
Turn from thine own bright world away,
And look upon that dungeon wild.
O God, O Jesus, see how dark

That den of woe, O Savior, mark
How angels weep, now hearken, hark!

"He will not, will not do it more;
Restore him to his throne again.
Oh open wide the dismal door
Which presses on the souls in pain;
So men and angels all will say
Our God is good; O day by day,
Pray for the devil, Jesus, pray!"

All night Aquinas knelt alone—
Alone with black and dreadful sight,
Until before his pleading moan
The darkness ebbed away in light.
Then rose the saint, and "God" said he,
"If darkness change to light with thee,
The devil yet may angel be!"

Aquinas says:

The punishment will not be absolutely removed by absolution, but while it lasts pity will work by diminishing it.

Johann Tauler.—A. D. 1290–1361.

All beings exist through the same birth as the Son, and therefore shall they all come again to their original, that is God the Father.

Let the reader consult Whittier's poem, "Tauler," to learn the spirit of this ancient saint.

Martin Luther.—A. D. 1483–1546.

Though the great German reformer seems to have

held and taught the opposite doctrine, yet, in his best moments he rose above it. In his letter to Hansen von Rechenberg, in his later life (1522), he says:

> God forbid that I should limit the time for acquiring faith to the present life. In the depths of the divine mercy there may be opportunity to win it in the future state.

Francis Bacon.—A. D. 1561–1626.

The celebrated Lord Verulam, who has been called the wisest of mankind, endorses the sentiment of Plutarch, already quoted in this volume:

> It were better to have no opinion of God at all than such an opinion as is unworthy of him; for the one is unbelief, the other is contumely; and certainly superstition is the reproach of the Deity. Plutarch saith well to that purpose, "Surely," saith he, "I had rather a great deal men should say there was no such man at all as Plutarch, than that they should say that there was one Plutarch that would eat his children as soon as they were born;" as the poets speak of Saturn. And as the contumely is greater towards God, so the danger is greater towards men.—*Essay of Superstition.*

William Shakspere.—A. D. 1564–1616.

The greatest of poets sang the very soul of our faith, in his description of mercy. Shylock, a portrait of the partialist's God, demands his just due, even though it be the pound of flesh nearest the heart. Portia replies:

> The quality of mercy is not strained;
> It droppeth, as the gentle rain from heaven,
> Upon the place beneath; it is twice blessed;
> It blesseth him that gives, and him that takes;
> 'Tis mightiest in the mightiest; it becomes
> The thronéd monarch better than his crown;
> His sceptre shows the force of temporal power,
> The attribute to awe and majesty,
> Wherein doth sit the dread and fear of kings;
> But mercy is above this scepter sway,—
> It is enthronéd in the hearts of kings:
> It is an attribute to God Himself;
> And earthly power doth then show likest God's,
> When mercy seasons justice. Therefore, Jew,
> Though justice be thy plea, consider this—
> That in the course of justice, none of us
> Should see salvation: we do pray for mercy,
> And that same prayer doth teach us all to render
> The deeds of mercy!

Hamlet gives expression to the great truth that God's punishments are reformatory, in the words of the ghost:

> I am thy father's spirit,
> Doomed for a certain time to walk the night;
> And for the day confinéd fast in fires
> Till the foul crimes done in my days of nature,
> Are burnt and purged away.

Sir Henry Wotton.—A. D. 1568–1639.

The author of the immortal hymn, "How Happy is He Born or Taught," expresses the spirit of the true faith thus:

Well, then, my soul, joy in the midst of pain,
Thy Christ, that conquer'd hell, shall from above
With greater triumph yet return again,
And conquer his own justice with his love,
Commanding earth and seas to render those
Unto his blisse, for whom he paid his woes.

Now have I done, now are my thoughts at peace,
And now my joyes are stronger than my griefs;
I feel those comforts that shall never cease,
Future in hope, but present in beliefe;
Thy words are true, thy promises are just,
And thou wilt find thy dearly-bought in dust.

John Selden.—A. D. 1584–1654.

Selden's "Table Talk" is one of the most delightful of books. We make this extract:

Salvation. We can best understand the meaning of σωτηρία, salvation, from the Jews, to whom the Savior was promised. They held that themselves should have the chief place of happiness in the other world; but the Gentiles that were good men, should likewise have their portion of bliss there, too. Now, by Christ the partition-wall is broken down, and the Gentiles that believe in him are admitted to the same place of bliss with the Jews; and why, then, should not that portion of happiness still remain to them, who do not believe in Christ, so they be morally good? This is a charitable opinion.

Thomas Hobbes.—A. D. 1588–1679.

Usually classed as a deist, it is probable that the views of Hobbes on the subject of human destiny were what put him under the ban. Rev. John Hunt, in his "Religious Thought in England," insists that it is absurd to call Hobbes a deist. He declares that he was "a believer in the most orthodox form of Christianity." But he rejected endless punishment, and held that

> There will be a final restitution, and no more going to Hades.

Francis Quarles.—A. D. 1592–1644.

The quaint old poet, Quarles, has left a statement of his religious thought. It is unique, but fine:

> Earth is an island, parted round with fears;
> Thy way to heaven is through a sea of tears;
> It is a stormy passage, where is found
> The wreck of many a ship, but no man drowned.

Sir Thomas Browne.—A. D. 1605–1682.

The "error" which Sir Thomas Browne so happily describes, in his words seems to wear the garb of truth:

> The second [error] was that of Origen, that God would not persist in his vengeance forever, but after a definite time of his wrath he would release the damned souls from torture; which error I fell into upon a serious contemplation of the great attribute of God, his mercy; and did a little cherish it

in myself, because I found therein no malice, and ready weight to sway me from the other extreme of despair, whereunto melancholy and contemplative natures are too easily disposed.—*Religio Medici, Sec. 7, p. 17, of Boston Edition.*

John Milton.—A. D. 1608–1674.

In 1853 Rev. Abel C. Thomas visited Leigh Hunt, who spoke of Milton. Hunt said, "In his later life Milton became an Arian—and he went farther than that before he died. How sorrowful must have been his reflection that in 'Paradise Lost' he had immortalized false and mischievous fables, and thus contributed to the perpetuation of monstrous and dishonorable thoughts of the Supreme Being."

Although Milton has embodied the popular theology of his day, it is very doubtful whether he regarded punishment as endless. Jeremy White, Cromwell's chaplain, an intimate of Milton, wrote a book defending universal salvation, and Milton's theology was progressive throughout his life. And certainly he frames an argument in the following lines that he not only does not attempt to answer, but that can only be answered on the ground that punishment is limited and corrective.

> O Father! gracious was that word that closed
> Thy sovereign sentence, that man should find grace
> For which both heaven and earth should high extol
> Thy praises, with the innumerable sound

Of hymns and sacred songs, wherewith thy throne
Encompassed, shall resound thee ever blessed.
For should man finally be lost, should man,
Thy creature late so loved, thy youngest son,
Fall circumvented thus by fraud, though joined
With his own folly?   That be from thee far,
That far be from thee, Father, who art judge
Of all things made, and judgeth only right.
Or shall the adversary thus obtain
His end, and frustrate thine?   Shall he fulfill
His malice, and thy goodness bring to naught?
Or proud return, though to his heavier doom,
Yet with revenge accomplished, and to hell
Draw after him the whole race of mankind,
By him corrupted?   Or wilt thou thyself
Abolish thy creation, and unmake
For him, what for thy glory thou hast made?
So should thy goodness and thy greatness both
Be questioned, and blasphemed without defence.

"Endless punishment," says Milton, "questions and blasphemes God's goodness and greatness, and leaves them without defence." Can he have believed it true?

Sir Henry Vane.—A. D. 1612–1662.

Bishop Burnet says of "Harry Vane":—"His friends told me he leaned to Origen's notion of an universal salvation of all, both of devils and the damned." These are his words:

Death, instead of taking away anything from us, gives us all, even the perfection of our natures; sets us at liberty both from our own bodily desires, and others' domination. It brings us out of a dark dungeon, through the crannies whereof our sight of light is but weak and small, and brings us into an open liberty, an estate of light and life unveiled and perpetual.

Jeremy Taylor.—A. D. 1613–1667.

Coleridge gives Jeremy Taylor as authority for the following story. In Vaughn's "Hours With the Mystics" it is ascribed to Taylor's sermon on "The Mercy of the Divine Judgment":

Bishop Ivo, going on an embassy for St. Louis, meets by the way a grave, sad woman, with fire in one hand and water in the other, and when he inquires what these symbols mean, she answers, "My purpose is with fire to burn paradise, and with water to quench the flames of hell, that men may serve God without the incentives of hope and fear, and purely for the love of God."

De Joinville, in his life of St. Louis, gives the probable original of the story:

When the king was at Acre, the sultan of Damascus despatched envoys to the king, and complained to him bitterly of the emirs of Egypt, who had put to death his cousin, the sultan; and he promised the king that if he would help him, he would give over to him the kingdom of Jerusalem, which was in his hands. The king decided upon sending an answer to the sultan of Damascus by the mouth of his own envoys, whom he dispatched to the sultan. With these envoys he sent brother Yves (Ivo?) the patron of the order of the Dominican friars, who understood Saracen. While they were going from their own lodgings to the sultan's palace, brother Yves saw an old woman crossing the street, who carried in her right hand an open vessel full of fire, and in her left hand a vial full of water. Brother Yves asked her, "What do you mean to do with that?" She replied, that with the fire she meant to burn paradise, and with the water extinguish hell, so that there should be no more of either. And he asked her, "Why do you wish to do that?" "Because I do not wish that any one henceforth shall do what is right for the sake of the rewards of paradise, or from fear of hell, but simply from love of God, who is so worthy of it, and who can do for us all possible good."

Ralph Cudworth.—A. D. 1617–1688.

The great philosopher and divine is emphatic in rejecting the Pagan error of endless torment:

There are two ways by which men may avoid the eternity of hell torments; by the cessations of their beings or of their torments. See Pearson on article of "Life Everlasting." Now, though the cessation of being is what I dislike more than the other, though entertained by Smalcius, yet I must confess that I cannot conceive how a man can endure pain of sense eternally with knowledge and consciousness of his fate, when any violent tortures so disorder our understanding, that we can't be called ourselves; and, since all pain of sense must arise from union of the soul with the body, and the material fire preys always on the body, how the body can naturally subsist. For if you have recourse to supernatural means or miracles to conserve it, then I see no reason why God may not as well change the course of nature, and work a miracle for man's salvation as well as for his destruction.

We shall therefore show what authority this opinion has from Scripture, for what reasons it was generally received and understood in the literal sense, what has been the opinion of the ancients of those places, how advantageous it is to religion and virtue, and the equity and justice of God in this design; and then show what inconveniences will arise from the removal of this belief, as also what inconveniences and also absurdities are likely to flow from the contrary opinion and notion. And on the other side we shall give a just and reasonable interpretation of those places of Scripture which seem to favor this opinion, and show that there is no necessity to understand them in the literal sense. We shall show that several of the ancients have rejected it; that it is inconsistent with the attributes of God, with his justice, wisdom and goodness; that the power of God, which they seem to elevate so much by this design, is in reality vilified, lessened and disparaged; we shall prove its inconsistency with the plain and visible designs of God in the forming human nature; we shall also make it manifest that the design of religion is not really promoted or advanced by this opinion, but that it is rather hindered and obstructed by it; that it is not the best motive to virtue and morality; and whereas it is pretended several inconveniences will arise from it, we shall show that there is no inconvenience or disadvantage in it, but that there is just and reasonable encouragement to virtue without it; and leave it to every man's judgment and apprehension to conclude or determine whether he thinks it eternal or no.

After reverting briefly to Tillotson, he considers the "Argument from the Necessity of it to Religion":

This implies that religion and virtue are only secured by eternal torments, that this is the only or at least the principal motive and enforcement of virtue and righteousness, * * * that that virtue has all its binding force, its authority and influence, from fear and terror. * * * We have plain experience that men may be virtuous without it; witness the Jews, all those who died before our Savior Jesus Christ, and all that believe not the eternity of hell torments.

He remarks that

He loves neither God nor goodness that loves him only out of dread and fear.

La Fontaine.—A. D. 1621–1695.

Along with the names of Owen, Wright, and others who have rejected the Scriptures because they supposed them to contain the doctrine of endless punishment, must be recorded the name of the eminent French fabulist, La Fontaine, who says:

I have lately taken to read the New Testament, which, I assure you, is a very good book; but there is one article to which I cannot accede; it is that of the eternity of punishment. I cannot comprehend how this eternity is compatible with the goodness of God!

John Tillotson.—A. D. 1630–1694.

Archbishop Tillotson occupied the very singular position of teaching that God threatens endless torment for the purpose of restraining men from sin, without intending to execute it, just as he threatened the overthrow of Nineveh. He says:

The primary end of all threatenings is not punishment, but the prevention of it. The higher the threatening runs, so much the more goodness and mercy there is in it; because it is so much the more likely to hinder men from incurring the penalty that is threatened.

In other words, he preached and would have men believe the doctrine of endless torment, though he held it to be false! He cautiously observes:

If it be anywise inconsistent either with righteousness or goodness, to make sinners miserable forever, that he will not do it.

Sir Isaac Newton.—A. D. 1642–1727.

Whiston, a Universalist, declares that Newton's views and his own, were the same. In his paraphrase of Rev. xiv: 10-11, Newton says:

The degree and duration of the torment of these degenerate and anti-Christian people, should be no other than would be approved of by those angels who had ever labored for their salvation, and that Lamb who had redeemed them with his most precious blood.

Daniel Defoe.—A. D. 1661–1731.

In the world-renowned "Robinson Crusoe," De Foe has put language into the mouth of his good man Friday, which would become many a good man, Sunday, better than the horrible caricatures of Deity that are presented. Can the reader reconcile it with the idea that sin is endless? When Friday was told that God was stronger than the devil, he says:

"If God much strong, much might as the devil, why God not kill the devil, so make him no more wicked?"

Sure enough. But the Christian replies, humorously, we think, that God reserves him to everlasting fire in the bottomless pit. But Friday, not to be put off, says:

"Reserve at last? Me no understand; but why not kill the devil now?" Crusoe says, "God does not kill you and me, when we do wicked things here that offend him." To this, Friday says, (mighty affectionately,) "Well, well, that well. So you, I, devil, all wicked, all preserve, repent, God pardon all."

Joseph Addison.—A. D. 1672–1719.

In his "Cato" Addison utters language that only a Universalist can consistently employ:

> The stars shall fade away, the sun himself
> Grow dim with age, and nature sink in years;
> But thou shalt flourish in immortal youth,
> Unhurt amidst the war of elements,
> The wreck of matter and the crush of worlds.
>   *   *   *   *   *
> Else whence this pleasing hope, this fond desire,
> This longing after immortality?
> Or whence this secret dread, and inward horror
> Of falling into nought? Why shrinks the soul
> Back on itself, and startles at destruction?
> 'Tis the divinity that stirs within us;
> 'Tis heaven itself that points out an hereafter,
> And intimates eternity to man.

Isaac Watts.—A. D. 1674–1748.

Though Dr. Watts is not known as a believer in universal salvation, yet how frequently he transcended the narrow limits of a partial creed, and expressed the sentiments of the widest faith. He says:

> The work that wisdom undertakes
> Eternal wisdom ne'er forsakes.

His soul revolted at the cruel statements of error, and his heart outran his head, which, as will be seen below, followed after. He says in one of his sermons:

> Whensoever any such criminal in hell shall be found making such a sincere and mournful address to the righteous and merciful Judge of all; if at the same time he is truly humble and penitent for his past sins, and is grieved at his heart for having offended his Maker, and melts into sincere repentance, I cannot think that a God of perfect equity and rich mercy will continue such a creature under his vengeance, but rather that the perfections of God will contrive a way for escape, though God has not given us here any revelation or discovery of such special grace as this. I grant that the eternity of God himself before this world began, or after its consummation, has something in it so immense and so incomprehensible, that in my most mature thoughts, I do not choose to enter into those infinite abysses; nor do I think we ought, usually, when we speak concerning creatures, to affirm positively, that their existence shall be equal to that of the blessed God, especially with regard to the duration of their punishment.

John Foster says Watts was "in the same parallel of latitude with respect to orthodoxy" as himself, "in the late maturity of his thoughts." These words are certainly unequivocal:

There is not one place of Scripture that occurs to me where the word death necessarily signifies a certain miserable immortality of the soul.

Whether he meant it, we cannot say, but surely this stanza expresses the largest faith:

> Why do we start and fear to die?
>   What timorous worms we mortals are
> Death is the gate of endless joy,
>   And yet we dread to enter there.

Nor is this a narrower sentiment:

> Why do we mourn departed friends,
> Or shake at Death's alarms?
> 'Tis but the voice that Jesus sends,
> To call them to his arms.

Do not the foregoing lines find an interpretation in these words:

If the blessed God should at any time, in consistence with his glorious and incomprehensible perfections, release these wretched creatures (suffering future punishment) from the acute pains and long imprisonment, I think I ought cheerfully to accept the appointment of God for the good of millions of my fellow creatures, and add my joys and praises to all the songs and triumph of the heavenly world, in a day of such divine and glorious release of these prisoners. This will indeed be such a new and such an astonishing and universal jubilee both for evil spirits and wicked men, as must fill heaven, earth and even hell with joy and hallelujahs.

Dr. Edward Young.—A. D. 1684–1765.

Dr. Young represents the lost soul as saying:

> Why burst the barriers of my peaceful grave?
> Ah, cruel Death, that would no longer save,

> But grudg'd me e'en that narrow, dark abode,
> And cast me out into the wrath of God!
> Where shrieks the roaring flame, the rattling chain,
> And all the dreadful eloquence of pain
> Our only song; black fires malignant light,
> The sole refreshment of the blasted sight.
> Must all those powers heaven gave me to supply
> My soul with pleasure, and bring in my joy,
> Rise up in arms against me, join the foe,
> Sense, reason, memory, increase my woe?
> And shall my voice, ordained on hymns to dwell,
> Corrupt to groans, and blow the fires of hell?
> Oh, must I look with terror on my gain,
> And with existence only measure pain?
> What! no reprieve, no least indulgence given,
> No beam of hope from any point of heaven?
> Ah! Mercy! Mercy! art thou dead above?
> Is Love extinguished in the source of Love?

Why did not the Doctor answer his question? He must have stated it as an objection to the very thing he described. In his "Night Thoughts" he says:

> Pain is to save from pain; all punishment
> To make for peace, and death to save from death:
> And second death to guard immortal life!
> By the same tenderness divine ordained,
> That planted Eden, and high bloomed for man
> A fairer Eden endless in the skies.
> Great Source of Good alone, how kind in all!
> In vengeance kind! Pain, Death, Gehenna, save!

Young could not have believed the future state of punishment endless. The fact that he recommended Hartley's and Clarke's Universalist publications, establishes this. He condemns endless punishment in these words:

> Father of Mercies! why from silent earth
> Didst thou awake, and curse me into birth?
> Tear me from quiet, ravish me from night!
> And make a thankless present of thy light?
> Push into being a reverse of thee,
> And animate a clod with misery?

The damned soul may well ask this question. But it proceeds to call God "My help, my God," and to say:

> And canst thou, then, look down from perfect bliss,
> And see me plunging in the dark abyss?
> Calling thee Father in a sea of fire,—
> Or pouring blasphemy at thy desire?

Does it not seem that these lines were written that the reader might say, "No! No!"

Chevalier Ramsay.—A. D. 1686–1743.

This remarkable man, a Scotch Catholic, was an avowed Universalist. He says:

Almighty power, wisdom and love cannot be eternally frustrated in his absolute and ultimate designs; therefore, God will at last pardon and reëstablish in happiness all lapsed beings.

In his "Travels of Cyrus," an imaginary work intended to show the superiority of the Christian religion over Paganism, published in Albany in 1814, he says:

"But what," said Cyrus, "is the design of this law, dictated by God himself with so much pomp, preserved by your forefathers with so much care, renewed and confirmed by your prophets with so many miracles? In what does it differ from the religion of other nations?"

"The design of the law and the prophets," replied Daniel, "is to show that all creatures were pure in their original; that all men are at present born distempered, corrupt and ignorant, even to the degree of not knowing their disease, and that human nature will one day be restored to its perfection. The miracles and prodigies of which I have made you a recital, are, so to speak, but the play of wisdom to lead men into themselves, and make them attend to those three truths, which they will find written in their own hearts, upon all nature, and in the whole plan of providence. The law of Moses is but an unfolding of the law of nature; all its moral precepts are but means more or less remote, to carry us to what may strengthen divine love in us, or to preserve us from what may weaken it. The burnt-offerings, the purification, the abstinences, all the ceremonies of our worship, are but symbols to represent the sacrifice of the passions, and to shadow out the virtues necessary to reëstablish us in our primitive purity; those who stop at the letter find expressions in our sacred books that seem to humanize the Deity; promises that do not appear to have any relation to immortality; and ceremonies which they think unworthy of the sovereign reason. But the true sage penetrates into their hidden meaning, and discovers mysteries in them of the highest wisdom. The foundation of the whole law, and of all the prophecies, is the doctrine of a nature pure in its original, corrupted by sin, and to be one day restored. These three fundamental truths are represented in our history under various images. The bondage of the Israelites in Egypt, their journey through the desert, and their arrival in the promised land, represent to us the fall of souls, their sufferings in this mortal life, and their return to their heavenly country."

William King.

William King, Archbishop of Dublin, wrote a famous book in 1729, "De Origine Mali," which is full of the principles of our faith. Wm. Law, author of "The Serious Call," himself a Universalist, translated it, and the preface, written by Rev. Mr. Gay, started Hartley on his way to the doctrine of universal redemption.

William Law.—A. D. 1686–1761.

Very few have known that the author of "The Serious Call" was a Universalist. Not only does Southey, in his "Life of Wesley," declare this, but Law himself says:

You say all partial systems of salvation are greatly derogatory to the goodness of God, but that you would say this to very few but myself. But, dear soul, why should you say this to me? I have, without any scruple, openly declared to all the world, that, from eternity to eternity, nothing can come from God but mere infinite love. In how many ways have I proved and asserted that there neither is, nor can be, any wrath or partiality in God; but that every creature must have all that happiness which the infinite love and power of God can help him to. As for the purification of all human nature, I fully believe it, either in this world, or some after ages.

Except Baxter, there are few men more prized to-day among the orthodox, than Law,—and yet, referring to the doctrine above announced, he says in his "Way to Divine Knowledge":

Let no man take offence at the opening of this mystery as though it brought anything new into religion, for it has nothing new in it; it alters no point of Gospel doctrine, but only sets each article of the old Christian faith upon its true ground. Every number of destroyed sinners must, through the all-working, all-redeeming love of God, which never ceaseth, come at last to know that they had lost and have found again such a God of love as this.

Alexander Pope.—A. D. 1688–1744.

The "Essay on Man" is a Universalist poem, in spirit, and this extract specifically expresses the great idea:

To him no high, no low, no great, no small,
He fills, he bounds, connects, and equals all.
    *   *   *   *   *
All nature is but art unknown to thee;
All chance, direction which thou canst not see,
All discord, harmony not understood,
All partial evil, universal good.
    *   *   *   *   *   *
God loves from whole to parts; but human soul
Must rise from individual to the whole.
Self-love but serves the virtuous mind to wake,
As the small pebble stirs the peaceful lake;
The center moved, a circle straight succeeds,
Another still, and still another spreads;
Friend, parent, neighbor, first it will embrace;
His country next; and next all human race;

Wide and more wide, th' o'erflowings of the mind
Take every creature in, of every kind;
Earth smiles around, with boundless bounty blest,
And heaven beholds its image in his breast.

Samuel Richardson.—A. D. 1689–1761.

The author of "Pamela" and "Sir Charles Grandison," in both of those unrivalled works avows Universalism. He says:

How much nobler to forgive, and even how much more manly to despise, than to resent an injury!

In detached passages the sentiment of universal salvation is expressed many times in the two works above mentioned.

William Duncombe.—A. D. 1690–1769.

The author of "Lucius Junius Brutus" wrote to a friend:

Vindictive justice in the Deity, is, I own, no article in my creed. All punishment in the hands of an infinitely wise and good being, I think must be medicinal, and what we call chastisement. What St. Paul speaks more directly of the reconciliation of both Jews and Gentiles to God, I am willing to understand in a more extensive sense, of the general redemption of mankind, at the consummation of all things.

Bishop Joseph Butler.—A. D. 1692–1752.

The immortal author of the "Analogy" writes this sentence, which Canon Farrar says first set him seriously thinking, while yet a boy:

And from hence we conclude that virtue must be the happiness, and vice the misery of every creature; and that regularity, and order, and right cannot but prevail finally in a universe under his government.

He protests against the idea that

None can have the benefit of the general redemption, but such as have the advantage of being made acquainted with it in the present life.

The following passage is printed with approbation, and underscored, by **Prof. Plumtre**, of King's College, London:

Virtue, to borrow the Christian allusion, is militant here; and various untoward accidents contribute to its being often overborne; but it may combat with greater advantage hereafter, and prevail completely, and enjoy its consequent rewards, in some future states. Neglected as it is, perhaps unknown, perhaps despised and oppressed here, there may be scenes in eternity, lasting enough, and in every other way adapted to afford it a sufficient sphere of action, and a sufficient sphere for the natural consequences of it to follow in fact. One might add, suppose all this advantageous tendency of virtue to become effective among one or more orders of creatures in any distant scenes and periods, and to be seen by any orders of vicious creatures throughout the universal kingdom of God; this happy effect of virtue would have a tendency by way of example, and possibly in other ways, to amend those of them who are capable of amendment, and of being recovered to a just sense of virtue.

John Donne.—A. D. 1573–1631.

John Donne, one of the earliest of English poets, did not believe in the "old wives' fables" which fill modern creeds. [Chronologically this extract belongs on page 33]:

> What if the present were the world's last night?
> Mark, in my heart, O Lord! where thou dost dwell,
> The picture of Christ crucified, and tell
> Whether his countenance can thee affright;
> Tears in his eyes quench the amazing light,
> Blood fills his frowns, which from his pierced head falls,
> And can that tongue adjudge thee unto hell,
> Which prayed forgiveness for his foes' fierce spite?
> No! No!

James Thompson.—A. D. 1700–1740.

The poet of the seasons has spoken "words fitly chosen," and they are indeed as "apples of gold in baskets of silver." He says:

> The great eternal scheme,
> Involving all, and in a perfect whole
> Uniting, as the prospect wider spreads,
> To reason's eye refined clears up apace;
> Ye vainly wise! ye blind presumptuous! now,
> Confounded in the dust, adore that Power,
> And Wisdom oft arraigned: see now the cause
> Why unassuming worth in secret lived,
> And died, neglected; why the good man's share
> In life was gall and bitterness of soul;
> Why the lone widow and her orphans pined
> In starving solitude, while Luxury,

In palaces, lay straining her low thought,
To form unreal wants; why heaven-born truth,
And moderation fair, wore the red marks
Of superstition's scourge; why licensed pain,
That cruel soldier, that embosomed foe,
Embittered all our bliss. Ye good distressed!
Ye noble few! who here unbending stand
Beneath life's pressure, yet bear up a while
And what your bounded view, which only saw
A little part, deemed evil, is no more;
The storms of wintry time will quickly pass,
And one unbounded Spring encircle all.

* * * * *

'Tis naught to me:
Since God is ever present, ever felt,
In the void waste as in the city full;
And where he vital breathes, there must be joy.
When even at last the solemn hour shall come,
And wing my mystic flight to future worlds,
I cheerful will obey; there, with new powers,
Will rising wonders sing; I cannot go
Where Universal Love smiles not around,
Sustaining all yon orbs and all their suns;
From seeming evil still educing good,
And better thence again, and better still,
In infinite progression.

Dr. Philip Doddridge.—A. D. 1702–1751.

Dr. Doddridge, one of the canonized among popular Christians, must have doubted endless misery. He says:

We cannot pretend to decide *a priori*, or previous to the event, so far as to say that the punishments of hell must and will certainly be eternal.

John Wesley.—A. D. 1703–1791.

Wesley quotes this from the Moravian literature of his time, apparently without disapprobation:

The name of the wicked shall not be so much as mentioned on the great day.—*Seven Discourses.* By his (Christ's) name all can and shall obtain life and salvation.—*Sixteen Discourses.*

Peter Bohler, Wesley's intimate friend, wrote (see Whitfield's Life):

All the damned souls shall yet be brought out of hell.

Bohler was afterwards made Bishop of American Moravians, next in rank to Zinzendorf. These quotations show how far Wesley was, in his sympathies, from many of his followers.

Soame Jenyns.—A. D. 1704–1787.

This author, in his "Origin of Evil," gives us some fine passages on the final triumph of Good. He says:

If there's a power above us,
(And that there is, all nature cries aloud
Through all her works,) he must delight in virtue,
And that which he delights in must be happy.

Death, the last and most dreadful of all evils, is so far from being one, that it is the infallible cure of all others.

To die is landing on some silent shore,

Where billows never beat, nor tempests roar;
Ere well we feel the friendly stroke, 'tis o'er. * *
How little they [ministers] God's counsels comprehend,
The universal parent, guardian, friend!
Who forming by degrees to bless mankind,
This globe our sportive nursery assigned.
Scarce any ill to human life belongs,
But what our follies cause, or mutual wrongs,
Or if some stripes from Providence we feel,
He strikes with pity, and but wounds to heal!

O would mankind but make these truths their guide,
And force the helm from prejudice and pride,
Were once these maxims fixed, that God's our friend,
Virtue our good, and happiness our end,
How soon must reason o'er the world prevail,
And error, fraud, and superstition fail.
None would hereafter, then, with groundless fear,
Describe the almighty cruel and severe
Inflicting endless pain for transient crimes,
And favoring sects or nations, men or climes.
None would fierce zeal for piety mistake,
Or malice, for whatever tenet's sake,
Or think salvation to a few confined,
And heaven too narrow to contain mankind.

Bishop Newton.—A. D. 1704–1782.

Bishop Newton, of the English church, thus puts himself on record against the doctrine of eternal punishment:

Imagine such a doctrine, you may; but seriously believe in it you never can. The thought is too shocking even to human nature; how much more abhorrent, then, must it be from divine perfection. The creator must have made all his creatures finally to be happy; and could never form any one whose end he foreknew would be misery everlasting. We can be sure of nothing, if we are not sure of this.

David Hartley.—A. D. 1705–1757.

Dr. Samuel Johnson one day observing a friend laying aside the volumes of Dr. Hartley's "Observations on Man" as companions for a country trip, said in his *ex cathedra* way:—"Sir, you do right to take Dr. Hartley with you." Dr. Priestley is also on record as giving approval to Hartley, and as saying that he "had learned more from Hartley, than from any book he had ever read except the Bible." Dr. Hartley was a confessed believer in final restoration. His great work, "Observations on Man, His Frame, His Duty and His Expectations," abounds in passages in which this faith is expressed. In the closing chapter, after arguing the final happiness of all from reason and the Scripture, he adds:

> I have now gone through with my observations on the frame, duty and expectations of man, finishing them with the doctrine of ultimate unlimited happiness to all. This doctrine, if it be true, ought at once to dispel all gloominess, anxiety and sorrow from our hearts; and raise them to the highest pitch of love, adoration and gratitude towards God, our most bountiful Creator and merciful Father, and the inexhaustible source of all happiness and perfection. Here self-interest, benevolence and piety all concur to move and exalt our affec-

tions. How happy in himself, how benevolent to others, and how thankful to God ought that man to be, who believes both himself and others born to an infinite expectation!

Dr. Hartley's opinion as to the practical influence of this faith is given in the following words:

If we embrace the opinion of universal restoration, then all the exhortations contained both in the word and the works of God will produce their genuine effects and concur to work in us dispositions fit to receive happiness ultimately.

I thank God that he has at last brought me to a lively sense of the infinite goodness and mercy to all his creatures, and that I see it in all his works, and in every page of his word. This has made me much more indifferent to this world than ever, at the same time that I enjoy it more; it has taught me to love every man and to rejoice in the happiness which our Heavenly Father intends for all his creatures; and has quite dispersed all the gloomy and melancholy thoughts which arise from the apprehension of eternal misery for myself or friends.

How long, or how much God will punish wicked men, he has nowhere said, and therefore I cannot tell; but this I am sure of, that in judgment he will remember mercy; that he will not be extreme to mark what is done amiss; that he chastens only because he loves; that he will not return to destroy, because he is God and not man; that is, has none of our foolish passions; that his tender mercies are over all his works, and that he is even love itself. I could almost transcribe the whole Bible, and the conclusion I draw from the whole is this: —First,—That no man can ever be happy till he is holy; till his affections are taken off from this vain world, and set upon a better; and till he loves God above all things, and his neighbor as himself. Secondly,—That all the evils and miseries which God sends upon us, are for no other purpose but to bring us to himself, to the knowledge and practice of our duty, and that as soon as that is done they will have an end.

Many men are so foolish as to fight against God all their lives, and to die full of obstinacy and perverseness. However, God's method of dealing with them in another world is still full of mercy, though it is severe. He will force them at last to comply, and make them happy whether they will or no. In the meantime, those who are of an humble and contrite heart, have nothing to fear, even here. God will conduct them through all the afflictions which he thinks fit to lay upon them for their good, with infinite tenderness and compassion.

Benjamin Franklin.—A. D. 1706–1790.

The great sage who "snatched fire from heaven and the scepter from tyrants," had no sympathy with the gloomy and dreadful theology of his times. His daughter, at whose house he died, tells us that Franklin thought

No system in the Christian world was so well calculated to promote the interests of society, as the doctrine which showed a God reconciling a lapsed world unto himself.

On the death of his brother he wrote:

Our friend and we were invited abroad on a party of pleasure which is to last forever. His chair was ready first; and he has gone before us. We could not all conveniently start together, and why should you and I be grieved at this: since we are soon to follow, and know where to find him?

In a letter to George Whitefield, he wrote:

You will see in this, my notion of good works,—that I am far from expecting to merit heaven by them. By heaven we understand a state of happiness infinite in degree, and eternal in duration. I can do nothing to deserve such a reward. He that for giving a draught of water to a thirsty person should expect to be paid with a good plantation, would be modest in his demands compared with those who think they deserve heaven for the little good they do on earth. For my part, I have not the vanity to think I deserve it, the folly to expect it, or the ambition to desire it, but content myself in submitting myself to the disposal of that God who made me, who has hitherto preserved and blessed me, and in whose fatherly goodness I may well confide that he will never make me miserable, and that the affliction I may at any time suffer, may tend to my benefit.

When the celebrated Rev. Elhanan Winchester renounced the Baptist faith and became a Universalist, several of the first men in the city gave him encouragement to preach his new doctrine. Among these were Dr. Franklin, Dr. Rush, Dr. Priestley, Dr. William Shippen, Dr. Caspar Wistar, and others.

Thomas Say.

Thomas Say was a Philadelphia Friend, but a very decided and outspoken Universalist. We find evidence of his faith in his "Life," which was printed by Budd & Bartram, Philadelphia, 1776. On page 44 he says:

And now, having showed by a few arguments that the variety of God's dispensations to man is alone the effect of his universal omnipotent and never ending love to his creatures, and which in the end, must and will accomplish the salvation "of all men, especially of those that believe."

On page 5 he writes:

Some writers have thought that the promulgation of the doctrine of universal benevolence and restoration of man, might do injury at this time, but I believe differently, and think that every soul which can be made fully sensible of this extraordinary divine love to the creation will be a humbled creature, and often have to adore the great, powerful, condescending mercy and love.

In his "Essay on the Impartiality of God," he considers the case of Moses and Pharaoh, and of the Jews and the Egyptians, to show that, though their treatment was different, God was not partial to either; but treated them according to their different necessities, for the good of both, and the benefit of the human race through the lessons thus taught in their histories. He then says:

Let no man stop me here, and object to this, by saying that God drowned the Egyptians in the Red Sea, while he caused the Israelites to pass over safely; for if he does I will answer that God overthrew those very Israelites, whom he carried safe through the Red Sea, in the wilderness, destroying them with as great a destruction there, as he did the Egyptians in the Red Sea; and I moreover add, that those Israelites and those Egyptians who fell, had lived as long upon earth as the dispensations of God, in this world, could benefit either of them; and therefore, they were both carried into another state and more effectual dispensation, where they will, in the end, receive the adoption of sons; for "when God shall bring again the captivity of Sodom and her daughters, and the captivity of Samaria and her daughters, then will he bring again the captivity of these captives in the midst of them; for he will remember his covenant with them, in the days of their youth, and will establish unto them an everlasting covenant," (Ezek. xvi: 53, etc.) making them partake, by those more powerful dispensations, of the same good which their children and the whole world received by the dispensation which brought death to them.

After this manner reasons the apostle in his epistle to the Romans, mentioned above. While he beautifully opens the mystery of the divine goodness in the different dispensations of his providence, he concludes that the choosing of the Jews, would, in the end, prove the salvation of the Gentiles, and again that the choosing of the Gentiles would end in the salvation of the Jews; and that God has concluded all in unbelief that he might have mercy upon all; (Romans, Chap. xi) thus making their fall in turns prove the rising of both; thereby showing incontestably that his ways are not as our ways, neither are his thoughts as our thoughts; but as the heavens are above the earth, so are his ways above our ways, and his thoughts above our thoughts; making what we think ends in damnation, to land in salvation. "Therefore, let no man henceforth judge after the appearance, but judge righteous judgment." * * *

Charles Wesley.—A. D. 1708–1788.

The great achievement of the Methodist movement of the last one hundred and fifty years has been the utter defeat of Calvinism. If the brother of the founder of Methodism hated anything with a righteous hatred it was the Calvinistic theology. "The horrible decree!" was one of his most frequent exclamations as he attuned his tongue to sing the glories of free grace.

The doctrines of election and reprobation were to him the sum of all that was satanic.

> Horror, to think that God is hate,
>   Fury in God can dwell!
> God could an helpless world create
>   To thrust them into hell!
>
> Doom them an endless death to die,
>   From which they could not flee!
> No, Lord! Thine inmost bowels cry
>   Against the dire decree!
>
> Believe who will that human pain
>   Pleasing to God can prove;
> Let Moloch feast him with the slain;
>   Our God, we know, is love.
>
> Lord, if indeed without a bound
>   Infinite love thou art,
> The horrible decree confound;
>   Enlarge thy people's heart.

Samuel Johnson.—A. D. 1709–1784.

Dr. Johnson wrote twenty-five sermons for his friend Dr. John Taylor, Prebendary of Westminster, which were preached by the latter, and published at his death as the compositions of the great moralist. In one of them is this explicit language:

> In our present state, it is impossible to practice this or any other duty, in perfection. We cannot trust God as we ought because we cannot know him as we ought. We know, however, that he is infinite in wisdom, in power, and in goodness;

that therefore he designs the happiness of all his creatures; that he cannot but know the proper means by which this end may be obtained; and that, in the use of these means, as he cannot be mistaken because he is omniscient, so he cannot be defeated because he is almighty.

In the sermon on the text, "The Lord is good to all, and his tender mercies are over all his works," Dr. Johnson thus speaks:

Without goodness, what apprehensions could we entertain of all the other attributes of the Divine Being? Without the utmost extent of benevolence and mercy, they would hardly be perfections or excellences. And what would a universal administration produce in the hand of an evil, or a partial, or malevolent direction, but scenes of horror and devastation? Not affliction and punishment for the sake of discipline and correction, to prevent the offense and reform the sinner; but heavy judgments and dreadful vengeance to destroy him; or implacable wrath, or fiery indignation, to prolong his misery, and extend the duration of his torture through the revolving periods of an endless eternity.

No bounds can be fixed to the Divine presence, nor is any part of illimitable space without his inspection and active influence. There is nothing remote or obscure to him, nor any exception to his favor among all the works of his hands. Far and wide as is the vast range of existence, so is the divine benevolence extended; and both in the previous trial and final retribution of all his rational and moral productions, "the Lord is good to all, and his tender mercies are over all his works."

We can only reconcile these admirable sentiments with the universal goodness of God. And they explain why Dr. Johnson placed "Hartley's Observations," a Universalist work, next to the Bible. He told Boswell, "Some of the texts of Scripture, on this subject, are as you observe, indeed strong, but they may admit of a mitigated construction." These facts interpret his immortal lines:

> O thou whose power o'er moving worlds presides,
> Whose voice created and whose wisdom guides,
> On darkling man in pure effulgence shine,
> And clear the clouded mind with light divine.
> 'Tis thine alone to calm the pious breast,
> With silent confidence and holy rest;
> From thee alone we spring, to thee we tend,
> Path, motive, guide, original and end!

George Stonehouse.—A. D. 1710–1780.

George A. Stonehouse, fellow of Oxford with the Wesleys, in "Universal Restitution Further Defended," says:

> We understand the Scriptures as affirming that not only all men, but also all creatures that are in this world are purposed of God to be subordinated or restored by our common creator.

Jean Jacques Rousseau.—A. D. 1712–1778.

The great French genius thus writes:

> I now plainly see that an intolerant spirit must by degrees become obdurate. For what charity can be long preserved for those we think must inevitably be damned? To love

them would be to hate God for punishing them. To act, then, on principles of humanity, we must take upon ourselves to condemn actions only, and not men. Let us not assume the horrible functions of devils. Let us not lightly throw open the gates of hell to our fellow creatures. Alas, if all those are destined to be eternally miserable who deceive themselves, where is the mortal who can avoid it?—*Elouisa.*

The God I serve is a merciful being—a father whose goodness only affects me and surpasses all his other attributes. His power astonishes me; his immensity confounds my ideas; his justice—he has made man weak, and though he be just, he is merciful. An avenging God is the God of the wicked. I can neither fear him on my own account, nor pray for his vengeance to be exerted against any other. It is the God of peace, the God of goodness, I adore. I know, I feel, I am the work of his hands and trust to see him at the last day, such as he has manifested himself to my heart during my life.—*Elouisa.*

Frederic the Great.—A. D. 1712-1788.

The sympathies of the great Prussian can be gathered from a well known anecdote. Petitpierre, a minister of the National church, was complained of by other clergymen, for preaching universal salvation, and Frederic was asked to forbid him. He replied:

Let the man alone, but since the Neuchâtel ministers desire to be damned eternally, let him not prevent them. They have entire liberty.

Charles Bonnet.—A. D. 1720–1793.

The great French genius, Charles Bonnet, in his "Philosophic Pangenesis," expresses this truth:

> The progress that we shall have made here below in knowledge and virtue will determine our point of departure in another life, and the place we shall occupy there.

Henry Brooke.—A. D. 1720.

This author was the associate of Pope, Swift, and Chatham. His "Fool of Quality" was published a century ago. Frequently, the Universalist theory glows with divine beauty in the picturesque sentiment of the then popular book.

> And thus, on the grand and final consummation, when every will shall be subdued to the will of good to all, our Jesus will take in hand the resigned chordage of our hearts, he will tune them as so many instruments, and will touch them with the finger of his own divine feelings. Then shall the wisdom, the might, the goodness of our God, become the wisdom, might and goodness of all his intelligent creatures; the happiness of each shall multiply and overflow in the wishes and participation of the happiness of all; the universe shall begin to sound with the song of congratulation, and all voices shall break forth in an eternal hallelujah of paise transcending praise, and glory transcending glory, to God and the Lamb.

Mark Akenside.—A. D. 1721–1770.

From the "Pleasures of the Imagination," one of the purest poems ever written, we extract:

> From the birth
> Of mortal man, the sovereign maker said
> That not in humble, nor in brief delight,—
> Not in the fading glories of renown,
> Power's purple robes, nor pleasure's flowery lap,
> The soul should find enjoyment, but from these
> Turning disdainful to an equal good,
> Thro' all the ascent of things enlarge her view,
> Till every bound at length should disappear,
> And infinite perfection close the scene!

Immanuel Kant.—A. D. 1724–1804.

In his "End of all Things," after objecting to endless damnation, as a "dual system," he says:

> Why were a few, or a single one, made at all, if only to exist in order to be made eternally miserable, which is infinitely worse than non-existence?

Thomas Gainsborough,—A. D. 1727–1788.

When Gainesborough, the great painter, and the hating and hated rival of Vandyke, was dying, he cried out:

> We are all going to heaven, and Vandyke is of the party.

William Cowper.—A. D. 1731–1800.

It is not pretended that poor Cowper saw God as he is, and his beneficent dealings with men as they are. His heart was broken, his mind was shattered, and his whole existence was under a pall of gloom, in consequence of his conviction that God was a monster, and eternity a calamity to countless millions of immortal souls. But it must be that once, at least, there was a rift in the clouds, and that the beautiful gates were ajar even to his tear-blinded eyes, when he wrote:

> God moves in a mysterious way
>   His wonders to perform:
> He plants his footsteps in the sea
>   And rides upon the storm.
> Deep in unfathomable mines
>   Of never-failing skill,
> He treasures up his bright designs,
>   And works his sovereign will.
>
> His purposes will ripen fast,
>   Unfolding every hour;
> The bud may have a bitter taste,
>   But sweet will be the flower.
> Blind unbelief is sure to err,
>   And scan his work in vain,
> God is his own interpreter,
>   And he will make it plain.

Had Cowper realized the sublime philosophy of this poem, he would have found sweet solace where he experienced life-long agony, in the contemplation of the character and dealings of God. And certainly in his sane moments he rose to the altitude of the genuine faith, as toward the close of Book VI of "The Task:"

Thus heavenward all things tend. For all were once
Perfect, and all must be at length restored.
So God has greatly purposed, who would else
In his dishonored works himself endure
Dishonor, and be wronged without redress.

James Necker,—A. D. 1732–1804.

The great French financier, and father of Madame de Stael, says:

Eternal punishment! Power Almighty! can they who entertain such an idea know thee? Thy goodness precedeth our birth, it still subsists after we are cut off by the hand of death.

Dr. Joseph Priestley,—A. D. 1733–1804.

This distinguished scholar and genius, the day before he died, desired his son to reach him a pamphlet,—John Simpson's work against eternal punishment. He then remarked:

It will be a source of great satisfaction to you to read this pamphlet. It contains my sentiments, and a belief in them will be a support to you in the most trying circumstances, as it has been to me. We shall all meet finally; we only require different degrees of discipline, suited to our different tempers, to prepare us for final happiness. * * We shall all meet again, in another and a better world.

James Beattie.—A. D. 1735-1803.

Beattie, the once famous poet, sings:

Shall I be left abandoned in the dust,
When Fate, relenting, lets the flowers revive?
Shall Nature's voice, to man alone unjust,
Bid him, though doomed to perish, hope to live?
Is it for this fair virtue we must strive
With disappointment, penury and pain?
No! heaven's immortal Spring shall yet arrive,
And man's majestic beauty bloom again,
Bright through th' eternal year of Love's triumphant reign.

Ferdinand Oliver Petitpierre.—A. D. 1740-1790.

This eloquent Swiss clergyman's "Plan of God with Respect to Man," is entirely devoted to the advocacy of the final redemption of all. The reader is referred to his work, one of the Universalist classics.

Jung Stilling.—A. D. 1740-1817.

The famous mystic declares:

Not a single soul will be lost, they will all—all be saved at last. The Holy Scriptures do not in one instance say the contrary, and they cannot say it, and if it even seems so, we then must choose the most reasonable construction. But they do not even seem to say it, for all the passages wherewith some are essaying to prove the infinity of hell torments, prove nothing further than that they shall continue a long, undefined time. The Hebrew word *olam*, and the Greek *aiōnios*, which Luther has translated by *ewig* (eternal), signify nowhere an infinite, but a very long, an indefinite time.

John Frederick Oberlin.—A. D. 1740–1826.

From the model village pastor, and world-renowned philanthropist, we have no quotations to present, but we can say, on the authority of his biography, translated by Halsey, that the belief in universal salvation animated this remarkable man, and was the spur of his benevolence. His biographer says:

It may here be considered necessary, for the sake of biographical clearness, to observe that upon some points he certainly held very fanciful and unwarranted notions, more particularly upon those relative to a future state. He seemed to hope that the passage I. Cor. xv: 28, where it is said that "all things" shall be subjected unto the Almighty, and the Son also himself shall be subjected, "that God may be all in all," might include not only the little flock of Christ's immediate followers, but ultimately, at some almost indefinite period, through the boundless mercy of God, and the blood of Jesus, which was shed for the sins of the whole word, all the race of mankind. And he was strengthened in this belief by understanding in another than the ordinary sense, that "as in Adam all die, even so in Christ shall all be made alive." It is needless to say of these doctrines that they are fanciful and mistaken, etc.

An adequate biography of this great man has never been written. If it shall ever appear, we venture to prophesy that his discourses will reveal the fact that his faith in universal good inspired him to labor as he did, that he might accelerate the consummation he anticipated.

Alison Rutherford Cockburn.

Mrs. Cockburn (pronounced Coburn), a well known authoress, who wrote one of the versions of "The Flowers of the Forest," a most excellent woman, and an accomplished leader of society in Edinburgh in the last century, in a letter to Lady Anne Barnard, author of "Auld Robin Gray," says:

The almighty maker of souls has various methods of restoring them to the divine image; it is impossible his power can fail; it is impossible for his image to be entirely obliterated; it is impossible that misery, sin, and discord can be eternal! Look, then, on the erring sons of men as on wretched prisoners bound in fetters for a time; but recollect that they are and must be eternal as well as you, and that in the endless ages of eternity they will be restored to order. This faith, which is sincerely mine, makes me see things in very different lights from what others do, and perhaps is the key to my whole conduct. Clean and unclean are welcome to my pity; I know that with all our thousand errors flesh is heir to, we will one day be all right.

Sir Walter Scott says of this friend of Hume, Mackenzie, and Lord Lindsay:—"Her active benevolence kept pace with her genius, and rendered her equally an object of love and admiration."

Johann Kasper Lavater.—A. D. 1741–1801.

Johann Kasper Lavater, the great Swiss, uttered the following evangelical aspiration:

My prayers were comprehensive. My family, my friends, my fellow-citizens, my enemies, all Christians, all men were included in them. I flew to the most distant seas; I penetrated into the deepest mines and dungeons. I embraced in my heart all that is called man, present and future times and nations; the dead, the damned, yea, Satan himself; I presented them all to God, with the warmest wishes that he would have mercy upon all.

It is enough, my creator, that thou art love. Love seeketh not her own; thou seeketh the happiness of all, and shouldest thou not then find what thou seekest?

Anna Letitia Barbauld.—1743–1825.

This most amiable and talented writer, who lived to the ripe age of 82, was full of the impartial Gospel. It was her open profession, and inward faith. Leigh Hunt, who knew her well, declares the fact. She says, among other things:

No one who embraces the common idea of future torments, together with the doctrine of election and reprobation, the insufficiency of virtue to escape the wrath of God, and the strange absurdity which, it should seem, through similarity of sound alone, has been admitted as an axiom, that sins committed against an infinite being, do therefore deserve infinite punishment, no one, I will venture to assert, can believe such tenets, and have them often in his thoughts, and yet be cheerful. The God of the Assembly's Catechism is not the same God with the Deity of Thomson's Seasons. We often boast, and with reason, of the purity of our religion, as opposed to the grossness of the theology of the Greeks and Romans; but we should remember that cruelty is as much worse than licentiousness, as a Moloch is worse than a satyr.

The age which has demolished dungeons, rejected torture, and given so fair a prospect of abolishing the iniquity of the slave trade, cannot long retain among its articles of belief, the heart-withering perspective of cruel and never-ending punishments.

Benjamin Rush.—A. D. 1745–1813.

The eminent Dr. Rush, who was a firm friend of Elhanan Winchester, in a letter dated May 11, 1791, wrote to Winchester, then in London:

The universal doctrine prevails more and more in our country, particularly among persons eminent for their piety, in whom it is not a mere speculation, but a new principle of action in the heart, prompting to practical goodness.

If Christ died for all, as Mr. Wesley taught, it will soon appear a necessary consequence, that all shall be saved. * * * The benevolent spirit which has lately appeared in the world, in its governments, in its numerous philanthropic and humane societies, and even in public entertainments, reminds me of the first efforts of a child to move its body, or limbs. These efforts are strong, but irregular, and often in a contrary direction to that which is intended. * * * At present we wish liberty to the whole world, but the next touch of the celestial magnet upon the human heart will direct it into wishes for the salvation of all mankind.

John Prior Estlin, LL.D.—A. D. 1747–1817.

"An elegant scholar," says the *Monthly Review*, and voluminous writer on moral philosophy, thus records his sentiments:

It certainly argues a greater degree of benevolence in the governor of the world, after the punishment of his creatures, to restore them to his favor, than either to preserve them in misery, or to blot them out of existence. * * * * To a belief in the doctrine of the eternity of hell torments, I impute more absurdity, more misery, and more un-Christian conduct, than to all other false opinions put together. It is impossible that a mind of any benevolence should be able to look round on a race of beings, to whom it is connected by nearest ties, the greater part of whom are doomed to eternal misery, without feeling existence itself insupportable. The effects of this doctrine, when a person applies it to himself, are gloom and despair, often terminating in mental derangement; when he applies it to others, pride, cruelty, hatred, and all the worst passions of human nature. * * *

The firm belief in the doctrine of final universal restoration, has afforded much consolation to myself during a large portion of my life; has rendered advanced years placid and serene, and enables me to contemplate death itself, notwithstanding its gloomy appearance, as one of the most essential blessings of the whole plan of Providence.

I would as a friend, advise every one to take this subject into his most serious consideration. I would wish him to experience during the remainder of his life, all the happiness which results from the full persuasion of this delightful doctrine. I pray to God that others may experience that perpetual sunshine of the mind, that superiority of the passing events of this ever-varying scene, that universal philanthropy, that joy in the divine administration, that serenity through life, and that cheering prospect in the hour of death, which the belief in this doctrine does so manifestly inspire.

Christopher Marshall.

This gentleman was editor of the "Remembrancer," which appeared in five volumes; one of the most respectable citizens of Philadelphia, who died in 1797. He was on friendly and confidential terms with many leading men in the Continental Congress, and was a man of deep religious feeling. The following extract from his will shows what were his religious opinions:

He (Jesus) will, in the ages to come, put an end to sin, finish transgression, and bring in everlasting life unto all lapsed beings, as it stands recorded in the scriptures.

He was a member of the Society of Friends, but in consequence of his views on the lawfulness of defensive warfare, he was expelled. He offered to pay sixty guineas toward the expense of printing a new edition of the "World Unmasked" and Paul Siegvolk's "Everlasting Gospel"—Universalist publications.

Samuel Parr.—A. D. 1747–1825.

The wise Parr, a man of great learning and wisdom, and the spiritual adviser of Queen Caroline, was a Universalist. His biographer, Rev. Wm. Field, says:

Several of Dr. Parr's friends will recollect a long, learned and elaborate sermon delivered by him in Hatton Church, on Good Friday, 1822, in which he traversed the whole field of theological controversy and decided almost all the great leading points against the *dicta* of modern orthodoxy. He particularly discussed Christian reconciliation; stated and asserted his own view of it; and exposed and impugned the high satisfaction scheme with all the strange notions connected with it—such as infinite offenses committed by finite creatures, inexorable justice; vicarious punishment, imputed guilt and imputed righteousness. *   *   *   *   *

With most divines, he held the doctrine of different degrees of future rewards and punishments, proportioned to the merits or demerits of every individual character, but in opposition to the prevailing notions, he contended * * that future punishments are properly corrections, intended and fitted to produce moral reformation in the sufferer; and to prepare ultimately for the gradual attainment of greater or less degrees of happiness.

J. W. Goethe,—A. D. 1749–1832.

Says the *New Quarterly Magazine*, "As the politicians accused Goethe of want of patriotism, because his mind soared above the mists of party feeling and international jealousies, so theologians charged him with irreligion and unbelief because he denounced priestcraft in whatever form it appeared, and refused to sacrifice his right of judgment to the arbitrary dicta of rival churches." He says:

I ever believed in God and nature, and in the victory of good over evil, but this was not enough for the pious souls. I must also believe that three are one, and that one is three, and this the truthfulness of my soul rebels against, nor do I see what possible help it would be to me. * * * At seventy-five years of age one cannot but think of death sometimes. The thought leaves me perfectly at peace, for I entertain a firm conviction that man's spirit is an essence of an indestructible nature, working on from eternity to eternity. It is like the sun, that to human eyes appears to go down, but which does not go down, but shines on forever. * * Man believes in immortality; he has a right to the belief, for it is in accord with his nature, and he may, if he will, rest this belief on religious teachings; but for a philosopher to attempt to argue the immortality of the soul from a legend, would be weak and come to nothing. My own conviction of a continuous existence springs from my consciousness of personal energy, for I work incessantly to the end. Nature is bound to assign to me another outward form of being as soon as my present one can no longer serve my spirit.

Thomas Belsham.—A. D. 1750-1829.

The eternity of hell-torments is a doctrine from which Christianity revolts; to which it gives not the slightest countenance; and of which there is not the slightest trace either in the Old Testament or the New. * * * I will venture to affirm that there is not in the whole voluminous code of the Jewish and Christian Scriptures, from the beginning of Genesis to the end of Revelation, one single passage, one solitary text, in which the doctrine is taught. I will add, that there is not a single sentence in which the very idea of a human individual existing through eternity in a state of torment is even expressed distinctly and unequivocally.

If the main design of punishment be to reclaim the offender to virtue and happiness, this grand difficulty (endless misery) is removed. We see the triumph of benevolence in restoring the dead transgressor to life; in visiting him with suffering in exact proportion to the greatness of his offences and the inveteracy of his vicious habits; and finally, in his ultimate purification from moral stain, and his restoration to virtue, to happiness, and to God. This is indeed a result infinitely worthy of infinite benevolence; it clears up at once all the difficulties of the divine dispensations; all the mysteries of the divine government; and the belief of it fills the pious and contemplative mind with unspeakable satisfaction and delight. * * *

Rev. Robert Aspland.

We regard the doctrine of endless punishment as so utterly incompatible both with the goodness and justice of God, that we think it ought not to be received upon any evidence whatever. To affirm that the Almighty will render any of his creatures miserable to all eternity, and especially, when these creatures, like mankind, are frail and ignorant, and exposed to numerous temptations, is but saying in other words, that he is neither merciful nor just: and to such a doctrine what evidence ought to obtain an assent? It can scarcely be reprobated in terms sufficiently strong.

George Crabbe.—A. D. 1754–1832.

The eminent poet of "the short and simple annals of the poor," an Episcopal clergyman, was a Universalist. His heart and head outran his narrow creed. He said, long before his death:

We have, it seems, who teach, and doubtless well,
Of a chastening, not awarding hell;
Who are assured that an offended God
Will cease to use the thunder and the rod;
A soul on earth, by crime and folly stained,
When here corrected has improvement gained;
In other state still more improved to grow,
And nobler powers in happier world to know;
New strength to use in each divine employ,
And, more enjoying, looking to more joy.

A pleasing vision! could we thus be sure
Polluted souls would be at length so pure;
The view is happy, we may think is just,
It may be true—but who shall add it must?
To the plain words and sense of Sacred Writ,
With all my heart I reverently submit;
But where it leaves me doubtful, I'm afraid
To call conjecture to my reason's aid;
Thy thoughts, thy ways, great God! are not as mine,
And to thy mercy I my soul resign.

Dr. T. Southwood Smith says:

I have a letter from a son of Crabbe, informing me that my treatise was his father's daily companion in the close of life, and that the poet declared on his death bed, that he had received more solace from that book than from all other human compositions.

The book referred to is one of the best expositions of Universalism ever written, "Illustration of Divine Government."

Robert Burns.—A. D. 1759-1796.

This poet of nature, in many places on his undying pages, has recorded his horror and detestation of popular error, and his ardent aspirations for the higher faith. Allan Cunningham says:—"To a love of human nature he (Burns) added an affection for the flowers of the valley, the fowls of the air, the beasts of the field; he acknowledged the tie of social sympathy which bound his heart to all created things, and carried his universal good-will so far as to entertain hopes of universal redemption, and the restoration of the doomed spirits to power and lustre."

In harmony with the above sentiment he says:

> To give my counsels all in one,
> Thy tuneful flame still careful fan;
> Preserve the dignity of man
>   With soul erect;
> And trust the universal plan
>   Will all protect!

So again he says:

> Sure thou, Almighty, canst not act
> From cruelty or wrath!

Again:

> Where with intention I have erred,
>   No other plea I have,
> But, thou art good; and goodness still
>   Delighteth to forgive!

None of his readers can be ignorant of his horror of what was and is so falsely styled evangelical religion. For illustration:

> Ye'll get the best o' moral works,
> 'Mang black Gentoos and Pagan Turks,
> Or hunters wild of Ponotaxi,

Wha never heard of Orthodoxy.
That he's the poor man's friend in need,
The gentleman in word and deed,
It's through no terror o' damnation;
It's just a carnal inclination.
Morality! thou deadly bane,
Thy tens o'thousands thou hast slain;
Vain is his hope whose stay and truth is
In moral mercy, truth, and justice,
No; stretch a point to catch a plack,
Abuse a brother to his back,
Be to the poor like onie whunstane,
And haud their noses to the grunstane
Ply every art o' legal thieving;
No matter; stick to sound believing.
Learn three-mile prayers, and half-mile graces,
Wi' weel-spread looves, and lang, wry faces,
Grunt up a solemn, lengthened groan,
And damn a' parties but your own;
I'll warrant, then, ye're nae deceiver,
A steady, sturdy, staunch believer!

In the same strain are "Holy Willie's Prayer," and the "Kirk's Alarm." Elsewhere, referring to popular error, he says:

Auld Orthodoxy lang did grapple,
But now she's got an unco rapple,
Haste, gie her name up i' the chapel,
 Nigh unto death;
See how she fetches at the thrapple,
 And gasps for breath.

Enthusiasm's past redemption,
Gaen in a galloping consumption;
Not all the quacks wi' a' their gumption,
 Will ever mend her;
Her feeble pulse gies strong presumption
 Death soon will end her.

He also wrote those beautiful lines ending with:

> No wanderer lost,
> A family in Heaven.

Other verses accordant with the language ascribed to him by Cunningham, may be found. Thus:

> Lord, help me thro' this world o' care,
> I'm weary, sick o't, late and air,
> Not but I have a richer share
>   Than many others;
> But why should one man better fare,
>   And all men brothers?

Again:

> Let me, oh Lord, from life retire,
> Unknown each guilty, worldy fire,
> Remorse's throb, or loose desire;
>   And when I die,
> Let me in this belief expire—
>   To God I fly.

> The fear o' hell's a hangman's whip,
>   To haud the wretch in order;
> But where ye feel your honor grip,
>   Let that aye be your border:
> Its slightest touches, instant pause—
>   Debar all side pretences;
> And resolutely keep its laws,
>   Uncaring consequences.

His address to the Prince of Evil indicates his indulgence of the larger hope:

> O wad ye tak a thocht and men',
> Ye aiblins might, I dinna ken,
>   Still hae a stake;
> I'm loath to think upon yon den
>   E'en for your sake.

Burns wrote in 1789:

I trust that in Jesus Christ shall "all the families of the earth be blessed," by being yet connected together in a better world, where every tie that bound heart to heart in this state of existence shall be far beyond our present conception, more enduring.

Johann C. F. von Schiller.—A. D. 1759–1805.

Goethe's great associate, and next to him the genius of German song, thus sings:

> We speak with the lip, and we dream in the soul
>   Of some better and fairer day;
> And our days, the meanwhile, to that golden goal,
>   Are gliding and sliding away.
> Now the world becomes old, now again it is young,
>   But "The Better" is ever the word on the tongue.
>
> At the threshold of life Hope leads us in——
>   Hope plays round the mirthful boy;
> Though the best of its charms may with youth begin,
>   Yet for age it reserves its toy.
> When we sink at the grave, why the grave has scope,
>   And over the coffin man planteth—HOPE.
>
> And it is not a dream of fancy proud,
>   With a fool for its dull begetter;
> There's a voice at the heart which proclaims aloud,
>   "We are born for something better!"
> And that voice of the heart, oh, ye may believe,
>   Will never the hope of the soul deceive!

Joanna Baillie.—A. D. 1762–1851.

This celebrated writer has left a few traces of her love for this benevolent faith.

In "The Second Marriage," Beaumont, a benevolent clergyman, replies to a disparaging remark by his wife on the step-mother:

"Nay, my dear, you are prejudiced and severe. She has an ungracious countenance, to be sure, but now and then, when it relaxes, she looks as if she had some good in her.

Mrs. B. Yes, Charles, you find always some good in every one of God's creatures.

Mr. B. And there is some good in every one of God's creatures, if you would but look for it.

In another place the sentiment is repeated:

Mrs. B. Poo, Mr. Beaumont! the wickedest creature on earth has always your good word for some precious quality or other.

Mr. B. Well, my dear, and the wickedest creature in the world always has something about it that shows whose creature it is,—that shows we were all meant for a good end—and that there is a seed—a springing place—a beginning for it, in everybody.

In "The Election," a comedy, Baltimore saves the life of a hated rival, Freeman, under strong temptations to leave him to perish; whereupon, Mrs. Baltimore, on hearing it, exclaims:

Thy master—ay, and my husband! and God Almighty's good creature, who has formed everything good! Oh, yes, he has made every being with good in it, and will at last make everything perfectly so, in some way or other, known only to his wisdom!

Samuel Rogers.—A. D. 1763-1855.

James Freeman Clarke, in his "Eleven Weeks in Europe," describes an interview with Samuel Rogers, the banker poet, who recited passages from "Paradise Lost," and said:

> Milton had put an argument into the mouth of Adam, complaining of his punishment, which he had not answered. "There's no answering that, indeed, except we admit that all punishment is corrective."

This shows plainly what were the feelings of the author of "The Pleasures of Memory," on this subject. [See Milton, page 35.]

Sir James Mackintosh.—A. D. 1765-1832.

The ablest of England's scholars, Sir James Mackintosh, wrote,—see "Life by his Son":

> The fear of hell or the desire of reward for ourselves, may, like the fear of the gallows, prevent crimes; but at most it can only lead to virtue, it can never produce it. I leave below me those coarse notions of religion which degrade it into a supplement to police and criminal law. All such representations are more practically atheistical, more derogatory from the grandeur of religious sentiment, than any speculative system called atheism.
>
> There is nothing in this world so right as to cultivate and exercise kindness—the most certainly evangelical of all doctrines—the principle of Jesus Christ.

"These precepts," says his biographer, "led him to look forward with ardent hope and humble faith to the day when tears shall be wiped from all eyes."

Alexander von Humboldt.—A. D. 1767–1835.

Humboldt, the great German scientist, declared:

The conviction—arising from a firm confidence in Almighty goodness and justice—that death is only the termination of an imperfect state of being, whose purpose cannot be fully carried out here, and that it is the passage to a better and a higher condition, should be so constantly present to us, that nothing should be able to obscure it, even for a moment; it is the groundwork of inward peace, and of the loftiest endeavors, and is an inexhaustible spring of comfort in affliction.

Samuel Taylor Coleridge.—A. D. 1770–1834.

Southey, the poet, having apologized for Wesley's theory of endless misery, Coleridge, the deepest, subtlest, and perhaps most wonderful mind England saw for a century, thus protested:

Dear and honored Southey! All this is very plausible; The picture is frightful, and a recoil is at first inevitable by any sane mind. But what have you to substitute, or, rather what had Wesley, who still believed in everlasting (that is, endless) torments? for so he understood the word eternal.

I boldly answer, and appeal to Taylor's letters on original sin, a mere paltry evasion; a quibble, (and one that is quite absurd when applied to an omniscience and omnipotence perpetually creative,) between decreeing and permitting. If any one, it should be a Spanish theologian to treat on this subject; for the Spaniards only combine depth with subtlety. I feel and I think as you do, Southey. How could it be otherwise? In this only I differ, that the controversy is between Whitefield and Wesley, and men like them. And is it not fair to take the question abstractedly from the total creed of both parties? Not simply, what is there in reprobation so horrible? To this you have returned a fit answer. But what is there in it that Mr Wesley could with consistency affect horror at? Let him turn the broad road round before it comes to the everlasting fire lake, and then he may reprobate reprobation as loudly as he lists.

This great philosopher, metaphysician and poet, never assented to that gross caricature of God whom he called in derision

> That Deity, Accomplice Deity,

who,

> In the fierce jealousy of awakened wrath
> Will go forth with our armies, and our fleets,
> To scatter the red ruin on their foes.
> O Blasphemy! To mingle fiendish deeds
> With blessedness.

His soul was cheered with the sublime thought:

> There is one Mind, one omnipresent mind,
> Omnific. His most holy name is Love.
> Truth of subliming import! with the which
> Who feeds and saturates his constant soul,
> He from his small, particular orbit flies
> With bless'd outstarting. From himself he flies,

> Stands in the Sun, and with no partial gaze
> Views all creation; and he loves it all,
> And blesses it, and calls it very good!
> This is indeed to dwell with the Most High!
> Cherubs and rapture-trembling seraphim
> Can pass no nearer to the Almighty Throne.
>   'Tis the sublime of man,
> Our noontide majesty, to know ourselves
> Parts and proportions of one wondrous whole!
> This fraternizes man, this constitutes
> Our charities and bearings. But 'tis God
> Diffused through all, that doth make all one whole.

He expresses the same idea in other words:

> He prayeth well, who loveth well,
> Both man, and bird, and beast.
> He prayeth best, who loveth best
> All things, both great and small,
> For the dear God who loveth us;
> He made and loveth all.

It was the confidence caused by such thoughts that enabled him to pen the most beautiful description of silent prayer that ever was written:

> Ere on my bed my limbs I lay,
> It hath not been my use to pray
> With moving lips, or bended knees;
> But silently, by slow degrees,
> My spirit I to love compose,
> In humble trust mine eyelids close,
> With reverential resignation,
> No wish conceived, no thought express'd!
> Only a sense of supplication,
> A sense o'er all my soul impress'd
> That I am weak, yet not unblest,
> Since in me, round me, everywhere,
> Eternal strength and wisdom are.

His faith relating to the future he expresses in this sublime passage:

> Believe thou, O my soul
> Life is a vision shadowy of truth:
> And vice, and anguish, and the wormy grave,
> Shapes of a dream.   The veiling clouds retire,
> And lo! the Throne of the Redeeming God,
> Forth flashing unimaginable day,
> Wraps in one blaze, earth, heaven, and deepest hell!

Crabb Robinson in his diary, 1836, says:

On a visit to Cottle, I was shown a letter by Coleridge on the future state, with a strong bearing against the idea of eternal suffering.

John Foster.—A. D. 1770–1843.

The celebrated English essayist and Baptist theologian was a good example to modern Baptists. In a "Letter to a Young Clergyman," he writes:

But endless punishment! hopeless misery, through a duration to which the enormous terms above imagined will be absolutely nothing! I acknowledge my inability (I would say it reverently) to admit this belief, together with a belief in the divine goodness—the belief that "God is love," that "his tender mercies are over all his works."

But, after all this, we have to meet the grave question, What say the Scriptures? There is a force in their expression at which we well may tremble. On no allowable interpretation do they signify less than a very protracted duration and formidable severity. But I hope it is not presumption to take advantage of the fact that the terms everlasting, eternal, forever, original or translated, are often employed in the Bible, as well as other writings, under great and various limitations of import; and are thus withdrawn from the predicament of necessarily and absolutely meaning a strictly endless duration. The limitation is often, indeed, plainly marked by the nature of the subject. In other instances the words are used with figurative indefiniteness, which leaves the limitations to be made by some general rule of reason and proportion. They are designed to magnify, to aggravate, rather than to define. My resource, in the present case, then, is simply this: that since the terms do not necessarily and absolutely signify an interminable duration—and since there is, in the present instance, to be pleaded for admitting a limited interpretation, a reason in the moral estimate of things, of stupendous, of infinite urgency, involving our conceptions of the divine goodness and equity, and leaving those conceptions overwhelmed in darkness and horror, if it be rejected, I therefore conclude that a limited interpretation is authorized. Perhaps there is some pertinence in the suggestion, which I recollect to have seen in some old and nearly unknown book in favor of universal restitution, that the great difference of degrees of future punishment, so plainly stated in Scripture, affords an argument against its perpetuity: since, if the demerit be infinite, there can be no place for a scale of degrees, apportioning a minor infliction to some offenders; every one should be punished up to the utmost that his nature can sustain; and the same reason of equity there may be for a limited measure, there may consistently be for a limited duration. The assignment for an unlimited duration would seem an abandonment of the principle of the discriminating rule observed in the adjustment of degrees.

If it be asked, how could the doctrine have been more plainly and positively asserted than it is in the Scripture language, in answer I ask, how do we construct our words and sentences to express it in an absolute manner, so as to leave no possibility of misunderstanding doctrine, and yet, pressed to the strength of the Scripture language, have had recourse by a literal interpretation of a threatened destruction, to eternal death, as signifying annihilation of existence after a more or less protracted penal infliction. Even this would be a prodigious relief; but it is an admission that the terms in question do mean something final, in an absolute sense. I have not directed much thought to this point; the grand object of interest being a negation of the perpetuity of misery. I have not been anxious for any satisfaction beyond that; though certainly one would wish to indulge the hope, founded on the divine attribute of infinite benevolence, that there will be a period somewhere in the endless futurity, when all God's sinning creatures will be restored by him to rectitude and happiness.

William Wordsworth.—A. D. 1770–1850.

The most philosophical, and one of the greatest of English poets, shows us, that Christian "faith is the substance of things hoped for."

> As men from men
> Do, in the constitution of their souls,
> Differ, by mystery not to be explained;
> And as we fall by various ways, and sink
> One deeper than another, self-condemned,
> Through manifold degrees of guilt and shame,
> So manifold and various are the ways
> Of restoration, fashioned to the steps
> Of all infirmity, and tending all
> To the same point,—attainable by all,—
> Peace in ourselves and union with our God.
>
>   'Tis nature's law
> That none, the meanest of created things,

Of forms created the most vile and brute,
The dullest or most noxious, should exist
Divorced from good,—a spirit and pulse of good,
A life and soul, to every mode of being
Inseparably linked.   Then be assured
That least of all can aught that ever owned
The heaven-regarding eye and front sublime
Which man is born to,—sink, howe'er depressed,
So low as to be scorned without a sin;
Without offence to God cast out of view
Like the dry remnant of a garden flower
Whose seeds are shed, or as an implement
Worn out and worthless.

One adequate support
For the calamities of mortal life
Exists, one only;—an assured belief
That the procession of our fate, howe'er
Sad or disturbed, is ordered by a being
Of infinite benevolence and power,
Whose everlasting purposes embrace
All accidents, converting them to good.

January 5, 1843, a walk with Wordsworth and Faber, Wordsworth denied transubstantiation on grounds "on which," says Faber, "I should deny the Trinity." Wordsworth declared, in strong terms, his disbelief of eternal punishment, which Faber did not attempt to defend.—*From Crabb Robinson's Diary.*

Hosea Ballou.—A. D. 1771–1852.

This eminent theologian was also a poet.

In God's eternity
There shall a day arise,

When all the race of man shall be
   With Jesus in the skies.

As night before the rays
   Of morning flees away,
Sin shall retire before the blaze
   Of God's eternal day.

As music fills the grove
   When stormy clouds are past,
Sweet anthems of redeeming love
   Shall all employ at last.

Redeemed from death and sin
   Shall Adam's numerous race,
A ceaseless song of praise begin,
   And shout redeeming grace.

James Montgomery.—A. D. 1771–1854.

James Montgomery wrote a jubilate which we can not interpret in harmony with the doctrine that Christ shall be defeated. Can the reader?

Hark! the song of jubilee,
   Loud as mighty thunders roar,
Or the fullness of the sea,
   When it breaks upon the shore:—
Hallelujah! for the Lord
   God omnipotent shall reign!
Hallelujah! let the word
   Echo round the earth and main.

Hallelujah!—hark! the sound
   Heard thro' earth and through the skies,
Wakes above, beneath, around,
   All creation's harmonies;

See Jehovah's banner furled,
  Sheathed his sword; he speaks—'tis done!
And the kingdoms of this world
  Are the kingdoms of his Son.

He shall reign from pole to pole
  With illimitable sway;
He shall reign when, like a scroll,
  Yonder heavens are passed away;
Then the end;—beneath his rod
  Man's last enemy shall fall;
Hallelujah! Christ in God,
  God in Christ, is all in all!

Again:

O'er every foe victorious,
  He on his throne shall rest,
From age to age more glorious,
  All blessing, and all blest,
The tide of time shall never
  His covenant remove;
His name shall stand forever;
  That name to us is Love.

While we lay no claim to Montgomery, we do not know how universal salvation could be more clearly stated in rhyme.

Thomas Dick.—A. D. 1772–1857.

In January, 1833, Rev. A. C. Thomas held a conversation with Dr. Dick, in the course of which the latter said:

I see not how the universality and unchangeability of the first and great commandment can be admitted without implying the final salvation of all mankind.

In a letter to J. E. Miles, February 22, 1849, he wrote:

When I consider the boundless nature of eternity, and when I consider the limited nature of man, I can scarcely bring myself to believe that the sins of a few fleeting years are to be punished throughout a duration that has no end, more especially when it is declared more than a score of times that "the mercy of the Lord endureth forever," and that "his tender mercies are over all his works." If his mercy endures forever, it appears scarcely consistent with the idea that punishment will be inflicted throughout unlimited duration. * * I think it more consistent with the goodness of God to suppose that the punishments he inflicts upon the wicked are intended for their ultimate benefit; and to prepare them for restoration to the happiness they had lost.

James Hogg.—A. D. 1772–1835.

The "Ettrick Shepherd" was among the most popular of Scottish poets and authors three quarters of a a century ago. The "Pilgrims of the Sun" was written apparently to show that all souls are God's, that all punishment is disciplinary, and that at last all will achieve holiness. We present a passage, sent to us, and quoted from memory, by Rev. G. W. Lawrence:

> These grosser regions yield
> Souls thick as blossoms of the vernal field,

Who after death, in relative degree,
Fairer or darker, as their lives may be,
To other worlds are led to learn and strive,
Till to perfection all at last arrive.
This once conceived, the ways of God are plain,
But thy unyielding race in error will remain,
And would, presumptuous, the eternal bind
Either perpetual blessings to bestow,
Or plunge the souls he framed in endless woe.

Nor more nor less, for the Almighty still
Suits to our life the goodness and the ill.

Robert Southey,—A. D. 1774–1843.

The poet laureate of England has given this testimony :

What though at birth we bring with us the seed
Of sin, a mortal taint—in heart and will
Too surely felt, too plainly shown in deed,
Our fatal heritage; yet are we still
The children of the All-Merciful; and ill
They teach, who tell us that from hence must flow
God's wrath, and then his justice to filfull,
Death everlasting, never-ending woe!
O miserable lot of man, if it were so!
Falsely and impiously they teach, who thus
Our Heavenly Father's holy will misread!
In bounty hath the Lord created us,
In love redeemed. From this authentic creed
Let no bewildering sophistry impede
The heart's entire assent, for God is good:
Hold firm this faith, and in whatever need,

Doubt not but thou wilt find thy soul endued
With all-sufficient strength of heavenly fortitude.

In the "Life of Wesley" he refers to a controversy which had taken place between the great champion of Arminianism and the Calvinist, Whitefield. The latter wrote to Wesley:

I am sorry, honored sir, to hear, by many letters, that you seem to own a sinless perfection in this life attainable. I think I cannot answer you better than a venerable minister of these parts answered a Quaker:—"Bring me a man that has really arrived at this, and I will pay his expenses, let him come from whence he will." Besides, dear sir, what a fond conceit is it to cry up perfection, and yet to cry down the doctrine of final perseverance. But this, and many other absurdities, you will run into, because you will not own election; and you will not own election, because you cannot own it without believing in reprobation. What, then, is there in reprobation so horrid?

In the biography, Southey is sufficiently explicit in reference to Calvinism. Taken in connection with the first quotation, it gives us Southey's estimate of that sum of all monstrosities:

That question might have been easily answered. The doctrine implies that an almighty and all-wise Creator has called into existence the greater part of the human race, to the end that, after a short, sinful, and miserable life, they should pass into an eternity of inconceivable torments, it being the pleasure of their Creator that they should not be able to obey his commands, and yet incur the penalty of everlasting damnation for disobedience. In the words of Mr. Wesley, who has stated the case with equal force and truth, "The sum of all this is, one in twenty, suppose, of mankind are elected, nineteen in twenty are reprobated." The elect shall be saved, do what they will; the reprobate shall be damned, do what they can. This is the doctrine of Calvinism, for which diabolism would be a better name; and in the worst and bloodiest idolatry that ever defiled the earth, there is nothing so horrid, so monstrous, so impious as this.

    Here we see
The water at its well-head; clear it is,
Not more transpicuous the invisible air;
Pure as an infant's thoughts; and here to life
And good directed all its uses serve.
The herb grows greener on its brink; sweet flowers
Bend o'er the stream that feeds their freshened roots:
The redbreast loves it for his wintry haunts,
And, when the buds begin to open forth,
Builds near it, with his mate, their brooding nest;
The thirsty stag with widening nostrils there
Invigorated draws his copious draught;
And there amid its flags the wild-boar stands,
Nor suffering wrong nor meditating hurt.
Through woodlands wide and solitary fields
Unsullied thus it holds its bounteous course;
But when it reaches the resorts of men,
The service of the city there defiles
The tainted stream; corrupt and foul it flows
Through loathsome banks and o'er a bed impure,
Till in the sea, the appointed end to which
Through all its way it hastens, 'tis received,
And, losing all pollution, mingles there
In the wide world of waters. So is it
With the great stream of things, if all were seen;
Good the beginning, good the end shall be,
And transitory evil only makes
The good end happier. Ages pass away,
Thrones fall, and nations disappear, and worlds
Grow old and go to wreck; the soul alone

Endures, and what she chooseth for herself,
The arbiter of her own destiny,
That only shall be permanent.

Henry Crabb Robinson says in his Diary, "Mr. Gurney read me some letters from Southey. In one written in 1826, Southey thus expressed himself:"

I cannot believe in an eternity of hell. I hope God will forgive me if I err; but in this matter I cannot say, "Lord, help my unbelief." (See the same opinion in a "Tale of Paraguay," Canto II, verses 15, 16, 17.)

F. E. Schleiermacher.—A. D. 1768–1834.

The great Berlin professor writes:

The figurative language of Christ has led men to accept over against the doctrine of eternal blessedness, that of a state of unabatable misery for those who die out of fellowship with Christ; but this language will be found hardly sufficient for such a conclusion if we examine it more closely. (Matt. xxv: 46; Mark ix: 44; John v: 20.) These passages for one thing can only by very arbitrary treatment be separated from others which of necessity point to something previous. Further, other passages stand over against them which do not allow us to think of a definitive victory of evil over a part of the human race, which rather oblige us to conclude that even before the general resurrection, evil shall be wholly destroyed. (Comp. Matt. xiv: 30-34 and John v: 24-15, I. Cor. xv: 26.) Still less can the idea of an eternal damnation, whether considered in and by itself, or in reference to eternal blessedness, bear close examination. For if one but reflects that by eternal damnation there cannot be understood condemnation to bodily pain and suffering, since, unless human nature is to be wholly destroyed, we cannot think away the mitigating power of habit, and if one further reflects that even the consciousness of being able to bear what is imposed brings with it a certain satisfaction, one will find it impossible to deduce the conception of a pure misery susceptible of no abatement; and so there scarcely remains a bit of firm ground to stand upon. If we suppose the misery to pertain to the soul, and to consist chiefly in the pangs of conscience, then the damned would be much better in damnation than they were in this life, and so would be more miserable because of being better. This we cannot conceive, for even if this were consistent with divine righteousness, still there would be nothing to hinder the self-approbation of the awakened and sensitive conscience from forming a counterbalance to the misery; yea, we cannot conceive that the awakened conscience as a living inward movement should not even produce something good. Should it be said in reply that it is not the sensitiveness of conscience to the contrast between good and evil that is to be regarded as the source of eternal suffering, but solely the thought of despised blessedness: still even this could only be a living thing in so far as the blessedness is at least conceived of in the consciousness, and could only be tormenting in so far as a capability may still exist to take part in that blessed condition. But this capability implies a bettering, and that conception of blessedness would be an enjoyment lessening the misery. Let us consider now eternal damnation in reference to eternal blessedness. It is easy to see that the existence of the latter is incompatible with that of the former. For although the two domains are outwardly quite separate, yet a state of blessedness in itself so elevated is incompatible with a complete ignorance of the misery of others, all the more when the separation itself is the result of a general judgment at which both divisions were present—each aware of the other's presence. If, then, we attribute to the blessed a knowledge of the condition of the damned, this knowledge cannot be conceived as destitute of sympathy. For sympathy, unless the perfecting of our nature is to be retrogressive, must embrace the whole human race, and sympathy for the damned must necessarily trouble blessedness all the more that it will not, like every similar feeling in this life, be tempered by hope.

For however much we may reflect that if damnation is eternal it must be right that it should be so, and that when we see God we shall see also the righteousness of God, such reflection can never destroy sympathy, since even here we rightly require a deeper sympathy for deserved than for undeserved suffering. But if to our future existence there belongs in any form at all the recollection of that previous condition in which some of us were always associated with some of them in ordinary life, then must the sympathy be so much the stronger, as in that space of time there was a period when we were as little renewed as they. For since in God's government of the world all things are inseparably mixed, we shall not be able to hide from ourselves the fact that the arrangements that were so helpful to us were determined by that same world-plan, in which no similar advantages were assigned to them. Our sympathy, therefore, must have this further poignant element which can never be awanting when we become aware of the connection between our benefit and another's injury.

Looked at, then, from either side, there are great difficulties in the way of conceiving the final result of redemption to be, that some shall be partakers of the highest blessedness, but that others, and these according to the common conception the greater part of the human race, shall be lost in irretrievable misery. Therefore we should not hold such a conception, without proof that Christ himself foresaw this issue—proof of such decisive character as we certainly are not in possession of. Hence we may at the least put in an equal claim on behalf of that milder view that through the power of redemption a general restoration of all human souls shall at some time be accomplished.—*Der Christliche Glaube, II. 503.*

Paul Chatfield.

Paul Chatfield, the author of "The Tin Trumpet, or Heads and Tails for the Wise and Waggish, a new

American edition, with alterations and additions, New York: D. Appleton & Co., 1859," says:

FUTURITY—what we are to be, determined by what we have been. An inscrutable mystery, of which we can only guess at a solution, by referring to the past and present. These assure us, by millions of incontestible proofs, that the benevolent Creator sympathizes with our happiness; then he must sympathize more tenderly with our sufferings. To suppose that he would scatter all sorts of delights around us in this evanescent world, and yet doom the great mass of mankind to everlasting anguish in the next, is an irreconcilable contradiction. The earth, upon which we are merely flitting passengers, is everywhere enameled with flowers, equally exquisite for varied beauty and perfume, but useless, except for the purpose of diffusing pleasure; and yet our eternal abode is to be horrent with fire and agony! The best way of combatting the terrors with which superstition has darkened futurity, is to appeal from the unknown to the known—from the unseen to the visible—from imaginary torment to real enjoyment—from the frightfulness and stench of Tophet to the beauty of a tulip, and the fragrance of a rose.

OPTIMISM—a devout conviction that, under the government of a benevolent and all-powerful God, everything conduces ultimately to the best, in the world he has created; and that mankind, the constant objects of his paternal care, are in a perpetual state of improvement and increased happiness. This is a great and consoling principle, the summary of all religion and all philosophy, the reconciler of all misgivings, the source of all comfort and consolation. To believe in it, is to realize its truth, so far as we are individually concerned; and, indeed, it will mainly depend upon ourselves, whether or not everything shall be for the best. Let us cling to the moral of Parnell's "Hermit," rather than suffer our confidence in the divine goodness to be staggered by the farcical exaggerations of Voltaire's "Candide." If the theory of the former be a delusion, it is at least a delightful one; and for my own part,

—*malim cum Platone errare, quam cum aliis recte sentire*—where the error is of so consolatory and elevating a description. An optimist may be wrong, but presumption and religion are in his favor; nor can we directly pronounce anything to be for final evil, until the end of all things has arrived, and the whole scheme of creation is revealed to us. Does not every architect complain of the injustice of criticising a building before it is half finished? Yet who can tell what volume of the creation we are in at present, or what point the structure of our moral fabric has attained? Whilst we are all in a vessel that is sailing under sealed orders, we shall do well to confide implicitly in our government and captain.

Helen Maria Williams.

Crabb Robinson, in his Diary, mentions Helen Maria Williams, the aunt of Athanase Coquerel, as a Universalist. This fact enables us to "read between the lines," and thus interpret her immortal lyric as the author intended it to be understood, "While Thee I Seek, Protecting Power."

H. W. Haber.—A. D. 1773–1854.

In the use of the Scripture argument the triumph is completely and most remarkably on the milder side. [See Coleridge, Wordsworth and Crabb Robinson, in this volume.]

Charles Lamb.—A. D. 1775–1834.

The good and gentle "Elia," the immortal essayist and poet, embodies the popular idea of Satan, derived from Milton:

> Sabbathless Satan! he who his unglad
> Task ever plies, 'mid rotary burnings,
> That round and round incalculably reel,—
> For wrath divine hath made him like a wheel,
> In that red realm, from which are no returnings,
> Where toiling and turmoiling ever and aye,
> He and his thoughts keep pensive working day!

But he thus ignores it:

> Fancy, most licentious on such themes,
> Where decent reverence well had kept her mute,
> Hath o'erstocked hell with devils, and brought down
> By her enormous fablings and mad lies,
> Discredit on the Gospel's serious truths
> And salutary fears. The man of parts,
> Poet, or prose declaimer, on his couch
> Lolling like one indifferent, fabricates
> A heaven of gold, where he, and such as he,
> Their heads encompasséd with crowns, their heels
> With fine wings garlanded, shall tread the stars
> Beneath their feet, heaven's pavement, far removed
> From damnéd spirits, and the torturing cries
> Of men, his brethren, fashioned of the earth
> As he was, nourished with the self-same bread,
> Belike his kindred or companions once,
> Through everlasting ages now divorced,
> In chains and savage torments to repent
> Short years of folly upon earth. Their groans unheard
> In heaven, the saint nor pity feels, nor care
> For those thus sentenced, pity might disturb

> The delicate sense and most divine repose
> Of spirits angelical. Blessed be God,
> The measure of his judgments is not fixed
> By man's erroneous standard. He discerns
> No such inordinate difference and vast
> Betwixt the sinner and the saint, to doom
> Such disproportioned fates.

Mrs. Mary M. Sherwood.—A. D. 1775–1851.

This delightful authoress, in her day the most popular who had ever written, developed the great idea, abundantly. Her works were in all the Sunday schools in England and America, and were acknowledged as the best of books, when the lynx-eyed censors of the church began to see the tracks of heresy. At first they denied the genuineness of the books which held the idea of a final reconciliation, but at length the evidence could not be resisted, and she is now classed with "the sect everywhere spoken against." The "Monk of Cimies," "Henry Milner," "Shanty the Blacksmith," and perhaps others, develop the great truth. Here is a passage from "Henry Milner":

> Lord H—— then proceeded to remark, that there are no means of accounting for the ways of God with man, but by what Scripture in its truth tells us respecting the work of salvation by Christ. "When we do not add to or diminish from the words of Scripture, but take them as they are delivered to us, then immediately such a light bursts upon us that we are no longer perplexed with the dealings of God with man.

Consider only two passages which this moment occur to me:—
'And he is the propitiation for our sins; and not for ours only, but also for the sins of the whole world.' 'But we see Jesus, who was made a little lower than the angels, for the suffering of death, crowned with glory and honor; that he by the grace of God should taste death for every man.' Can words be plainer than these passages? Is it not giving God the lie, then, to doubt his purposes toward man, and to assert, as some do, that he has made creatures to be eternally miserable? Yet," continues Lord H——, "these are subjects of such infinite solemnity, that we cannot contemplate them with too much awe, and ought ever to pray that we may not be permitted to decide lightly upon them, or to be suffered, in the opinions which we adopt respecting them, to lean upon our own understanding."

"I do think so," replied Henry, "we cannot be too cautious when we speak of things of such vast importance. But, sir, if the visible church, and the professors of all descriptions, have made a mistake respecting the extent of the work of salvation, have they not committed a grievous offence against their God and Savior, by substituting vengeance when infinite love only is displayed, and making it appear that either the will or the power of the Redeemer was wanting to complete the work of salvation?"

"If Scripture was not so clear on this point as it is," replied Lord H——, "we ought to put our mouths in the dust and be silent; but even allowing for argument's sake, that the intentions of God toward those who die in a hardened state are doubtful; supposing that the texts on either side are so balanced, as not to admit of decision upon the point, the one party, at least, ought to be as careful as the other in hazarding its opinions. The one party ought to be as much afraid of giving offence by asserting that the misery of the wicked is eternal in the face of such texts as these:—'This is a faithful saying, and worthy of all acceptation, for therefore we both labor and suffer reproach, because we trust in the living God, who is the Savior of all men, especially of them that believe;'—

I repeat, that the one party should at least be equally cautious with the other, and that there is the same reason for silencing one party as another by the plea that they are meddling with things too high for them, and coming to conclusions, which they cannot do, even by their own statements, without forcing some passages and adding words to others not found in the original text."

"You think, my lord, then," said Henry, "that we may sum up all the purposes of God toward man in one word, and that is love; and that all the follies, all the pains, all the sorrow, and even all the offences of man, are permitted for his ultimate good."

"I do," replied Lord H——, "and I am assured that I have not been suffered to expect too much; this is not an error which has ever been charged on a child of God from the beginning of time."

In another passage, referring to a former writer, she says:

The Gospel, by the grace of God, bringeth salvation to all men; but few, in comparison, have seen this, so as cordially to fall in with and confess it, when by all men is to be understood, every individual of the human race. Some, indeed, in every period of the Christian church, have seen and acknowledged this, but by one means or other, this excellency of the Gospel has been hidden from the eyes of the generality of both preachers and hearers. * * *

In "Shanty the Blacksmith" the great truth is fully stated:

"And so," continued the old man, "when it was given me to see and accept this one passage first, in its completeness, all other parts of Scripture seemed to fall at once in their places; and the prophecies, the beautiful prophecies of future peace and joy to the earth, of the destruction of death and of hell, all opened out to me, as being hidden and shut up in Christ—

for Christ is all; and as I desired the treasure, so I was drawn more and more toward him who keeps the treasure, and all this," he would add, "was done for me, through no deserts or deservings of my own; for, till this light was vouchsafed me, I was as other unregenerate men, living only to myself, and for myself; and more than this," he would say, "were it the divine will to withdraw the light, I should turn again to be dead and hard, as iron on the cold anvil." In this way, Shanty often used to talk to Mrs. Margaret, and after a while to Tamar; but the old lady for many years remained incapable of entering so entirely as he could wish, into his views of the sufficiency of the Redeemer. She could not give up entirely her notions of the need of some works, not as evidences of the salvation of an individual, but as means of ensuring that salvation, and accordingly she never met with Shanty for many years, without hinting at this discrepancy in their opinions, which hints seldom failed of bringing forward an argument.

In 1839, she wrote a letter to Rev. Dr. Thom, of Liverpool, Eng., avowing herself a Universalist.

F. W. J. Schelling,—A. D. 1775–1854.

The great metaphysician thus speaks in "Remarks on I. Cor. xv: 24." (Original translation.)

To the Son, then, is Being away from God, alienated from God and the Father, given over, that he may reconcile it again to the Father. He has received Being as away from and unacceptable to the Father, that he may give it back to him again, as Godlike, again acceptable and reconciled to him. This will be completely realized only at the end of the World-time. Then shall Being which was away from God and wholly alienated from him be in the Father.—*Sämmtliche Werke iv: 62.*

Sarah Flower Adams.

"Nearer My God to Thee," is the composition of a Universalist woman. So says Henry Crabb Robinson, her friend, in his famous "Diary."

Walter Savage Landor.—A. D. 1775–1864.

No English writer has ever surpassed Landor for purity, strength and beauty of style. His "Imaginary Conversations" and other publications are classic. He often asserts, and far oftener implies his belief in the final restoration, notably in the conversations between Melancthon and Calvin, and between the emperor of China and his ambassador. He observes:

Our blessed Lord himself in his last hours, ventured to express a wish before his heavenly Father that the bitter cup might pass away from him. I humbly dare to implore that a cup much bitterer may be removed from the great body of mankind; a cup containing the poison of eternal punishment, where agony succeeds to agony, but never death.

"Sometimes I have been ready to believe," says Bocaccio to Petrarca in Landor's "Pentameron," "so far as our holy faith will allow me, that it were better our Lord were nowhere than torturing in his inscrutable wisdom to all eternity so many myriads of us poor devils, the creatures of his hands."

If God's first love was hell making, we might almost wish his affections were as mutable as ours are.

Henry Crabb Robinson,—A. D. 1775–1867.

This English lawyer and *litterateur*, was the intimate friend of Wordsworth, Southey, Lamb, Lady Byron, etc. His "Diary and Correspondence" published in London, and in this country republished by Field, Osgood & Co., in 1869, is full of the most pronounced Universalism on his part, and on that of many of his contemporaries and friends, as Wordsworth, Coleridge, Southey, Lamb, Lady Byron, Helen Maria Williams, Sarah Flower Adams, Clarkson, and others. He says:

> I had with Anthony Robinson a long and serious talk on religion, and on that inexplicable riddle, the origin of evil. He remarked that the amount of pain here justifies the idea of pain hereafter, and so the popular notion of punishment is authorized. But I objected that evil or pain here may be a mean towards an end. So may pain inflicted as a punishment. But endless punishment would be itself an end in a state where no ulterior object could be conceived. Anthony Robinson declared this to be a better answer to the doctrine of eternal punishment than any given by Price or Priestly. Leibnitz, who in terms asserts eternal punishment, explains away the idea by affirming merely that the consequences of sin must be eternal, and that a lower degree of bliss is eternal punishment.
>
> Speaking of Benecke, whom he calls a "most remarkable German," he says his speculation was that every one had taken part in the great rebellion in a former state, and that we were all ultimately to be restored to the divine favor, and then adds, "this doctrine of the final restoration was the redeeming article of his creed."

"I was not aware," says Robinson in a letter to his brother, "that John Wesley had ever said anything so bold as your quoted words, that 'Calvin's God was worse than his devil.'"

Thomas Campbell.—A. D. 1777–1844.

The famous author of the "Pleasures of Hope," seems to have obtained a glimpse of "eternal hope":

> Eternal hope! when yonder spheres sublime,
> Peal'd their first notes to sound the march of Time,
> Thy joyous youth began—but not to fade,—
> When all the sister planets have decay'd;
> When wrapt in fire the realms of ether glow,
> And heaven's last thunder shakes the world below;
> Thou, undismayed, shalt o'er the ruins smile,
> And light thy torch at Nature's funeral pile.

Thomas Moore.—A. D. 1779–1852.

"The Bard of Erin" has uttered the ultimate optimism in many passages, both prose and poetry. In "The Epicurean," one of the most eloquent prose poems in the language, he says:

> Passing, then, in review, the long train of inspired interpreters whose pens and whose tongues were made the echoes of the divine voice, he traced through the events of successive ages, the gradual unfolding of the dark scheme of Providence —darkness without, but all light and glory within. The glimpses of a coming redemption, visible even through the

wrath of heaven; the long series of prophecy through which this hope runs, burning and alive, like a spark along a chain;—the slow and merciful preparation of the hearts of mankind for the great trial of their faith and obedience that was at hand, not only by miracles that appealed to the living, but by prophecies launched into the future to carry conviction to the yet unborn; "through all these glorious and beneficent gradations we may track," said he, "the manifest footsteps of a creator, advancing to his grand ultimate end, the salvation of his creatures."

Here is another passage:

"Such," continued the hermit, "was the mediator, promised through all time, to 'make reconciliation for iniquity,' to change death into life, and bring 'healing on his wings' to a darkened world. Such was the last crowning dispensation of that God of benevolence, in whose hands sin and death are but instruments of everlasting good, and who, bringing all things 'out of darkness into his marvellous light,' proceeds watchfully and unchangingly to the great, final object of his providence, the restoration of the whole human race to purity and happiness!"

In the Appendix to the work is the following note:

"The restoration of the whole human race to purity and happiness." This benevolent doctrine—which not only goes far to solve the great problem of moral and physical evil, but which would, if received more generally, tend to soften the spirit of uncharitableness, so fatally prevalent among Christian sects—was maintained by that great light of the early church, Origen, and has not wanted supporters among more modern theologians. That Tillotson was inclined to the opinion, appears from his sermon, preached before the queen. Paley is supposed to have held the same amiable doctrine; and Newton (the author of the work on "Prophecies") is also among the supporters of it. For a full account of the arguments in favor of this opinion, derived both from reason, and the express language of Scripture, see Dr. Southwood Smith's very interesting work, "On the Divine Government."

Moore's poetry is more explicit than his prose. In the "Loves of the Angels," the poet proceeds to describe an angel as standing and breathing:

> Inwardly a voiceless prayer,
> Unheard by all but Mercy's ear,
> And which if Mercy did not hear,—
> Oh, God would not be what this bright
> And glorious universe of his,—
> This world of beauty, Gospel light
> And endless love, proclaims he is!

This is the poetry of Universalism. What, then, shall we say of this?

> But not alone the wonders found,
>   Thro' Nature's realm—the unveiled, material,
> Visible glories that hung round,
>   Like lights, through her enchanted ground—
>   But whatsoe'er unseen, etherial,
> Dwells far away from human sense,
> Wrapped in its own intelligence,—
> The mystery of that Fountain Head,
>   From which all vital spirit runs,
> All breath of life, where'er 'tis shed,
>   Through men or angels, flowers or suns—
> The workings of the Almighty Mind,
> When first o'er chaos he designed
> The outlines of this world; and through
>   That spread of darkness—like the bow,
> Called out of rain-clouds, hue by hue,
>   Saw the grand, gradual picture grow!—
> The covenant with human kind,
>   Which God has made—the chains of Fate,
> He round himself and them hath twined,

'Till his high task he consummate—
'Till good from evil, love from hate,
  Shall be worked out through sin and pain
And Fate shall loose her iron chain,
And all be free, be bright again.

Horace Smith.—A. D. 1779–1849.

Horace and James—the brothers Smith—are among those who testify against error:

Religions—from the soul deriving breath,—
  Should know no death;
Yet do they perish, mingling their remains
  With fallen fanes.
Creeds, canons, dogmas, councils, are the wrecked
And mouldering masonry of intellect.

Apis, Osiris, paramount of yore
  On Egypt's shore,—
Woden amd Thor, through the wide North adored,
  With blood outpoured,—
Jove, and the multiform divinities
To whom the Pagan nations bowed their knees,—

Lo! they are cast aside, dethroned, forlorn,
  Defaced, out-worn,
Like the world's childish dolls, which but insult
  Its age adult,
Or prostrate scarecrows, on whose rags we tread
With scorn proportioned to our former dread.

Is there no compass, then, by which to steer
  This erring sphere?
No tie that may indissolubly bind
  To God, mankind?

No code that may defy Time's sharpest tooth?
No fixed, immutable, unerring truth?
There is! there is! One primitive and sure,
    Religion pure,
Unchanged in spirit, though its forms and codes
    Wear myriad modes,
Contains all creeds within its mighty span:
The love of God displayed in love of man.
This is the Christian's faith when rightly read;
    Oh! may it spread,
Till earth redeemed from every hateful leaven
    Makes peace with heaven;
Below one blesséd brotherhood of love,
One Father—worshiped with one voice—above!

    Father and God! whose love and might
    To every sense are blazoned bright
On the vast three-leaved Bible—earth—sea—sky,
    Pardon th' impugners of thy laws,
    Expand their hearts, and give them cause
To bless th' exhaustless grace they now deny.

The brothers, James and Horace Smith, in "Rejected Addresses," have said:

The present and the past assure us, by millions of incontestable proofs, that the benevolent Creator sympathizes with our happiness; then he must sympathize more tenderly with our sufferings. To suppose he would scatter all sorts of delights around us in this evanescent world, and yet doom the great mass of mankind to everlasting anguish in the next, is an irreconcilable contradiction.

William Ellery Channing.—A. D. 1780–1842.

The great Unitarian accepted and announced principles wholly at war with endless evil, and that logically result in universal salvation, but he nowhere, that we remember, explicitly announces that great truth on which the Unitarians are now substantially agreed. He declares:

> We consider the errors which relate to Christ's person as of little or no importance compared with the error of those who teach that God brings us into life wholly depraved and wholly helpless, that he leaves multitudes without that aid which is indispensably necessary to their repentance, and then plunges them into everlasting burnings and unspeakable torture for not repenting. This we consider as one of the most injurious errors which ever darkened the Christian world, and none will pretend that we have anything to fear from exposing this error to our people.

Rev. L. Carpenter, LL.D.—A. D. 1780–1840.

Dr. Lant Carpenter, eminent among English Unitarians, observes:

> As nothing approaching to the feelings of vindictive vengeance can have place in the Divine mind, and as the best notions of punishment we are able to form, require us to keep in view the reformation of the offender,—to me it appears necessary to follow, not only from the paternal, but even from the judicial and rectorial character of God, that when suffering has done its work, and the deep stains of guilt have been removed, as by fire, suffering will be no longer required. When unholy desires, malignant passions, sordid selfishness, causeless impiety and neglect of religion have been eradicated, and the once wicked being looks up with humble submission to him whose wisdom and goodness have appointed his unmingled, unalleviated anguish, with humble acknowledgment that his

ways are good as well as righteous, and with freedom from those bonds which made misery his home,—what Scriptural representation of God forbids the belief that the Father of spirits will thenceforwards commence that progress in holiness and consequent happiness, to which through his infinite mercy, he had before raised myriads of his frail children of mortality? That, by his almighty power and infinite wisdom, he can thus eradicate guilt and misery, who can doubt? and that he will do it, who can doubt, unless he have himself told us that he will not?

Those views of the divine character to which I refer, inevitably lead to the belief that there will be a time when all the rational creatures of God will have been purified from every pollution, and made fit for holiness and consequently, for happiness. Most of us believe that a period will come to each individual when punishment shall have done its work, when the awful sufferings with which the Gospel threatens the impenitent and disobedient, will have humbled the stubborn, purified the polluted, and eradicated the malignity, impiety, hypocrisy, and every evil disposition;—that a period will come (which it may be the unspeakable bliss of those who enter the joy of their Lord, to accelerate, which, at least, it will be their delight to anticipate), when he "who must reign till he hath put all enemies under his feet," "shall have put down all rule and all authority and power." "The last enemy, Death, shall be destroyed." "Every tongue shall confess that Jesus Christ is Lord, to the glory of God the Father," who wills that all men should be saved and come to the knowledge of the truth—that truth which sanctifies the heart, that knowledge which is "life eternal," and "God shall be all in all."

The Abbe La Mennais,—A. D. 1782–1854.

"The People's Own Book," by F. De La Mennais, is translated from the French by Nathaniel Greene,

Boston, 1840. The original is "Le Livre du Peuple," by Abbe F. De La Mennais.

If suffering was eternal, the malady of which it was the punishment would be so, also, consequently moral evil; and that evil eternal, would constitute, in opposition to the good principle, the evil principle of the dualistic systems, we should be compelled to conceive of it as independent, as subsisting by itself, or to admit something still more monstrous, for if it was not self-existent, if it depended on the divine will, God would be the direct author of evil. * * *

We, ourselves, constitute our hell, our purgatory, our heaven, according to the state of the soul, on which necessarily depends the state of the body, and however low may be that point from which they start, all souls tend towards heaven, and all will arrive there with more or less labor, because God draws all to himself, because God is love, and love is stronger than death.

People, guard against incarnating your sublime hopes in the dust which you trample under your feet. During your short earthly pilgrimage you are surrounded but by phantoms, by vain shadows; the realities are invisible to you, the eye of flesh cannot seize them, but God, who has given to man his invincible desire for them, has also planted in his heart the infallible presentiment of their attainment.

Apart from the mortal appendages with which it has been confounded, Christianity is the first and last law of humanity; for beside God nothing can be proposed as the goal of man; nor is there any other way of approaching God, any other means of becoming united with him, than by love; nor will this great commandment of love ever be exhausted, either upon earth, where its effect will be to form of all individuals, all families, all people, one sole unity, that of the human race,—or in heaven, where it will find its accomplishment in the constantly more and more perfect union of all creatures with the creator. And thus what Christ said is now and ever will be true:—"Come unto me, all you that labor and are heavy laden, and I will give you rest." And one day all will come unto him, and that day is not distant; already it dawns in the bosom of futurity. We now walk as by a feeble twilight, when the radiant star shall rise, the world, deluged with light, and feeling within itself, with the revival of hope, the revival also of faith and love, shall salute it with songs of joy.

Washington Irving.—A. D. 1783–1859.

The entire spirit of Irving's cheerful works is the spirit of our faith. Rev. I. D. Williamson, D. D., relates in the *Herald and Era*, that on a voyage across the Atlantic, in April, 1842, in the ship Independence, he preached a sermon from the text, "As many as I love I rebuke and chasten," a thoroughly Universalistic discourse, since published in Dr. Williamson's volume, "Endless Misery Refuted." At its close Mr. Irving took Dr. Williamson by the hand, and said:

> I thank you, sir, for that sermon. There was more of sound sense in it than I often hear in a discourse. That is the doctrine I believe and want to practice.

Bernard Barton.—A. D. 1784–1849.

The genial Quaker poet denies that "too late" will ever be heard in heaven.

> Bitter the anguish with these two words blended,
> For those contemplating their hopeless lot,

Who find life's Summer past,—its harvest ended,
  And Winter nigh, while they are gathered not.

Yet do thou, Lord, by thy supreme conviction,
  Give them to feel that, though their sins are great,
Thy love and mercy own not our restriction,
  But that with thee, it never is too late!

Leigh Hunt.—A. D. 1784–1859.

One of the most voluminous and elegant of the poetical and prose writers of England has exerted a vast influence in favor of the belief in a world's salvation. In a review of the writings of Hannah More, he says:

It is time for philosophy and true religion to know one another, and not hesitate to follow the most influential truths into their consequences. If "a small unkindness is a great offence," what would Miss Hannah More have said to the infliction of eternal punishment? Or are God and his ways eternally to be represented as something so different from the best attributes of humanity, that the wonder must be, how humanity can survive in spite of the mistake? The truth is, that the circulation of Miss More's own blood was a better thing than all her doctrines put together; and luckily it is a much more universal inheritance. The heart of man is continually sweeping away the errors he gets into his brain.

Elsewhere he says:

Heaven and earth should petition to be abolished, rather than one such monstrosity (a victim of infinite suffering) should exist;—it is the absurdest, as well as the most impious of all fears.

He is most explicit in his autobiography, declaring:

My father, though a clergyman of the Established Church, had settled, as well as my mother, into a Christian of the Universalist persuasion, which believes in the final restoration of all things. It was hence that I learned the impiety (as I have expressed it,) of the doctrine of eternal punishment. In the present day, a sense of impiety, in some way or other, whether of doubt or sophistication, is the secret feeling of nine-tenths of all churches; and every church will discover, before long, that it must rid itself of the doctrine, if it would not cease to exist. Love is the only creed destined to survive all others.

* * * * * * * *

This palpable revelation, then, of God, which is called the universe, contains no evidence whatsoever of the thing called eternal punishment; and why should I admit any assertion of it that is not at all palpable? If an angel were to tell me to believe in eternal punishment I would not do it; for it would better become me to believe the angel a delusion, than God monstrous; and we make him monstrous when we make him the author of eternal punishment, though we have not the courage to think so. For God's sake, let us have piety enough to believe him better.

Such are the doctrines, and such only, accompanied by expositions of the beauties and wonders by God's great book of the universe, which will be preached in the temples of the earth, including those of our beloved country, England, its beautiful old ivied turrets and their green neighborhoods, then, for the first time, thoroughly uncontradicted and heavenly; with not a sound in them more terrible than the stormy yet sweet organ, analogous to the beneficent winds and tempests; and no thought of here or hereafter, that can disturb the quiet aspect of the graves, or the welcome of the new-born darling.

And that such a consummation may come, slowly and surely, without intermission in its advance, and with not an injury to a living soul, will be the last prayer, as it must needs be among the latest words, of the author of this book. * * * *

Leigh Hunt delights to bear his testimony in behalf of the truth. Universalism is with him a definite theory. And the cheerful, and moral, and sublime sentiments his works inculcate, are natural results. Rev. A. C. Thomas relates a most interesting interview with the venerable man, enjoyed in the year 1853. The evangelist had presented the poet with a copy of his "Autobiography." "Oh, what pleasure would this have imparted to my father and my mother!" was the recorded outpouring of the heart of Leigh Hunt.

"It was worth a long journey to spend an evening with Leigh Hunt. So genial in his spirit, so kindly in his every thought, so completely is he imbued with the spirit of Universalism, that you feel yourself in conversation with 'Abou Ben Adhem.' I mentioned his poem with that title, and told him how repeatedly it had been quoted and printed, until it had become a household word in all circles of the United States. He was greatly pleased with the information, not so much, he said, because he had put the sentiment into an acceptable shape (though he was not indifferent to his reputation as an author), as because the sentiment itself had found a sympathetic answer so generally in the human heart despite the hard training of sectarian creeds. 'The heart,' he continued, 'is, after all, the final judge of religious truth, and it is a melancholy thing that so many Christian people, who have personally been redeemed from barbarism, should have brought along with them the gods of barbarism!'

"We spoke of Dante. 'In my early life,' said he, 'I wrote a series of papers on the Italian poets. While making a prose version of Dante's "Hell," I could but love the real spirit of the man, while I abhorred the thoughts he invested with the attractions of poesy. And I felt persuaded that he must have had an angel for his mother and a devil for his father.'"

> Death is a road our dearest friends have gone;
> Why, with such leaders, fear to say "Lead on"?
> Its gate repels, lest it too soon be tried;
> But turns in balm on the immortal side.
> Mothers have passed it; fathers; children; men,
> Whose like we look not to behold again;
> Women, that smiled away their loving breath;—
> Soft is the traveling on the road of Death!
>
> But Guilt has passed it! Men not fit to die!
> Oh, hush—for he that made us all, is by!
> Human were all; all men; all born of mothers;
> All our own selves, in the worn shape of others;
> Our used and oh! be sure, not to be ill-used brothers!

"Abou Ben Adhem" breathes the very soul of the Universalist faith.

> Abou Ben Adhem (may his tribe increase!)
> Awoke one night from a deep dream of peace,
> And saw, within the moonlight of his room,
> Making it rich, and like a lily in bloom,
> An angel, writing in a book of gold;
> Exceeding peace had made Ben Adhem bold;

And to the presence in the room he said,
"What writest thou?" The vision raised his head,
And, with a look made of all sweet accord,
Answered, "The names of those who love the Lord."
"And is mine one?" said Abou. "Nay, not so,"
Replied the angel. Abou spake more low,
But cheerily still; and said, "I pray thee, then,
Write me as one that loves his fellow men."
The angel wrote and vanished. The next night
It came again with a great wakening light,
And showed the names whom love of God had blessed,
And lo! Ben Adhem's name led all the rest!

Thomas De Quincey.—A. D. 1785-1859.

In a treatise on the æonian words, De Quincey says:

If it be an excess of blindness which can overlook the *aionian* differences amongst even neutral entities, much deeper is that blindness which overlooks the separate tendencies of things evil and things good. Naturally, all evil is fugitive, and allied to death. I, separately, speaking for myself only, profoundly believe that the Scriptures ascribe absolute eternity to one sole being, viz:—to God—and derivatively to all others according to the interest which they can plead in God's favor. Having anchorage in God, innumerable entities may possibly be admitted to a participation in divine *aion*. But what interest in the favor of God can belong to falsehood, to malignity, to impurity? To invest them with *aionian* privileges, is, in effect, and by its results, to distrust and to insult the Deity. Evil would not be evil, if it had that power of self-subsistence which is imputed to it in supposing its *aionian* life to be co-eternal with that which crowns and glorifies the good.

John Pierpont.—A. D. 1785–1866.

Pierpont's exquisite poem," He is Not There," expresses the full measure of faith, and is as hostile to the idea of a partial salvation, as was the life of its author. It concludes:

> Yes, we all live to God;
> Father, thy chastening rod
> So help us thine afflicted ones, to bear,
> That, in the spirit land,
> Meeting at thy right hand,
> 'Twill be our heaven to find that he is there.

His celebrated hymn on Universal worship ends in these fitting words:

> Oh, thou, to whom, in ancient time,
> The lyre of prophet bards was strung,
> To thee at last in every clime,
> Shall temples rise, and praise be sung.

John Wilson.—A. D. 1785–1844.

"Kit North" has given the following testimonies:

> Oh! how oft
> In seasons of depression,—when the lamp
> Of life burned dim, and all unpleasing thoughts
> Subdued the proud aspirings of the soul,—
> When doubts and fears withheld the timid eye
> From scanning scenes to come, and a deep sense
> Of human frailty turned the past to pain,—
> How oft have I remembered that a world

Of glory lay around me,—that a source
Of lofty solace lay in every star;
And that no being need behold the sun
And grieve, that knew who hung him in the sky!
Thus unperceived I woke from heavy grief
To airy joy; and seeing that the mind
Of man, though still the image of his God,
Leaned by his will on various happiness,
I felt that all was good; that faculties
Though low, might constitute, if rightly used,
True wisdom, and when man hath here attained
The purpose of his being, he will sit
Near Mercy's throne, whether his course hath been
Prone on the earth's dim sphere, or, as with wing
Of viewless eagle round the central blaze.

    Like children for some bauble fair
      That weep themselves to rest,
    We part with life—awake! and there
      The jewel in our breast!

Professor Espy.—A. D. 1785.

In 1842, Prof. Espy, who was then called by way of derision, the "Storm King," was invited to lecture before the "Baltimore Murray Institute," on his favorite theory, which was the origin of the present signal service, etc., etc. A member of the Universalist parish was about to publish a portrait of the pastor of the church, and submitted the selection of the motto to Prof. Espy, giving him the choice of two passages of Scripture; one was, "As in Adam all die, even so in Christ shall all be made alive"; the other, "Have we not all one Father?" The professor remarked:

Both are good, but "Have we not all one Father?" is infinitely the better. It is a question which will induce men to think, and if men will only think they will very soon discard the idea of eternal punishment. If one Father, of course it follows one origin, and one destiny for all; I have not been a close student of the Bible, but of one thing I feel quite sure, the Universalists have both reason and philosophy on their side.

"Thus spoke Mr. Espy to me in 1842." So writes Rev. James Shrigley.

Allan Cunningham.—A. D. 1785–1842.

Besides mentioning the fact that Burns was a Universalist, Cunningham indicates his love for the doctrine, in his "Life and Writings of Burns," and in his novel, "Roldau," a copy of which I have been unable to consult.

John Young, LL.D.—A. D. 1788–1856.

This eloquent author of "The Christ of History," and "The Creator and the Creation," (Strahan & Co., London,) says in the preface to the third edition, that in the first issue, in 1857, he had not undertaken a solution of the mystery of evil, but that now, in 1870, he can see further. He adds:

It has seemed to me that a richer and more comprehensive meaning than I once was able to perceive lies in these apostolic words, "It pleased the Father that in him (Christ) should all fulness dwell, and * * * by him (Christ) to reconcile all things unto himself, by him I say, whether they be things on earth, or things in heaven" (Col. i: 19, 20). These words clearly convey that Christ is the chosen Redeemer of the whole universe of being. They teach that the reconciliation and restoration to God of the entire creation, throughout the eternal ages, was the grand end of our Lord's life and death and reign, the end of all the vast, complicated, and seemingly inexplicable movements of earthly Providence, and of all the sacred dispensations, economies and ministries of time. The conception is full of rapture, and it is as sanctifying as it is grand. Every pious soul could but exult in the belief (were it shown to be Scriptural, consistent and rational), that God-in-Christ shall yet reign over an entire, regenerated, holy and happy universe.

After quoting John iii: 17, xii: 32; Isa. xlv: 22; Rom. v: 18, 19, xii: 25; I. Cor. xv: 22; I. Tim. ii: 4, and iv: 10 to prove the doctrine of universal salvation Scriptural, he says:

Independently of the Scriptural evidence, there are two great principles, in which the belief of universal salvation is firmly grounded. First, the absolute inpreventability of moral evil, in free, finite beings. God alone is infallible and immutable, because he alone is self-existent and eternal. All finite beings, in the finity of their nature, which neither they nor their Maker could change, are fallible, and have actually fallen either as individuals or as races. Second, it is inconceivable, because it would uproot our deepest moral convictions and principles, that the infinitely loving, pure and blessed God could create a single being, foreknowing, and above all fore-ordaining, that that being should exist in eternal sin, the thing which he infinitely abhors, even if no eternal misery were entailed by it; much more when eternal sin must be also eternal misery.

To my co-religionists of the evangelical school, I humbly commend a conclusion, to which none of them can be more sternly averse than I once was, but which I now believe to be full of glory to the ever blessed Redeemer and to the great Father of all souls. (P. 213.) The solution of the confusions and troubles and vices of time, lies in the relation of time to eternity, and in the settled faith that the Great Father is ever doing the very best which is possible, for each and for all, even now, and that at last the Almighty Maker shall be the Almighty Redeemer and Restorer of all souls.

On one point it is impossible to feel the least hesitation; eternal punishment in the sense of conscious suffering, even in a single instance, is inconceivable and unendurable by any sound and sane conscience. With great reverence I venture to express the conviction that if the Great Being foreknew that even this eternal torpor, but much more that eternal misery, conscious suffering, would be the doom even of a single creature, it is incredible that he should have given existence to that creature.

This work is warmly commended by Sir Wm. Hamilton.

Anonymous.

In the *Philadelphian Magazine* for 1788 (London), these quaint words are printed; they are said to have been written by a blind girl:

> Could we with ink the ocean fill,
>   Were the whole earth of parchment made,
> Were every single stick a quill,
>   And every man a scribe by trade,
>   To write the love
>   Of God above,
> Would drain the ocean dry,
>   Nor could the scroll
>   Contain the whole,
> Though stretched from sky to sky.

Thomas Erskine, of Linlathen.—1788–1870.

Erskine was a country gentleman of large wealth, educated originally for the bar, but who never practiced, and the writer of several theological works of marked ability. Dr. Chalmers said of one of them, "The Unconditional Freeness of the Gospel," that it was "one of the most delightful books ever written." Erskine was a pronounced Universalist, and many passages in his books breathe the spirit and teachings of our faith.

He is mentioned by Dean Stanley in his "Lectures on the History of the Church of Scotland." See also "Contemporary Review," of 1878, Vol. XXXII, p. 457, "Present Day Papers," "Letters of Thomas Erskine," by Dr. Hanna, "Contemporary Review," May, 1870. Some of the works which he published, are:—"The Unconditional Freeness of the Gospel," "The Purpose of God in Creation," "An Essay on

Faith," "The Brazen Serpent," "Evidences of Revealed Religion." In a letter to Mr. Craig, author of a work called "Final Salvation," Mr. Erskine writes:

> I believe that the love and righteousness and justice of God, mean exactly the same thing, viz:—A desire to bring his whole moral creation into a participation of his own character, and his own blessedness. He has made us capable of this, and he will not cease from using the best means for accomplishing it in us all. When I think of God making a creature of such capacities, it seems to me almost blasphemous to suppose that he will throw it from him into everlasting darkness because it has resisted his gracious purposes toward it for the natural period of human life. No; he who waited so long for the formation of a piece of old red sandstone, will surely wait with much long-suffering for the perfecting of a human spirit.

In another letter to the same, he says:

> I cannot believe that any human being can be beyond the reach of God's grace, and the sanctifying power of his spirit. And if all are within his reach, is it possible to suppose that he will allow any to remain unsanctified? Is not the love revealed in Jesus Christ a love unlimited, unbounded, which will not leave undone anything which love could desire? It was surely nothing else than the complete and universal triumph of that love which Paul was contemplating when he cried out, "Oh, the depth of the riches both of the wisdom and knowledge of God!"

In a letter to Bishop Argyl he writes:

> I believe that God's purpose in my being is to teach me to receive himself, his own spirit, nature, character, into me; and I believe he has the same purpose for all spiritual beings. How long it may be before the end is attained, I don't attempt to conjecture; but of this I am sure, that his search after the lost sheep will not cease until he has found it. I believe that God's purpose in creating spiritual beings, is to educate them,

that they cannot be made good in the full sense of the word, and therefore, it is a great mistake to call our present state a state of probation, as if we were here on trial. This idea gives a wrong interpretation to conscience; it makes us feel as if we were continually standing before a judgment seat, instead of being in our Father's school.—*Present Day Papers, p. 35.*

The blessed hope that you and I cherish for the ultimate salvation of all, is, I think, fully borne out by distinct, unequivocal declarations in the Scriptures. (Romans, chaps. v and xi.) But the spirit of the whole Scripture, notwithstanding apparent superficial contradictions, is all in the same direction. The restitution of all things is the bright goal before us to animate exertion, whilst it gives the continual assurance that it is only through holiness that it can be reached. The consent of the mind to remain in suspense on such a point because of any supposed uncertainty in the word *aiōnios*, seems to me a sad phenomenon. "Be not overcome of evil, but overcome evil with good," ought, I think, to decide the question; it is the character of God. He is love, and created men to be partakers in his own holiness, and will he be overcome of evil?—*Present Day Papers, p. 40.*

One of his friends wrote, "Everything in you reminds me of God."

Dr. T. Southwood Smith.—A. D. 1788–1861.

Toward the close of his "Illustrations of the Divine Government," this celebrated author writes:

A firm persuasion that our Creator is possessed of every possible excellence, that he is our constant and best friend, that we are entirely at his merciful disposal, that he is conducting us, and all our brethren of mankind, by the wisest means, to the highest happiness, and that the natural and moral disorders which afflict us are the instruments by which he will eventually establish the universal and eternal reign of purity and bliss, cannot but tend to expand the heart, to cherish the benevolent affections, to soften the manners, and unite the whole human race in the tenderest bands of friendship and affection. Were it right to judge of the general effect which the frequent and serious contemplation of these sublime and cheering truths would have on the mind, by the feeling of which he who has made this humble attempt to illustrate and establish them, has been conscious while engaged in the pleasing task, with sincerity he might say, that it would be highly favorable to benevolence and to happiness. A more ardent love of the Supreme Being, a purer and warmer attachment to his fellow creatures, a more anxious desire to promote the attainment of genuine excellence, both in himself and others, has glowed in his heart while meditating on these delightful subjects. * * * And may the anticipation of the universal and everlasting reign of Purity and Happiness hasten his (the reader's) own attainment of both!

Lord Byron.—A. D. 1788–1824.

Dr. Kennedy, a Calvinistic Christian, in his conversations with Byron, represents him as speaking in the loftiest terms of that powerful defence of Universalism, T. Southwood Smith's "Divine Government," saying, among other things, that it contained the only views which could sustain Christianity against infidelity. In one of his letters he rebukes those who deride reason, and insist on blind belief. Indeed, none can read the words of the noble poet, without believing him to be disgusted with the miserable religion of his day, and longing for a realization of that, of which, in his inspired moments, he caught glimpses, and whose mingling harmonies broke in wonderful angel-cadence on his ears, in the times of his communion with the Spirit of Beauty. Byron had passed years in sin, but he never ascertained the alleged fact that sin hardens the heart of man to such a degree, that, although it is unpleasant at first, it becomes desirable. He found, in his own fearful experience, that

> The mind which is immortal, makes itself
> Requital for its good or evil thoughts,—
> Is its own origin of ill and end—
> And its own place and time.

So, also, he says:

> Oh, just God!
> Thy hell is not hereafter!

He satirically says:

> I know this is unpopular; I know
> It is blasphemous; I know one may be damn'd
> For hoping no one else may e'er be so.

When in Switzerland, he seized the imagery presented to his eye and described it as

> White and sulphury,
> Like foam from the roused ocean of deep hell,
> Whose every wave breaks on a living shore,
> Heaped with the damned like pebbles.

But at other times, when the problem of existence demanded a solution, he broke out into a declaration of the future, seldom surpassed:

> The eternal will
> Shall deign to expound this dream
> Of good and evil, and redeem
> Unto himself all times, all things,
> And gathered under his Almighty wings
> Abolish hell!
> And to the expiated earth,
> Restore the beauty of her birth,
> Her Eden in an endless paradise,—
> Where man no more can fall, as once he fell,
> And even the very demons shall do well!

We are far from quoting him as an example, but he was one of the gifted of earth, and we are glad to know that at times he could look so far into the infinite future. Often did the beauty of the Eden-land of truth open to his entranced vision. Those glimpses he has revealed to us.

Lady Byron.

The wife of the great poet is very explicit. In a letter to Henry Crabb Robinson—see his "Letters," Vol. II, p. 444,—she writes:

> I must confess to intolerance of opinion as to these two points,—eternal evil in any form, and (included in it), eternal suffering. To believe in these would take away my God, who is all-loving.

Sir James Stephen, K. C. B.—A. D. 1789-1859.

This eminent essayist, though an ardent defender of the Episcopal church, is one of the many thousands of her children who revolt from the dogma of endless hell torments. He tells us that the true Catholic belief and life are, God is Light, and God is Love. He speaks of the progress of the mythical system of Strauss, and then says:

The real, though often unavowed, ground of the doubts which are thus overclouding the spirits of so many of the nominal disciples of Christ, is the hopeless dejection with which they contemplate that part of the Christian scheme which is supposed to consign the vast majority of our race to a future state, in which woe, inconceivable in amount, is also eternal in duration. From this doctrine the hearts of most men turn aside, not only with an instinctive horror, but with an invincible incredulity; of those who believe that it really proceeded from the lips of Christ himself, many are sorely tempted by it either to doubt the divine authority of any of his words, or to destroy their meaning by conjectural evasions of their force.

With the exception of one dubious expression in the Book of Daniel, the Old Testament is entirely silent on the subject of the eternity of future punishment. The same thing is true of a very large majority of the books of the New Testament.

In reference to Matthew xxv: 46, he says:

No human being knows, or ever can know what were the very words which thus fell from the lips of Christ. They were spoken in a dialect of the Syro-Chaldaic. No one even knows with any certainty whether our extant Greek version of them proceeded from the pen of St. Matthew. On the hypothesis adopted by many high critical authorities, we must believe the contrary. Assuming, however, that the hand of an inspired writer did trace the very words *eis kolasin aiōnion* it will yet not necessarily follow that either of those words is a precise equivalent for the original which it represents, because for terms so abstract, perfectly precise equivalents can seldom, if ever, be found in languages so essentially dissimilar as the Syro-Chaldaic and Greek.

On the supposition, however, that Christ uttered the exact words, he says:

They might be rendered with literal accuracy "life-long punishment."

He thinks Christians should lean toward that interpretation which harmonizes with infinite love, and adds:

The angel who descended from heaven and proclaimed to the shepherds the incarnation of the Redeemer, announced himself as the herald "of good tidings of great joy which should be to all people." But if it be indeed true that he who was thus made incarnate, proclaimed an eternity of unutterable woe to the vast majority of those, who, from generation to generation throng our streets, our marts, and our churches, how shall we reconcile the angelic announcement with this awful proclamation? The Bible teaches us that Christ came into the world to bruise the serpent's head, to destroy the works of the devil, and to establish the kingdom of God; and Christ himself declared that he "saw Satan like lightning fall from heaven." Is it reasonable to accept any construction of the other words of Christ, which would seem to ascribe to the spirit of evil an eternal triumph over the spirit of good in the persons of the vast majority of the race whom he lived and died to redeem?

The Edinburgh Review.

The following definition of optimism is from the *Edinburgh Review*, and was perhaps written by the same brilliant essayist as the foregoing:

It is a devout conviction, that, under the government of a benevolent and all-powerful God, everything conduces ultimately to the best in the world he has created, and that mankind, the constant objects of his paternal care, are in a perpetual state of improvement and increased happiness. This is a great and consoling fact, the summary of all religion and all philosophy, the reconciler of all misgivings, and the source of all comfort and consolation.

Johann A. W. Neander.—A. D. 1789–1850.

Neander thinks that the apostolic declaration of universal confession of allegiance to Christ denotes the final salvation of all. He says:

The doctrine of such a universal restitution would not stand in contradiction to the doctrine of eternal punishment, as it appears in the Gospels; for although those who are hardened in wickedness are to expect endless unhappiness, yet a secret decree of the Divine compassion is not necessarily excluded, by virtue of which, through the wisdom of God revealing itself in the discipline of free agents, they will be led to a free appropriation of redemption.

Thomas Carlyle.—A. D. 1790.

In a letter to the *Edinburgh Scotsman*, 1848, September, Carlyle says:

The best philosophy teaches us that the very consequences (not to speak of the penalties at all) of evil actions die away and become abolished long before eternity ends; that it is only the consequences of good actions that are eternal—for these are in harmony with the laws of this universe, and add themselves to it, and coöperate with it forever, while all that is in disharmony with it must necessarily be without continuance, and soon fall dead—as perhaps you have heard in the sound of a Scottish psalm amid the mountains; the true notes alone support one another, all following the one true rule; the false notes each following its different false rule, quickly destroy one another, and the psalm, which was discordant enough near at hand, is a perfect melody when heard from afar.

H. H. Milman.—A. D. 1791–1868.

Dean Milman says in his "History of Latin Christianity," Vol. VIII, p. 225:

Purgatory, possible with St. Augustine, probable with Gregory the Great, grew up, I am persuaded (its growth is singularly indistinct and untraceable), out of the mercy and modesty of the priesthood. To the eternity of hell torments there is and ever must be—notwithstanding the peremptory decrees of dogmatic theology, and the reverential dread of so many religious minds of tampering with what seems to be the language of the New Testament—a tacit repugnance.

Percy Bysshe Shelley.—A. D. 1792–1822.

This child of genius, on whose name the accusation of infidelity has rested, was far from being the scoffer he has been called. He heartily detested the distorted caricature of Deity in human creeds, and his anathemas on superstition and false religion have been misconstrued by zealots and bigots, and Shelley has been called an infidel. He was well worthy to be called a Christian. Here are extracts from his worst poem—"Queen Mab,"—and we say, as we read, "If this be infidelity, let us have the world full of it!"

He describes what he despises:

> God, hell and heaven,
> A vengeful, pitiless and almighty fiend,
> Whose mercy is a nickname for the rage
> Of tameless tigers hungering for blood.
> Hell, a red gulf of everlasting fire,
> Where poisonous and undying worms prolong
> Eternal misery to those hapless slaves,
> Whose life has been a penance for its crimes,
> And heaven a meed for those who dare belie
> Their human nature, quake, believe, and cringe,
> Before the mockeries of earthly power!

True, every word of it; a correct description of popular error, as is this:

> Twin-sister of Religion, Selfishness!
> Not of the true, but of the false;—that
> Religion . . . . . prolific fiend,
> Who peopled earth with demons, hell with men,
> And heaven with slaves!

But because he hated such a religion, had he no hopes for the future? These are the thoughts which comforted his spirit:

> All tend to perfect happiness, and urge
> The restless wheels of being on their way

> Whose flashing spokes, instinct with infinite life,
> Bicker and burn to gain their destined goal;
> For birth but wakes the spirit to the sense
> Of outward shows, whose unexperienced shape
> New modes of passion to its frame may lend;
> Life is its state of action, and the store
> Of all events is aggregated there,
> That variegate the eternal universe;
> Death is a gate of dreariness and gloom,
> That leads to azure isles and beaming skies,
> And happy regions of eternal hope.

Says James Freeman Clarke:

Shelley thought himself an atheist because he refused to believe in the God of Calvin, but he worshiped God as the Spirit of Intellectual Beauty. He sang a hymn to this spirit, calling it "The Awful Shadow of an Unseen Power"; and says that, amid doubt and change, "Thy light alone gives grace and truth to life's unquiet dream." If Shelley had simply substituted the word "God" for the words "Intellectual Beauty," this hymn might be put in our collections of sacred poetry. He was really then worshiping God under another name. He devotes himself to his service, prays to him for help, blesses him for all good, and hopes from him triumph over all evil.

Symonds, in his "Shelley," observes:

We have only to read Shelley's "Essay on Christianity" in order to perceive what reverent admiration he felt for Jesus, and how profoundly he understood the true character of his teaching. That work, brief as it is, forms one of the most valuable extant contributions to a sound theology, and is morally far in advance of the opinions expressed by many who regard themselves as specially qualified to speak on the subject. It is certain that, as Christianity passes beyond its mediæval phase, and casts aside the husks of outworn dogmas, it will more and more approximate to Shelley's exposition.

Capt. Frederic Marryatt.—A. D. 1792–1848.

In "Japhet in Search of a Father" occurs this passage:

"Do you think that a great and good God ever created any being for its destruction and eternal misery?" * * * * "Then you suppose there is no such thing as eternal punishment?" "Eternal? No. Punishment there is, but not eternal. * * * This is certain, that no one was created to be punished eternally."

Dr. John Bowring.—A. D. 1792–1872.

Lord! when I seek thy face, I feel
I am but dust—the sprinkled dew
Of morning. But the towering will
That soars to heaven, is heavenly still
And man, though clay, is spirit, too.

Yes! I can feel that, though a clod
Of the dark vale, there is a sense
Of better things—the fit abode
Of something tending up to God—
A germ of pure intelligence.

I know not how the eternal hand
Has moulded man—but this I know,
That whilst 'mid earth's strange scenes I stand,
Bright visions of a better land
Go with me still, wher'er I go.

And surely dreams so pure, so sweet,
Friendly to hope and joy and worth,
  Are not the phantoms of deceit,

>   Delusions sent to blind, to cheat
>   The weary, wandering sons of earth.
>
>   My God! we are thine offspring—time
>   Is but our infancy—the earth
>   Our cradle—but our home's a clime
>   Eternal, sorrowless, sublime—
>   Heaven is the country of our birth!

The grand hymn, "God is Love, His Mercy Brightens," is the flowering of our faith in song.

>   Thy sun awakes and sets—the world grows old
>   And is renewed again. The seasons flow
>   Unchanging in their changes—joy and woe
>   Reside in turns—and then we are enrolled
>   Among the slumberers of the grave—but Thou,
>   To whom past, present, future, are as now,
>   Art still the same—still watching—still intent
>   On thy high purpose—from the labyrinth vast
>   Where good and evil, joy and grief are blent,
>   In common fate to perfect—and present
>   A future gathered from the checkered past,
>   Where bliss shall be predominant—and spread
>   Wider and wider—till it shall embrace
>   All the great family of the human race,
>   And give a crown of light to every head.

Felicia Dorothea Hemans.—A. D. 1794–1835.

We have somewhere read that Mrs. Hemans' son, then residing in this country, affirmed that his mother cherished the hope of universal redemption. We have been unable to find the testimony. Certainly the spirit of her amiable muse harmonizes with that of our faith.

In his "Recollections of a Busy Life," Horace Greeley quotes the following sonnet as a proof that the pure spirit of one of England's best and greatest women cherished the hope that the life beyond will amend the ills of time:

> O judge in thoughtful tenderness of those
>   Who richly dowered for life are called to die,
> Ere the soul's flame, through storms hath won repose.
>   In truth's divinest ether, still and high,
> Let their minds' riches claim a trustful sigh;
>   Deem them but sad, sweet fragments of a strain,
> First notes of some yet struggling harmony,
>   By the strong rush, the crowning joy and pain
> Of many inspirations, met and held
>   From its true sphere. Oh, soon it might have swelled
> Majestically forth! No doubt that he
>   Whose touch mysterious may on earth dissolve
> Those links of music, elsewhere will evolve
>   Their grand, consummate hymn from passion-gusts made free.

William Cullen Bryant.—A. D. 1794–1878.

The poet of America exhibits the soul of our religion in his perfect poems. He addresses his wife thus:

> How shall I know thee in the sphere which keeps
>   The disembodied spirits of the dead,
> When all of thee that time could wither, sleeps,
>   And perishes among the dust we tread?

For I shall feel the sting of ceaseless pain,
    If there I meet thy gentle presence not;
Nor hear the voice I love, nor read again
    In thy serenest eyes the tender thought.

Will not thy own meek heart demand me there?
    That heart whose fondest throbs to me were given;
My name on earth was ever in thy prayer,
    Shall it be banished from thy tongue in heaven?

In meadows fanned by heaven's life-breathing wind,
    In the resplendence of that glorious sphere,
And larger movements of the unfettered mind,
    Wilt thou forget the love that joined us here?

The love that lived through all the stormy past,
    And meekly with my harsher nature bore,
And deeper grew, and tenderer to the last,
    Shall it expire with earth, and be no more?

A happier lot than mine, and larger light
    Await thee there; for thou hast bowed thy will,
In cheerful homage to the rule of right,
    And lovest all, and renderest good for ill.

For me, the sordid cares in which I dwell,
    Shrink and consume my heart, as heat the scroll;
And wrath has left its scar—that fire of hell
    Has left its frightful scar upon my soul.

Yet, though thou wears't the glory of the sky,
    Wilt thou not keep the same beloved name,
The same fair thoughtful brow, and gentle eye,
    Lovelier in heaven's sweet climate, yet the same?

Shalt thou not teach me in that calmer home,
    The wisdom that I learned so ill in this—
The wisdom which is love—till I become
    Thy fit companion in the world of bliss?

He becomes entirely definite in his announcement of Universalism when he says:

> Each tie
> Of pure affection shall be knit again;
> Alone shall evil die,
> And sorrow dwell a prisoner in thy reign.

His "Lines to a Waterfowl" conclude thus:

> He who from zone to zone
> Guides through the boundless sky thy certain flight,
> In the long way that I must tread alone,
> Will guide my steps aright.

In the "Crowded Street," after surveying the rushing human torrent, the poet exclaims:

> Each, where his tasks or pleasures call,
> They pass and heed each other not;
> There is who heeds, who holds them all
> In his large love and boundless thought.
>
> These struggling tides of life that seem
> In wayward, aimless course to tend,
> Are eddies of the mighty stream
> That rolls to its appointed end.

And in his last great poem, he thus describes the scene of perfection beyond the "Flood of Years":

> In the room
> Of this grief-shadowed Present there shall be,
> A present in whose reign no grief shall gnaw
> The heart, and never shall a tender tie
> Be broken—in whose reign the eternal change
> That waits on growth and action shall proceed
> With everlasting concord hand in hand.

William Whewell.—A. D. 1794–1866.

In his "Philosophy of Discovery," this great scientist and divine, who enjoyed the reputation of "possessing more universal information than any other man in England," says his biographer, thus writes, pp. 389–393:

We are led to assume that there is in God an infinite love of man, a creature in a certain degree of a Divine nature. We must as a consequence of this, assume that the love of God to man, necessarily is, in the end and on the whole, completely and fully realized in the history of the world. But what is the complete history of the world? Is it that which consists in the lives of men such as we see them between their birth and their death? If the minds or souls of men are alive after the death of the body, that future life as well as the present life, belongs to the history of the world;—to that providential history, of which the totality, as we have said, must be governed by infinite Divine love. And in addition to all other reasons for believing that the minds and souls of men do thus survive their present life, is this:—that we thus can conceive, what otherwise it is difficult or impossible to conceive, the operation of infinite love in the whole of the history of mankind. If there be a future state in which men's souls are still under the authority and direction of the Divine Governor of the world, all that is here wanting to complete the scheme of a perfect government of intelligent love may thus be applied,—all seeming and partial evil may be absorbed and extinguished in an ultimate and universal good.

To complete the realization of the idea of justice as an element of the divine administration, there must be a life of man after his life in this present world. If man's mind and soul, the part of him which is susceptible of happiness and misery, survive this present life, and is still subject to the divine administration, the idea of Divine justice may still be completely realized, notwithstanding all that here looks like injustice or defective justice; and it belongs to the idea of justice to remedy and compensate, not to prevent wrong. And thus by this supposition of a future state of man's existence, we are enabled to conceive that, in the whole of the Divine goverment of the universe, all seeming injustice and wrong may be finally corrected and rectified, in an ultimate and universal establishment of a reign of perfect righteousness.

J. G. Percival.—A. D. 1795–1856.

This couplet was written by the poet, Percival:

We send these fond endearments o'er the grave,
Heaven would be hell, if loved ones were not there.

Horace Mann.—A. D. 1796–1859.

The great American educator thus testifies in a letter to his sister:

Though the whole offspring of the Creator, with the exception of one solitary being, were gathered into a heaven of unimaginable blessedness, while one solitary being, wide apart in some solitary region of immensity, however remote, were wedded to immortal pain, even then, just as soon as the holy principle of love sprang up in the hearts of the happy assembly, just so soon would they forget their joy, and forget their God, and the whole universe of them, as one spirit, gather around and weep over the sufferer. My nature revolts at the idea of belonging to a universe in which there is to be never-ending anguish. That nature never can be made to look on it with composure. * * * * What we learn from books, even what we think we are taught in the Bible, may be a mistake or misapprehension; but the lessons we learn from our own consciousness are the very voice of the Being who created us; and about it can there be any doubt?

Hartley Coleridge.—A. D. 1797–1849.

I need a cleansing change within—
My life must once again begin;
New hope I need, and youth renewed,
And more than human fortitude,—
New faith, new love, and strength to cast
Away the fetters of the past.

Ah! why did fabling poets tell
That Lethé only flows in hell?
As if, in truth, there was no river
Whereby the leper may be clean
But that which flows, and flows forever,
And crawls along, unheard, unseen,
Whence brutish spirits, in contagious shoals,
Quaff the dull drench of apathetic souls?

Ah, no! but Lethé flows aloft
With lulling murmur, kind and soft,
As voice which sinners send to heaven
When first they feel their sins forgiven;
Its every drop as bright and clear
As if indeed it were a tear
Shed by the lovely Magdalen
For him that was despised of men.

It is the only fount of bliss
In all the human wilderness—
It is the true Bethesda—solely

Endued with healing might, and holy;
Not once a year, but evermore—
Not one, but all men to restore.

J. G. Lockhart.—A. D. 1797–1854.

From lines on the death of his wife:

But, 'tis an old belief
  That on some solemn shore,
Beyond the sphere of grief,
  Dear friends shall meet once more;

Beyond the sphere of time,
  And sin, and fate's control;
Serene in endless prime
  Of body and of soul.

That creed I fain would keep,
  That hope I'll not forego;
Eternal be the sleep
  Unless to waken so.

Gerritt Smith.—A. D. 1797–1874.

Eternal Hell! No man does and no man can believe it. It is untrue if only because human nature is incapable of believing it. Moreover, were such a belief possible, it would be fatal. Let the American people wake up with it to-morrow, and none of them would go to their fields, and none to their shops, and none would care for their homes. All interest in the things of earth would be dead. The whole nation would be struck with paralysis and frozen with horror. Even the beginnings of such a belief would be too much for the safety of the brain; and every step in that direction is a step toward the mad-house. The orthodox preacher of an eternal hell would himself go crazy, did he believe his own preaching.

Theophilus Parsons.—A. D. 1797.

This distinguished American jurist, on one occasion listened to a discourse by an "orthodox" minister, and at its close, the preacher asked the lawyer's opinion of the discourse. "It was a very logical production," was the answer, "the premises and conclusion were perfect." "But," said the divine, "I had understood that you do not accept the evangelical views of the character of God?" "The character of God?" said the judge, "I supposed you were describing the devil."

Thomas Hood.—A. D. 1798–1845.

Hood's writings abound with the spirit of our faith. Instance his "Ode to Rae Wilson," one of the "Holy Willies" who had accused him of profaneness. He frankly confesses that he is

> Not one of those self-constituted saints,
> Those pseudo privy-counsellors of God,
> Who write down judgments with a pen hard nibb'd,
> Ushers of Belzebub's black rod,

> Who commend sinners, not to ice thick-ribbed,
> But endless flames, to scorch them up like flax,
> Yet sure of heaven themselves, as if they'd cribb'd
> The impression of St. Peter's keys in wax!

And he adds:

> Shun pride, O Rae! whatever sort beside
> You take in lieu, shun spiritual pride!
> A pride there is of rank, a pride of birth,
> A pride of learning, and a pride of purse,
> A London pride,—in short, there be on earth
> A host of prides, some better and some worse;
> But of all prides, since Lucifer's attaint,
> The proudest swells a self-elected saint.
> To picture that cold pride, so harsh and hard,
> Fancy a peacock in a poultry-yard.
> Behold him, in conceited circles sail,
> Strutting and dancing, and now planted stiff,
> In all his pomp of pageantry, as if
> He felt "the eyes of Europe" on his tail!
> "Look here," he cries, (to give him words,)
> "Thou feathered clay, thou scum of birds!"
> Flirting the rustling plumage in her eyes—
> "Look here, thou vile, predestined sinner,
> Doomed to be roasted for a dinner,
> Behold these lovely, variegated dyes!
> These are the rainbow colors of the skies,
> That heaven has shed upon me *con amore*—
> A bird of paradise! A pretty story!
> I am that saintly bird, thou paltry chick!
>   Look at my crown of glory!
> Thou dingy, dirty, drabbled, draggled jill!"
> And off goes Partlet, wriggling from a kick
> With bleeding scalp, laid open by his bill!
> That little simile exactly paints,
> How sinners are despised by saints, . . .
> The saints! the bigots that in public spout,

Spread phosphorus of zeal on scraps of fustian,
And go, like walking Lucifers about,
Mere living bundles of combustion. . . .
Thrice blessèd rather is the man with whom
The gracious prodigality of Nature,
The balm, the bliss, the beauty and the bloom,
The bounteous Providence in every feature
Recall the good Creator to his creature!
Making all earth a fane, all heaven its dome.
To his tuned spirit the wild heather bells
Ring Sabbath knells;
The jubilate of the soaring lark,
Is chant of clerk;
For choir, the thrush, and the gregarious linnet,
The sod's a cushion for his pious want,
And consecrated by the heaven within it,
    The sky-blue pool a font;
Each cloud-capp'd mountain is a holy altar;
An organ breathes in every grove;
    And the full heart's a psalter,
Rich in deep hymns of gratitude and love!

The "Bridge of Sighs" breathes the very soul of universal love and forgiveness. Though

    Perishing gloomily,
    Spurned by contumely,
    Cold inhumanity,
    Burning insanity,
      Into her rest,—
    Yet cross her hands humbly,
    As if praying dumbly,
      Over her breast!

    Owning her weakness,
    Her evil behavior,
    And leaving, with meekness,
    Her sins to her Savior!

Canon Farrar says of the foregoing passage:

Here again the Christian poets teach us a truer charity than the hard theologians.

In his prose works, Vol. II., p. 174:

Is there anything in common between the fierce, vindictive Creator, wrathfully consigning the creature he has made to everlasting and unutterable torment, as depicted by the gloomiest of fanatical sects, and the beneficent Jehovah, silently adored by the Quaker as the God of "peace and goodwill toward men?"

McDonald Clarke.—A. D. 1798.

The famous "mad poet," though he left no proof that he cherished the hope of universal redemption, gives this admirable statement of the true idea of retribution:

> How narrow are the bounds of hell,
>   Of blood and dust how small a part!
> The cloister of a forehead's clouded swell,
>   The dungeon of a loathing heart.
>
> The walls of hell may be the human skull—
>   The human breast its scorching base;
> There's a roar within, though man may lull
>   Its storms, ere its lightnings cross the face!

Robert Pollok.—A. D. 1799–1827.

We have no idea that the poet of orthodoxy,—par excellence—was a Universalist, for most of his poems are nightmares—the very delirium tremens of poetry, but he occasionally saw a gleam of light, as when he sang:

> Hail, holy love! thou word that sums all bliss,
> Gives and receives all bliss, fullest when most
> Thou givest! Spring-head of all felicity,
> Deepest when most is drawn! Emblem of God!
> O'erflowing most when greatest numbers drink!
> Essence that binds the uncreated Three,
> Chain that unites creation to its Lord,
> Center to which all being gravitates,
> Eternal, ever-growing, happy love!
> Enduring all, forgiving all;
> Instead of law, fulfilling every law.
>
> Breathe all thy minstrelsy, immortal Harp!
> Breathe numbers warm with love, while I rehearse
> Delighted theme, resembling most the songs
> Which, day and night, are sung before the Lamb!
> Thy praise, O Charity! thy labors most
> Divine; thy sympathy with sighs, and tears,
> And groans; thy great, thy godlike wish, to heal
> All misery, all fortune's wounds, and make
> The soul of every living thing rejoice.

Dr. K. Hase.—A. D. 1800.

Dr. Hase, professor of theology, Jena, Leipsic, 1870:

The restoration of every fallen being is an ideal floating before the history of the world, and its constant realization is conditioned by the moral freedom of all created spirits.—*Dogmatik, p. 478.*

Chauncey Hare Townshend.—A. D. 1800–1868.

This eminent Episcopal clergyman and graceful poet, is the author of a series of "Sermons in Sonnets," several of which we quote:

Give evil but an end—and all is clear!
Make it eternal—all things are obscured!
And all that we have thought, felt, wept, endured,
Worthless. We feel that e'en if our own tear
Were wiped away forever, no true cheer
Could to our yearning bosoms be secured
While we believed that sorrow clung uncured
To any being we on earth held dear.
Oh, much doth life the sweet solution want
Of all made blest in far futurity!
Heaven needs it too. Our bosoms yearn and pant
Rather indeed our God to justify
Than our own selves. Oh, why then drop the key
That tunes discordant worlds to harmony!

Let me not deem that I was made in vain,
Or that my being was an accident,
Which Fate, in working its sublime intent,
Not wished to be, to hinder would not deign.
Each drop uncounted in a storm of rain
Hath its own mission, and is duly sent
To its own leaf or blade, not idly spent
'Mid myriad dimples on the shipless main.
The very shadow of an insect's wing
For which the violet cared not while it stayed
Yet felt the lighter for its vanishing,
Proved that the sun was shining by its shade;
Then can a drop of the eternal spring,
Shadow of living lights, in vain be made?

Our sins from fire a dreadful emblem make
Of punishment, and woes that never tire;—
And yet how friendly—beautiful is fire!
Truth, dressed in fable, tells us it did wake
Man from brute sleep, heaven's bounty to partake,
And arts, and love, and rapture of the lyre.
The cottage hearth, the taper's friendly spire,
Have images to soften hearts that ache.
Virtuous is fire. The stars give thoughts of love,
And the sun chaseth ill desires away.
Fire cleanses too; by it we gold do prove,
And precious silver hath its bright assay.
Why then not deem the Bible's fires mean this—
Evil all melted, to make way for bliss?

The thought that any should have endless woe
Would cast a shadow on the throne of God,
And darken heaven. . . From the scarce warm clod
To seraphs, all him as a Father know;
He, all as children. Even with us below
The one rebellious son more thought and love
Than all the rest will in a parent move,
God stirring in us. Then how strong the glow
Of God's great heart our sorrows to relieve!
Could he be blest, beholding sufferings,
And not their end? His tenderness would grieve
If even the least of his created things
Should miss of joy. In its serenity
God's present happiness proves ours to be.

Evil! thou art a necessary good—
Fountain of Individualities,
Great tenure, thou, of all existences
That are not God. . . If rightly understood,

Thou art the lesson-book, and holy rood
Whereby, ascending up sublime degrees,
We know, and reconcile, and difference seize,
And change our earthly for a heavenly mood.
Ah, who can grieve that man has plucked the fruit
Of knowledge? . . Scarcely name we Innocence
The Virtue that is not Experience.
No! We our souls divinely must transmute
Out of the God-led instincts of the brute,
Into the loftier ways of Providence!

Oh no, great God! We feel thou canst not be
Spectator or upholder of distress,
So long, indeed, as it is objectless.
No! if thou lookst on sorrow, 'tis to see
Its benefit and end. If before thee
One hopeless ill could spread the smallest shroud,
Oh, wouldst thou not dissolve it as a cloud
In the mere fervors of thy radiancy?
'Tis so! And thou thy dearest Son didst send,
That message of a boundless love to make;
Not as a mockery—more the heart to rend,
If all were offered what but few could take!
Not as a thing of words—but as a meed,
Which, like thyself, is truth and love indeed.

Where is damnation?—
    Man-woven sadness!— •
Hark! all creation
    Answers in gladness!

Sin shall dissolve
    In goodness supernal!—
Beauty and joy
    Alone are eternal!

Edward Bouverie Pusey.—A. D. 1800.

The *New York Tribune*, in August, 1880, said:

Dr. Pusey agrees with Canon Farrar on an important question. He declares that it is not a dogma *de fide* that those who die in a state of sin cannot be reclaimed hereafter.

Coming from a Catholic source, this is an important item, indicating the direction of the theological breezes in the last quarter of the nineteenth century.

Frederika Bremer.—A. D. 1801–1865.

From the eloquent Swede we might quote pages:

Even in this life God wills that man shall partake of the fulness of this life, but what before all does Christianity say? God is love. He will, therefore, never cease to desire the delivery of every man; here, there, in eternity, he will labor for it. God is the only principle ever the same, ever active. Oh! certainly the time will come, when the Son, the eternal Word, shall have subdued all to the Father, to the eternal mind!

Again:

Let us, then, hope for all; the way may be more difficult for some natures than for others; but he who is light, and good, and eternally consistent, will sometime let his voice be heard, and raise them to light and harmony.

Again:

* * But now, wherever evil appears, it comes not as an organizing, always as a separating, destroying power. What, then, is evil? In its origin, probably a servant of good, as the shadow to the light, but which has wandered from its destina-

tion; a servant who has come to wear his master's clothes, and who, disguised in them, seeks to play his part. * * God, as the idea of God, as living goodness, must exclude all evil from his being. This exclusion, however, supposes the possibility of evil; hence follows a choice, the condition of free will. * * But God, the eternally good, the highest love, will he forsake his fallen, his wretched child? Will he do less than an earthly mother for her own? O, no; he will never turn away his face; he will seek his child; he will call him; he will suffer; he will give his heart's blood to win him again, to unite him again to himself. If God lives in holier worlds as a dispenser of blessedness, he must live on earth as a reconciler. The hymn of regret and homesickness which has arisen on earth from time immemorial,—this inward cry, "Come, Lord!" is from everlasting to everlasting answered with, "Here, my child!"

"Here, my child!"—Yes, O my God, in this world, in this futurity, thy child believes with his whole heart, and by the light of the doctrine of reconciliation, I see life and the world arrange themselves before my eyes. If I believe in God, the all good, and rich in love, I believe also in the Redeemer of the world, believe that the life which the heart seeks truly exists, and will gladly impart itself to us. I believe that it constantly comes nearer and nearer to us, until it has removed all obstacles, and unites itself with us fully and intimately. I believe that our God is no niggardly giver; I believe that he will give us all his fulness of life,—himself; I believe, that, as eternal love, he will suffer for and with us until he lives in us wholly. * * When we are again entered into God's eternal order, then our life will develop itself in undisturbed freedom and blessedness, and the drama will become, then, the unfolding of eternal love in every sphere of life.

Yes, I will preach of hope, and this in prison, by land and on sea. I will cry it in the ear of the dying malefactor, will shout it, even to the other side of death, to the other side of the grave,—I will cry it into endless eternity, "Hope ye! hope ye!"

Johann Peter Lange.—A. D. 1802.

We translate the following from Lange, the celebrated "orthodox" commentator, (Dogmatik, II., § 1294, Heidelberg, 1851). It will be a surprise in some quarters to learn that this great theologian cherishes so large a faith:

Throughout the New Testament the sway of divine grace is extolled as illuminating in its might the whole world, by Jesus himself, in his prayer, as High Priest. It is not merely his elect who shall recognize his glory, but the world also, until the world as world shall vanish in the contemplation of his glory (Jno. xvii: 22-24. See Lange's "Life of Jesus.") The Apostle Peter in his second Pentecostal speech teaches, certainly not the restitution of all things, but yet without doubt the realization of all the words which God has ever spoken, and therefore, particularly, of all divine promises. The apostle Paul closes his discussion of "Predestination" with the words, "God hath concluded all in unbelief that he might have mercy upon all" (Rom. xi: 32), and breaks out into the song of praise, "Of him, thro' him and to him are all things." His declaration that at the name of Jesus every knee shall bow, may of course be explained away to this—that a portion of men and of spirits shall be compelled against their will to bend the knee. But that the apostle intended such a meaning becomes very improbable when he adds, "Every tongue shall confess that Jesus Christ is Lord." For here we must remember his canon, "No man can call Jesus Lord but by the Holy Ghost." The mightiest word he has spoken is that concerning the destruction of death (I. Cor. xv: 26). Here, manifestly, the reference is to a new change, which takes place away beyond the general judgment. If death is wholly destroyed, then along with it must sin also be destroyed, for sin is death in essence. Yea, it is expressly announced that at some future time Christ shall have completed his work, and that then God shall be all in all. The Apostle

Peter has told us the means by which Christ reaches this goal (I. Peter 4: 6). The Apocalypse, however, says expressly that even the leaves of the tree of life which stand by the river of salvation serve for the healing of the heathen, and that there shall be no more any accursed thing.

The Apostle Paul has precisely expressed the special idea and purpose of excommunication from the church (I. Cor. v); —evidently a man may be given over to Satan that his soul may be saved. Nothing, then, seems more natural than that the purpose of the great and the greatest excommunication should be in the same line with that of the lesser. That the divine punishments even beyond the grave and deep in the realm of death have a tendency to conversion although they glorify God's righteousness and guard his rights, Peter has quite decisively shown. How, then, can it be regarded as a glorifying of God when the divine punishments which are awarded to the lost are considered solely as inflictions of vengeance, or of retribution? In such a case these punishments are to be no more punishment in the full meaning of the word, and in this penal region justice abandoned by grace is no more to stimulate, but only to kill. If men will separate in this way justice from grace they make a separation in God, and if in consequence they assign to justice through an endless eternity the office of tormenting in hell, so to speak, in a wholly isolated position, half severed from the whole living God, and sundered from grace and mercy, then in very deed they assign to justice a most painful office.

But God is everywhere present as God, even in hell. And if one acknowledges the article,—"I believe in God Almighty," one must feel that there is reference to the almightiness of his love also. But if his almightiness has eternal sway, it has also a corresponding eternal operation. People, therefore, should not think that they are zealous for the glory of God, when in spirit they bind man endlessly to the evil consequences of his unbelief in this world, and then endlessly bind the justice of God by itself alone to the endlessly bound man. In this case people are again in danger of making Time, the ancient Chronos, God, or at least the lost man's dying hour in which he abandoned hope forever. But God is greater than Time, and greater than the human heart. Certainly the human heart has in its freedom gained the power, even in its weakness, to carry on throughout the æons war with God to its own damnation. But the freedom of God stretches beyond the freedom of man, the freedom of the universe; and away there where the farthest æons of human rebellion are running out, the æon of God begins ever anew.

But God reigns in this æon in his eternal might. As the One, he will reflect himself in the unified organism of the spiritual world; and as the infinitely rich, in an organism which forms a kingdom of kingdoms, of many kingdoms, and whose Prince in every thought illuminates the whole organization. As the Lord of Kindness (Huld) God will brighten up out of its darkened condition his whole Kosmos till it be a full manifestation of the eternal beauty of his nature. As the Holy, he will bring it to appear in the perfected ideality of his spiritual sway. As the Righteous, he strives with fallen spirits, to throw them back on their conscience, that in their conscience they may be judged, destroyed and made alive again. And as he will bring them home to eternal right, so will he also have himself recognized by them in his eternal righteousness. For so long as they themselves are perverted, even the image of God in the perverted mirror of their consciousness seems a perverted thing. The perfect manifestation of the glory of God in his creature therefore demands the perfection of the world's mirror—consciousness. As the Loving One, also, he will see the personalities in that condition in which he planted them, and they shall utter his name as he utters theirs, in the reciprocal knowledge of personal life.

This sway of God demands an eternity, but for an eternity he does not lack; he himself is the Eternal. But that he is certain of his goal is to us made just as certain by the sway of Christ lasting after the final judgment, across the æons. He will destroy death as the last enemy. But how could he destroy death without destroying sin, which is the essential death,—the seed of death?

Dr. C. F. Kling.

Like most German theologians, Kling cherished the "eternal hope":

> Shall we then mistake, if we imagine that, even in the extra mundane sphere, that there are also fallen beings yet capable of salvation, and that into this sphere, whence came temptation and ruin into our race, there shall in return go forth blessed agencies of deliverance from this very race? *Lange's Commentary on I. Cor., vi: 2, p. 126.*

Lydia Maria Child.

In one of her New York letters, this gifted woman writes:

> But through this feeling arose the clear voice of Hope proclaiming that the tigers and snakes within man would finally be subdued, when this process is completed, man, being at peace with himself, will be in harmony with Nature, through the divine law of attraction.
>
> Let spirit change forms as it will, I know that nothing is really lost. The human soul contains within itself the universe. If the stars are blotted out, and the heavens rolled up as a scroll, they are not lost.
>
> If men applied half as much common sense to their theological investigations as they do to every other subject, they could not worship a God, who, having filled this world with millions of his children, would finally consign them all to eternal destruction, except a few who could be induced to believe in very difficult and doubtful explanations of prophecies, handed down to us through the long lapse of ages.

In her "Aspirations of the World," last lines of the book:

Let us all give each other cheerful assurance that we are all being guided through devious paths homeward by the universal Father.

Harriet Martineau.—A. D. 1802–1876.

Here are a few extracts from one of the most gifted women of modern times. In her old age she became a professed atheist. It seems that she occupied the same position earlier in life:

Here, where I once doubted whether I had a Maker, and whether, if there were such an one, men did anything but mock themselves in calling him Father, are the best witnesses of my avowal that I have found these doubts to be the result of human creeds, as far as they are impious, and that I have reached, through the very severity of the discipline, a refuge whence I can never again be driven forth, into the chaos of the elements, out of which my new life has been framed.

Had Doddridge known God only as a tender Father, Christ only as his holy and approved messenger, sin and sorrow as finite and limited influences, holiness and peace as the natural and ultimate elements of being, how serene, how exalted might have been his mortal life!

Here may we best reconcile our minds to the approach of the night of death, and exalt our conceptions of the eternal morning which shall unclose every eye, and restore the long suspended energies of every soul.

William Leggett.—A. D. 1802–1839.

This poet significantly asks, if we fail to find our loved ones, all of them, hereafter, will not heaven be impossible?

> If you bright stars, which gem the night,
>   Be each a blissful dwelling sphere,
> Where kindred spirits reunite,
>   Whom death has torn asunder here;
>
> How sweet it were at once to die,
>   And leave this blighted orb afar,
> Mixt soul and soul to cleave the sky,
>   And soar away from star to star.
>
> But oh! how dark, and drear, and lone,
>   Would seem the brightest world of bliss,
> If wandering through each radiant zone,
>   We failed to find the loved of this!

Thomas Guthrie.—A. D. 1803–1873.

In his "Life" he says:

St. John uses a very broad expression. "Jesus Christ," he says, "is the propitiation for our sins, and not for ours only, but also for the sins of the whole world." "The whole world. Ah," some would say, "that is dangerous language." It is God's language—John speaking as he was moved by the Holy Ghost. It throws a zone of mercy around the world. Perish the hand that would narrow it by a hand's breadth.

R. W. Emerson.—A. D. 1803.

Emerson employs the following language in an article on the system of Swedenborg:

Another dogma, growing out of this pernicious theological limitation, is this Inferno. Swedenborg has devils. Evil, according to old philosophers, is good in the making. That pure malignity can exist is the extreme proposition of unbelief. It is not to be entertained by a rational agent; it is atheism; it is the last profanation. Euripides rightly said,—

Goodness and being in the Gods are one,
He who imputes ill to them makes them none.

To what a painful perversion had Gothic theology arrived, that Swendenborg admitted no conversion for evil spirits! But the divine effort is never relaxed; the carrion in the sun will convert itself to grass and flowers; and man, though in brothels or jails, or on gibbets, is on his way to all that is good and true. Burns, with the wild humor of his apostrophe to "poor old Nickie Ben,"

O wad ye tak' a thought, and mend!

has the advantage of the vindictive theologian. Everything is superficial, and perishes, but love and truth only. The largest is always the truest sentiment, and we feel the more generous spirit of the Indian Vishnu, "I am the same to all mankind. There is not one who is worthy of my love or hatred."

Bishop Ewing.

This distinguished bishop of Argyll and the Isles —"the brightest and ablest of the Scotch prelates," according to Canon Farrar—says:

Unless this (the final restitution of all souls to God) be held as a matter of faith, and not as a speculative dogma, it is practically valueless. With me this final victory is not a matter of speculation at all, but of positive faith; and to disbelieve it would be for me to cease altogether either to trust or to worship God.

George Sand.—A. D. 1804–1876.

Amantine Lucille Aurore Dudevand (nee Dupin). This great genius says:

L'Église Romaine s'ést porté le dernier coup; elle a consommé son suicide le jour on elle a fait Dieu implacable et la damnation éternelle.—*Spiridion, p. 302.*

(The Romish church has dealt itself its death-blow. It consummated its own suicide when it made God implacable and damnation eternal.)

Edward Lytton Bulwer.—A. D. 1804–1872.

The distinguished novelist of England is author of this eloquent and truthful passage:

I cannot believe that earth is man's abiding place. It cannot be that our life is cast up by the ocean of eternity to float a moment upon its waves and sink into nothingness! Else, why is it that the aspirations which leap like angels from the temple of our hearts, are forever wandering about unsatisfied? Why is it that the rainbow and the cloud come over us with a beauty that is not of earth, then pass off, and leave us to muse upon their faded loveliness? Why is it that the stars who hold their festival around the midnight throne, are set above the grasp of our limited faculties, forever mocking us with their unapproachable glory? And, finally, why is it that bright forms of human beauty are presented to our view, and then taken from us, leaving the thousand streams of our affections to flow back in Alpine torrents upon our heart? We are born for a higher destiny than that of earth; there is a realm where rainbows never fade; where the stars will be out before us, like islets that slumber on the ocean; and where the beings that pass before us like shadows, will stay in our presence forever!

Not in the world without, but that within,
Revealed, not instinct—soul from sense can win!
And where the Natural halts, where cramped, confined,
The seen horizon bounds the baffled mind,
The Inspired begins—the onward march is given;
Bridging all space, nor ending ev'n in heaven!
There, veiled on earth, we mark divinely clear,
Duty and end—the There explains the Here!
We see the link that binds the future band,
Foeman with foeman gliding hand in hand;
And feel that Hate is but an hour's—the Son
Of earth, to perish when the earth is done—
But Love eternal; and we turn below,
To hail the brother where we loathed the foe;
There, in the soft and beautiful Belief,
Flows the true Lethé for the lips of Grief;
There, Penury, Hunger, Misery, cast their eyes,—
How soon the bright Republic of the Skies!
There, Love, heart-broken, sees prepared the bower,
And hears the bridal step, and waits the nuptial hour!
There, smiles the mother, we have wept! there bloom
Again the buds asleep within the tomb;
There, o'er bright gates inscribed, "No more to part,"
Soul springs to soul, and heart unites to heart!

So wonderful in equalizing all states and all times in the varying tide of life, are these two rulers yet levellers of mankind, Hope and Custom, that the very idea of an eternal punishment includes that of an utter alteration of the whole mechanism of the soul in its human state; and no effort of an imagination, assisted by past experience, can conceive a state of torture which custom can never blunt, and from which the chainless and immaterial spirit can never be beguiled into even a momentary escape.

Nathaniel Hawthorne.—A. D. 1804–1864.

In the *Atlantic Magazine*, speaking of the squalid and degraded poor of a great English city, Hawthorne observes:

Unless these slime-clogged nostrils can be made capable of inhaling celestial air, I know not how the purest and most intellectual of us can reasonably expect ever to taste a breath of it. The whole question of eternity is staked here. If a single one of these little ones be lost, the world is lost.

Mary Howitt.—A. D. 1804.

Mary Howitt, on the authority of Rev. A. C. Thomas, was a Universalist. So was William. Woman rarely defends the blasphemous errors of the church. What tender humanities and kind gentleness shine from the pages of Mrs. Heman's works,—the very soul of Universalism. Mary Howitt says:

Yes, than earth's mightiest mightier,
O Grave, thou hast thy vanquisher!
Long in thy night was man forlorn,
Long didst thou laugh his hope to scorn;
Vainly Philosophy might dream;—
Her light was but the meteor gleam,
Till rose the conqueror of Death,
The humble man of Nazareth;
He stood between us and despair;
He bore, and gave us strength to bear;
The mysteries of the grave unsealed,
Our glorious destiny revealed;
Nor sage nor bard may comprehend
The heaven of rest to which we tend.
Our home is not this mortal clime;
Our life hath not its bounds in time;
And death is but the cloud that lies
Between our souls and paradise.

J. P. Nichol, LL.D.—A. D. 1804.

In the vast heavens, as well as among phenomena around us, all things are in a state of change and progress; here, too, on the sky, in splendid hieroglyphics, the truth is inscribed, that the grandest forms of present being are only germs swelling and bursting with a life to come! And if the universal fabric is thus fixed and constructed, shall aught that it contains be un-upheld by the same preserving law? Is annihilation a possibility real or virtual—the stoppage of the career of any advancing being, while hospitable infinitude remains? No! let the night fall; it prepares a dawn when man's weariness shall have ceased, and his soul be refreshed and restored. To come! To every creature these are words of hope spoken in organ tone; our hearts suggest them, and the stars repeat them, and through the infinite aspiration wings its way rejoicingly, as an eagle following the sun.—*The Architecture of the Heavens.*

James Martineau.—A. D. 1805.

This learned and brilliant writer thus speaks in the *Westminster Review* for April, 1850:

No man who would hesitate to put Channing on the wheel, and object to burn Mrs. Fry, feeling that his reluctance comes from a good heart, can believe that God will do these things on a scale more terrible.

It requires indeed no great insight into character to discover that any reality in this eternal curse and penalty has for some time ceased. In proposing to rescue men from it, the church makes an offer which no one cares to accept. Have our lay readers ever practically met with a person—not under remorse for actual heinous sin, who wanted to be delivered from eternal torment? If ever a man does really apprehend such a thing for himself, and wring his hands and fix his eye in wild despair, how do we deal with him? Do we praise the clearness of his moral diagnosis and the logic of his orthodoxy? do we refer him to the font of baptism, or the keys for absolution? No, we send him to the physician rather than to the priest; we put cold sponges on his head, and bid his friends look after him. Nor does this doctrine any better bear application to the persons around us than to ourselves. If we sometimes act and speak by it, we never feel and rarely think of it. Who ever knew a mother to despair of her unbaptized and departed child? Let it only be considered what is the scene, what is the perspective, before her imagination, if she be at once sound and sincere in the faith; and it must be owned that even her most passionate grief never rises to the pitch of such piercing shrieks as she would hurl into the place of unutterable agony. The whole conduct and demeanor of the very persons who defend this doctrine afford the clearest proof that it is incredible. If we apply to it such tests of experience as would suffice in other cases, we produce results whose startling look distracts the attention from their logical consequentiality; and when we demand from men simple accordance with their profession, the thing itself is so impossible that we are apt to seem unreasonable, and become charged with the very extravagance which we impute. It is, however, notorious that a large number, even of the clergy, are fully conscious of their unbelief in this doctrine; and among the educated laity, the impression is general that no one, except here and there a dull curate or a pugnacious bishop, is sincere in his assent to it.

Hans Christian Andersen.—A. D. 1805–1875.

In the "True Story of my Life," he says:

Yet it is not so hard as people deem
  To see their souls' belovéd from them riven;
God has their dear ones, and in death they seem
  To form a bridge which leads them up to heaven.

Again, he says:

My whole life, the bright as well as the gloomy days, led to the best. It is like a voyage to some known point,—I stand at the rudder, I have chosen my path—but God rules the storm and the sea. He may direct it otherwise; and then happen what may, it will be the best for me. This faith is firmly planted in my breast, and makes me happy.

He declares:

I received gladly, both with feeling and understanding, the doctrine that God is love; everything which opposes this—a burning hell, therefore, whose fire endures forever—I could not recognize.

John Stuart Mill.—A. D. 1806.

This distinguished skeptic, though no Universalist, makes this declaration, to which most readers of this volume will fully assent:

If God will send me to hell for not loving a Being, many of whose traits are unlovely and abhorrent to my soul, then to hell I will go.

Rev. J. G. Street.

Mr. Street resides in Belfast, Ireland. He says:

We believe that all punishment, whether in this world or that which is to come, is designed by a wise and merciful God, for the reformation and restoration of the sinner; that every sin will receive its due punishment; that it must be cleansed away even as by fire; that it must be thoroughly eradicated from every soul throughout the universe before it can be said that Christ has subdued all things unto himself, and God become all in all. We believe the time will come when holiness will smile serenely above the grave of sin; when the dark lines will be chased from the moral landscape; when the sinner will have repented of every sin, and become purified by his chastisement; when the gates of Hades will be torn down, and the gloomy caverns of sin swept and garnished and glorified; when the smile of the All-Loving One will irradiate the countenance of every soul he has created; when the universe will be glorious with light and love; and eternal peace and joy will smile on all the children of God.

Rev. T. Latham.

Rev. T. Latham, of Bramfield, England, observes:

When the advocates of endless punishment have succeeded in proving God a God without goodness, a Father without compassion, a weak, a wavering, a false, a fickle, a changing, a disappointing, and a disappointed Deity; when they have proved Christ a useless, a worthless, an impotent, and merely a nominal Savior and restorer of the world; when they have proved the promises false, and made the Bible a mere fiction from beginning to end, they may then boast that they have established the horrible doctrine of eternal torments, and overthrown the final restoration of all mankind. And they may also at the same time prove the falsehood of the following statement, made by an eminent dignitary of the Church of England. [Bishop Newton in his "Dissertations on the Final State of Mankind."] " 'Known unto God are all his works from the beginning of the world.' He foresees what courses his rational creatures will take—their beginning, their progress, and their end, and nothing can be more contrary to the Divine Nature and attributes, than for a God all-wise, all-good, all-powerful, and all-perfect, to bestow existence on any being whose destiny he foreknew, and foreknows must terminate in wretchedness and misery, without respite or end. His goodness could never give birth to any one being, and much less to numberless beings whose end he foresaw would be irretrievable misery; nor could even his justice for short-lived transgressions, inflict everlasting punishment. Imagine a creature, nay, numberless creatures, produced out of nothing, and, therefore, guilty of no prior offence, sent into this world of frailty, which it is well known beforehand that they will so use as to abuse it, and then, for the excesses of a few years, delivered over to torments of endless ages, without the least hope or possibility of relaxation or redemption. Imagine it you may, but you can never seriously believe it. The thought is shocking even to human nature, and how much more abhorrent then it must be to the Divine Perfections? God must have made all his creatures finally to be happy; he could never make any whose end he foreknew would be misery everlasting.

"God is love; infinite benevolence alone prompted him to action, and infinite benevolence combined with unerring wisdom, and supported by irresistible power, will infallibly accomplish its purpose in the best possible manner."

With these views of the subject, then, till better views are given, let us joy and rejoice in the Lord, and give thanks at the remembrance of his holiness, faithfulness, goodness, justice, love, mercy and kindness, which all combine, with every perfection of his nature, to rescue and restore all his erring offspring from all error, and vice, and to bring them finally to inherit purity, peace, and a happy immortality.

Anonymous.

This epitaph on an infant, sufficiently condemns the absurd idea of native human depravity:

> He took the cup of life to sip,
>   But bitter 'twas to drain;
> He put it meekly from his lip,
>   And went to sleep again.

Emile Girardin.—A. D. 1806.

At the Peace Congress at Frankfort-on-the-Maine, in 1850, the compiler of these pages heard the great French journalist say:

The human race began in a unity, is governed as a unity, and must end in a unity.

Elizabeth Oakes Smith.—A. D. 1806.

In vain, in vain I turn the well known pages
For some authority, however brief,
For the hard doctrines which have been for ages
The substance of the Puritan's belief.
Father, forgive me, if with human blindness
I cannot see what may be plain to them;
Thy law to me is one of sacred kindness—
Thy love seems life's one priceless diadem.
The time will surely come when not in vain
Shall all thy children struggle with the wrong,
When angel forms shall walk the earth again,
And heavenly symphonies shall join with human song.
Then shall we learn, when sin lies cold and dumb,
The meaning of Christ's prayer, "Thy kingdom come."

N. P. Willis.—A. D. 1806–1867.

Oh, if we are not bitterly deceived—
If this familiar spirit that communes
With yours this hour—that has the power to search

All things but its own compass—is a spark
Struck from the burning essence of its God—
If, as we dream, in every radiant star
We see a shining gate through which the soul,
In its degrees of being, will ascend—
If, when these weary organs drop away,
We shall forget their uses and commune
With angels and each other, as the stars
Mingle their light, in silence and in love—
What is this fleshly fetter of a day
That we should bind it with immortal flowers!
How do we ever gaze upon the sky,
And watch the lark soar up till he is lost,
And turn to our poor perishing dreams away,
Without one tear for our imprisoned wings!

John Sterling.—A. D. 1806–1844.

 Still prayers are strong, and God is good;
  Man is not made for endless ill;
 Dear sprite! my soul's tormented mood
  Has yet a hope thou canst not kill.

 Repentance clothes in grass and flowers
  The grave in which the past was laid;
 And close to Faith's old minster towers
  The cross lights up the ghostly shade.

 Around its foot the shapes of fear,
  Whose eyes my weaker heart appall
 As sister suppliants thrill the ear
  With cries that loud for mercy call.

Thou, God, wilt hear! Thy pangs are meant
   To heal the spirit, not destroy;
And what may seem for vengeance sent,
   When thou commandest, works for joy.

In storm, and flood, and all decays of time,
   In hunger, plagues, and man-devouring war;
In all the boundless tracts of inward crime—
   In selfish hates, and lusts that deepliest mar,
In lazy dreams that clog each task sublime,
   In loveless doubts of truth's unsetting star;
In all—thy spirit will not cease to brood
With vital strength, unfolding all to good.

Fair sight it is, and med'cinal for man,
   To see thy guidance lead the human breast;
In life's unopen germ behold thy plan,
   Till 'mid the ripened soul it stands confest;
From impulse too minute for us to scan,
   Awakening sense with love and purpose blest;
And through confusion, error, trial, grief,
Maturing reason, conscience, calm belief.

This to have known, my soul, be thankful thou!—
   This clear, ideal form of endless good,
Which casts around the adoring learner's brow
   The ray that marks man's holiest brotherhood.
Thus e'en from guilt's deep course and slavish vow,
   And dreams whereby the light was long withstood;
Thee, Lord! whose mind is rule supreme to all,
Unveiled we see, and hail thy wisdom's call.

Bold is the life, and deep and vast in man—
   A flood of being poured unchecked from thee,
To thee returned by thy unfailing plan,
   When tried and trained thy will unveiled to see.

The spirit leaves the body's wondrous frame—
   That frame itself a world of strength and skill,
The noble inmate new abodes will claim,
   In every change to thee aspiring still.

Although from darkness born to darkness fled,
   We know that light beyond surrounds the whole,
The man survives though the weird corpse be dead,
   And he who dooms the flesh redeems the soul.

John F. D. Maurice.—A. D. 1806–1872.

The celebrated chaplain of Lincoln's Inn, and friend of Tennyson, has long been known as a defender of "the larger hope." In his "Unity of the New Testament," p. 257, he says of the language of Paul in Rom. v:

The justification is co-extensive with the condemnation; if all shared in one, all share in the other. . . . If only a certain portion of the human race had partaken of the sin of Adam, only a certain portion had partaken of the justification of Christ. But St. Paul affirms all to have been involved in one, all to be included in the other. . . . Since I look upon them (Christ's death and resurrection,) as revelations of the Son of God in whom all things had stood from the first, in whom God had looked upon his creature Man from the first, I give thanks for them as the most wonderful and blessed exposition of God's order in the universe, of man's disorder and transgression, of the method by which one has been used for the removal and cure of the other.

See Tennyson's "Sonnet to F. D. M."

H. W. Longfellow.—A. D. 1807.

There are many choice passages in the works of this elegant poet, which indicate that he agrees with the larger part of the denomination to which he is understood to belong, in rejecting the idea of the triumph of evil. He tells us, in the "Golden Legend".:

> It is Lucifer,
> The Son of Mystery;
> And since God suffers him to be,
> He, too, is God's minister,
> And labors for some good,
> By us not understood!

> The grave itself is but a covered bridge,
> Leading from light to light thro' a brief darkness.

> Some men there are, I have known such, who think
> That the two worlds—the seen and the unseen,
> The world of matter and the world of spirit,—
> Are like the hemispheres upon our maps,
> And touch each other only at a point.
> But these two worlds were not divided thus,
> Save for the purposes of common speech.
> They form one globe, on which the parted seas
> All flow together and are intermingled,
> While the great continents remain distinct.

"The Reaper and the Flowers," "Resignation," and many of the great poet's lines are saturated by the very spirit of universal love and redemption.

> There is no death! what seems so is transition,
>   This life of mortal breath
> Is but a suburb of the life elysian,
>   Whose portal we call Death.

Archbishop Trench.—A. D. 1807.

Dean Trench was not a Universalist, but these lines rise into the altitude of the Universal faith:

> I say to thee, do thou repeat
> To the first man thou mayest meet,
> In lane, highway, or open street,
>
> That he, and we, and all men move
> Under a canopy of love
> As broad as the blue sky above.
>
> And,—ere thou leave him,—say thou this
> Yet one word more,—they only miss
> The winning of that final bliss,
>
> Who will not count it true, that love,
> Blessing, not cursing, rules above—
> And that in it we live and move.
>
> And one thing farther make him know,
> That to believe these things are so,
> This firm faith never to forego,—
>
> Despite of all that seems at strife
> With blessing—all with curses rife—
> That this is blessing—this is life!

God's dealings still are love,—his chastenings are alone
Love, now compelled to take an altered, louder tone.
Mark how there still has run, enwoven from above,
Through thy life's darkest woof, the golden thread of love.

John Greenleaf Whittier.—A. D. 1807.

The spirit of our faith is the inspiration of Whittier's strains, and the animating impulse of his life. Once—in 1865—at his home, we listened to an animated conversation between the poet and a guest who was vindictive in her expressions against the rebels of the South. In his gentlest manner the poet said, "Thee is too orthodox." The woman replied, "But Andersonville must be avenged." To which Whittier made answer, "Andersonville was avenged when slavery was abolished." So sin will be avenged when the sinner shall have been converted,—and not till then.

Among the earliest of the utterances of New England's poet are these words from the "Stranger in Lowell":

> In the economy of God, no effort, however small, put forth for the right cause, fails of its effect. No voice, however feeble, lifted up for Truth, ever dies amidst the confused noises of Time. Through discords of Sin and Sorrow, Pain and Wrong, it rises a deathless melody, whose notes of wailing are hereafter to be changed to those of triumph as they blend with the great harmony of a reconciled universe.

His poetry is pervaded by the very spirit of our faith. "The Lost Soul," and "Eternal Goodness," are full of it. The utter impossibility that one soul can be happy, while others are wailing in endless torture, is set forth in "Divine Compassion," which asks:

> Is heaven so high
> That pity cannot breathe its air?

Its happy eyes forever dry,
Its holy lips without a prayer?
My God, my God, if thither led
By thy free grace unmerited,
No crown, no palm be mine, but let me keep
A heart that still can feel, and eyes that still can weep.

From the "Lost Soul":

Through sins of sense, perversities of will,
Through doubt and pain, through guilt and shame and ill,
Thy pitying eye is on thy creature still.

Wilt thou not make, eternal Source and Goal,
In thy long years life's broken circle whole,
And change to praise the cry of a lost soul?

In "The Grave by the Lake," the poet asks what has become of all the dead:

Desert-smothered caravan,
Knee-deep dust that once was man,
Battle-trenches ghastly piled,
Ocean-floors with white bones tiled,
Crowded tomb and mounded sod,—

* * * * * *

Where be now these silent hosts?
Where the camping-ground of ghosts?
Where the spectral conscripts led
To the white tents of the dead?
What strange shore or chartless sea
Holds the awful mystery?

And the poet's answer is,

Cast on God thy care for these;
Trust him if thy sight be dim;
Doubt for them is doubt of him.

* * * * *

> Still thy love, O Christ arisen,
> Yearns to reach these souls in prison,
> Through all depths of sin and loss
> Drops the plummet of thy cross!
> Never yet abyss was found
> Deeper than that cross could sound!
> Deep below as high above
> Sweeps the circle of God's love!

"The Brother of Mercy" prefers to be among the damned, rather than to sit unmoved in heaven. He truly says:

> If one goes to heaven without a heart,
> God knows he leaves behind his better part.
> I love my fellow-men; the worst I know
> I would do good to. Will death change me, so
> That I shall sit among the lazy saints,
> Turning a deaf ear to the sore complaints
> Of souls that suffer?
> Methinks (Lord, pardon, if the thought be sin!)
> The world of pain were better, if therein
> One's heart might still be human, and desires
> Of natural pity drop upon its fires
> Some cooling tears.

And the brother hears a voice assuring him:

> Never fear!
> For heaven is love, as God himself is love;
> Thy work below shall be thy work above!

"The Eternal Goodness" is the Universalist's church hymn. Addressing those who cherish a partial faith, he says:

> I trace your lines of argument;
> Your logic linked and strong,
> I weigh as one who dreads dissent,

And fears a doubt as wrong.
But still my human hands are weak
  To hold your iron creeds;
Against the words ye bid me speak,
  My heart within me pleads.
Who fathoms the Eternal thought?
  Who talks of scheme and plan?
The Lord is God, he needeth not
  The poor device of man.
I walk with bare, hushed feet the ground
  Ye tread with boldness shod,—
I dare not fix with mete and bound
  The love and power of God.
Ye praise his justice; even such
  His pitying love I deem.
Ye seek a king; I fain would touch
  The robe that hath no seam.
Ye see the curse which overbroods
  A world of pain and loss;
I hear our Lord's beatitudes
  And prayer upon the cross.
I see the wrong that round me lies,
  I feel the guilt within;
I hear, with groan and travail cries,
  The world confess its sin.
Yet, in the maddening maze of things,
  And tossed by storm and flood,
To one fixed stake my spirit clings,—
  I know that God is good!
Not mine to look where cherubim
  And seraphs may not see,
But nothing can be good in him,
  Which evil is in me.
The wrong that pains my soul below,
  I dare not throne above;
I know not of his hate,—I know
  His goodness and his love.

> I know not what the future hath
>   Of marvel or surprise,
> Assured alone that life and death
>   His mercy underlies.
> And so beside the silent sea
>   I wait the muffled oar;
> No harm from him can come to me
>   On ocean or on shore.
> I know not where his islands lift
>   Their fronded palms in air;
> I only know I cannot drift
>   Beyond his love and care.
> O brothers! if my faith is vain,
>   If hopes like these betray,
> Pray for me that my feet may gain
>   The sure and safer way.
> And thou, O Lord! by whom are seen
>   Thy creatures as they be,
> Forgive me if too close I lean
>   My human heart on thee.

In the same sublime spirit is "Tauler." The preacher is pondering the mysteries of life, when a stranger explains them to him in the light of the Divine Love. The preacher inquires:

> What if God's will consign thee hence to hell?
>   "Then," said the stranger, cheerily, "be it so.
>   What hell may be I know not; this I know—
>   I cannot lose the presence of the Lord:
>   One arm, Humility, takes hold upon
>   His dear Humanity; the other, Love,
>   Clasps his Divinity. So, where I go
>   He goes; and better fire-walled hell with him,
>   Than golden-gated Paradise without."
>   Tears sprang in Tauler's eyes. A sudden light
>   Like the first ray which fell on chaos, clove

Apart the shadow wherein he had walked
Darkly at noon.

* * * * * *

As he looked upward and saw the spire of the Strasburg Cathedral, its "stone lace-work" glowing in sunlight, while its base lay in gloomy shadow, he said:

>Behold
>The stranger's faith made plain before my eyes!
>As yonder tower outstretches to the earth
>The dark triangle of its shade alone
>When the bright day is shining on its top,
>So darkness in the pathway of man's life
>Is but the shadow of God's providence,
>By the great sun of wisdom cast thereon;
>And what is dark below is light in heaven!

The spirit of the great poet's philosophy and religion, he thus expresses:

>Bear up, bear on, the end shall tell
>The dear Lord ordereth all things well.

In a letter dated May 7, 1866, he writes:

God will do the best that is possible for all.

Rev. L. C. Marvin.—1807–1870.

Rev. L. C. Marvin was formerly a clergyman of the Universalist church. In his later years he was a physician. He died in Missouri at advanced age. On the death of the son of a friend, Dr. Marvin wrote:

>How could I tread that hallowed plain
>Where God and Christ and angels are,

Or how could heaven to me be gain,
Unless the lad were with me there?

* * * *

How could I join that wondrous throng,
'Mid burnished crowns and burning thrones,
And know his voice shall but prolong
Hell's dolorous, deep and dreadful groans?

* * * *

I'd join some rebel angel throng,
And power omnipotent defy,
The shout of war should be my song,
To sound rebellion through the sky.

* * * *

Far down through space, where Satan fell,
On strong immortal wings I'd fly,
And share the deepest, darkest hell,
Or bring the lad with me on high.

Yes, dearest boy! thy every woe
On earth 'tis given to me to share;
May God no other world bestow,
Unless that boon be granted there.

Abel C. Thomas.—A. D. 1807–1880.

One of the most eloquent of the divines of the Universalist church was also a poet. He says:

Thou whose wide-extended sway,
Suns and systems e'er obey!
Thou our Guardian and our Stay,
    Evermore obeyed;
In prospective, Lord, we see
Jew and Gentile, bond and free,

Reconciled in Christ to thee,
    Holy, holy, Lord!

Thou by all shalt be confessed,
Ever blessing, ever blest,
When to thy eternal rest
    In the courts above,
Thou shalt bring the sore oppressed,
Fill each joy-desiring breast,
Make of each a welcome guest,
    At the feast of love.

When destroying death shall die,
Hushed be every rising sigh,
Tears be wiped from every eye,
    Never more to fall;
Then shall praises fill the sky,
And angelic hosts shall cry
Holy, holy Lord, most high,
    Thou art all in all!

Christian Edward Baumstark.—A. D. 1807.

If we inquire after the wherefore of the creation of the world, or after the motive in the divine will for calling the world into existence, the question is identical with that regarding the design of creation. The New Testament gives to this question the answer:—The world is created at once by God and to God (*eis Theon*) Rom. xi: 36. In this general destination there lie implicitly two elements. If the world is created to God, this means, first:—That the aim of the creation of the world is the manifestation of the divine nature in outward time-being and space-being, the self-glorifying of God in created being. But as the divine will is no egoistic one, but is love, which, while it seeks itself, seeks by that very thing the good of others, the world cannot be merely the means of glorifying God; its design is at once the manifestation of the glory of God and also the highest well-being, the blessedness of the creatures. These, however, are not two elements standing apart from each other; the glorifying of God and the blessedness of the creatures are essentially one thing. The exhibition of the divine nature as absolute love is directly and at the same time the blessedness of the creatures; the self-manifestation of God in created existence is also as well the participation of creation in the divine fulness of life, i. e., its blessedness. What the analysis of the *eis Theon* thus tells us is expressly confirmed by those New Testament passages which speak of the design of redemption. The New Testament looks at creation with reference to redemption; the goal to be reached by the latter is presented as the design fixed by God in creation, just as according to the nature of the case, redemption can be only the means to the realization of the design in creation (Eph. i : 4-10-12). But the goal of redemption is that God may be all in all (I. Cor. xv : 28), by which is not meant a resolving and dissolving of the creature in God, but its being permeated with the divine fulness of life, while preserving its distinct and separate existence (Eph. iii : 19). In this, however, is involved just as much the glorifying of God as the blessed rest of the creatures in God. Heb. 4 : 9; Eph. i : 6, 12; Rev. xxi : 3, and following verses, II : 455, 6.—*Christliche Apologetik auf Anthropologischer Grundlage, Frankfurt-on-Main.* [Original translation.]

Caroline E. S. Norton.—A. D. 1808–1877.

Visiting a reform prison for youthful convicts, her heart is tenderly touched as she looks into their childish faces, where might be seen, probably, many traces of a depravity which they had sadly inherited; and thus she speaks of them as

The wrecked, round whom the threatening surges boomed,
   Borne in this life-boat far from peril's stress;
The sheltered, o'er whose head the thunder loomed;
   Convicts, (convicted of much helplessness)—
Exiles, whom mercy guides through guilt's dark wilderness.

Then in drawing a contrast between the wayward children of poverty, and those of highly favored conditions, she shows how love clings to its own, and will not let them go, even though low down in the degradation and wretchedness of sin.

   Are there no sons at college, "sadly wild?"
     No children, wayward, difficult to rear?
   Are they cast off by love? No, gleaming mild,
     Through the salt drops of many a bitter tear,
   The rainbow of your hope shines out of all your fear!

The spirit of our beautiful and comprehensive faith was in the heart of this gifted poet, to say the least,—and this, perhaps, is saying much—for the truest and best faith is of the spirit, much more than of the letter.

John R. Thompson.

John R. Thompson is widely and favorably known in the literary world. In a poem he read before the Alumni of the University of Virginia, at their annual meeting, July 1, 1869, he says:

And, casting off unwise regrets,
We yet may hope that time shall prove
　　Kind hearts are more than bayonets,
And force less strong than love;
　　We know that order shall appear,
　　When God has made his purpose clear,
　　The darkest riddle shall be understood,
And all the perfect world shall in his sight be good!

Ross Winans.

This gentleman was a highly respected citizen of Baltimore, who departed this life not long since. He was a gentleman of culture, and widely known as a successful business man. A few years ago he published a work of some 400 pages octavo, entitled "One Religion; Many Creeds."

Our belief is that man, being thus governed and trained through time and during eternity, a good and happy result must ensue to each individual. * * The idea of hell, hell fire, and eternal torment, when properly considered, is an idea that is alike blasphemous and illogical. Not so with the idea of eternal progress toward infinite knowledge and happiness, which is a natural deduction from our earthly experience. He (God) has ordained that every man shall sooner or later recognize and appreciate his blessing. Nothing less is consistent with God's determinate will and perfections. God is a God of infinite goodness, not of vengeance; to be loved, not feared; to be worshiped for love's sake, not through fear of everlasting punishment. We believe that every man will eventually love him, and strive more and more to serve him.

Oliver Wendell Holmes.—A. D. 1809.

Not only does this poet and man of genius repudiate the old abominations that have so long degraded the name of religion, but he rises to a high strain of exultation in setting forth the truth. When he describes "What We All Think," he speaks of

> That one unquestioned text we read,
>   All doubt beyond, all fear above,
> Nor crackling pile, nor cursing creed,
>   Can burn or blot it—God is love!

The "Crooked Footpath" describes the various paths of mortals, and concludes that

> No earth-born will
>   Could ever trace a faultless line;
> Our truest steps are human still,—
>   To walk unswerving were divine!

> Truants from love we dream of wrath;
>   O, rather let us trust the more!
> Through all the wanderings of the path,
>   We still can see our Father's door.

He vividly describes

> Those monstrous, uncouth horrors of the past,
> That blot the blue of heaven and shame the earth
> As would the saurians of the age of slime,
> Awaking from their stony sepulchers
> And wallowing hateful in the eye of day!

The English language contains few more eloquent denunciations of popular error, or grander statements of the truth, than are contained in "Love."

What if a soul redeemed, a spirit that loved
While yet on earth, and was beloved in turn,
And still remembered every look and tone
Of that dear earthly sister who was left
Among the unwise virgins at the gate,
Itself admitted with the bridegroom's train,—
What if this spirit redeemed, amid the host
Of chanting angels, in some transient lull
Of the eternal anthem, heard the cry
Of its lost darling, whom in evil hour
Some wilder pulse of nature led astray,
And left an outcast in a world of fire,
Condemned to be the sport of cruel fiends,
Sleepless, unpitying, masters of the skill
To wring the maddest ecstacies of pain
From worn-out souls that only ask to die,—
Would it not long to leave the bliss of heaven,—
Bearing a little water in its hand
To moisten those poor lips that plead in vain
With him we call our Father? Or is all
So changed in such as taste celestial joy,
They hear, unmoved, the endless wail of woe;
The daughter in the same dear tones that hushed
Her cradled slumbers; she who once had held
A babe upon her bosom, from its voice
Hoarse with its cry of anguish, yet the same?
No! not in ages when the Dreadful Bird
Stamped his huge footprints, and the fearful Beast
Strode with the flesh about those fossil bones
We build to mimic life with pigmy hands,—
Not in those earliest days when men ran wild,
And gashed each other with their knives of stone,
When their low foreheads bulged in ridgy roads,
And their flat hands were callous in the palm
With walking in the fashion of their sires,
Grope as they might, to find a cruel God
To work their will on such as human wrath

Had wrought its worst to torture, and had left
With rage unsated, white and stark and cold,
Could hate have shaped a demon more malign
Than him the dead men murmured in their creed,
And taught their trembling children to adore!
Made in his image! Sweet and gracious souls,
Dear to my heart by nature's fondest names,
Is not your memory still the precious mould
That lends its form to him who hears my prayer?
Thus only I behold him, like to them,
Long-suffering, gentle, ever slow to wrath,
If wrath it be that only wounds to heal,
Ready to meet the wanderer ere he reach
The door he seeks, forgetful of his sin,
Longing to clasp him in his father's arms,
And seal his pardon with a pitying tear.

* * * * *

Would that the heart of woman warmed our creeds!
Not from the sad-eyed hermit's lonely cell,
Not from the conclave where the holy men
Glare on each other as with angry eyes,
They battle for God's glory and their own,
Till, sick of wordy strife a show of hands
Fixes the faith of ages yet unborn,—
Ah, not from these the listening soul can hear
The Father's voice that speaks itself divine.
Love must be still our master; till we learn
What he can teach us of a woman's heart,
We know not his, whose love embraces all.

Alfred Tennyson.—A. D. 1809.

"In Memoriam," Tennyson's lament over the death of his friend—fibers from the heart are its eloquent lines—the great poem of this century, announces the high hopes inspired by a vision of the restitution of all things. Thus he sings:

> Oh, yes, we trust that somehow good
>   Will be the final goal of ill,
>   To pangs of nature, sins of will,
> Defects of doubt, and taints of blood:
>
> That nothing walks with aimless feet,
>   That not one life shall be destroyed,
>   Or cast as rubbish to the void,
> When God hath made the pile complete:
>
> That not a worm is cloven in vain,
>   That not a moth with vain desire
>   Is shrivelled in a fruitless fire,
> Or but subserves another's gain.
>
> Behold! we know not anything;
>   I can but trust that good shall fall
>   At last—far off—at last to all,
> And every Winter change to Spring.
>
> So runs my dream; but what am I?
>   An infant crying in the night;
>   An infant crying for the light;
> And with no language but a cry.

And again:

> That God which ever lives and loves,
>   One God, one law, one element,
>   And one far-off, divine event,
> To which the whole creation moves.

* * * * *

> The wish, that of the living whole

> No life may fail beyond the grave,
> Derives it not from what we have
> The likest God within the soul?

In the "Vision of Sin," after the poet has described his vision of evil, he sees hope of its final extinction:

> At last I heard a voice upon the slope
> Cry to the summit, "Is there any hope?"
> To which the answer pealed upon that high land,
> But in a tongue no man could understand,
> And on the glimmering summit far withdrawn,
> God made himself an awful rose of dawn.

Addressing Rev. F. D. Maurice as

> Being of that honest few
> Who give the fiend himself his due,

He continues,—

> Should eighty thousand college councils
> Thunder "anathema," friend, at you,
> Should all our churchmen frown in spite,
> At you so careful of the right,
> Yet one lay hearth would give you welcome,—
> Take it and come to the Isle of Wight.

The chief offence of Maurice is, that he advocates the doctrine of Tennyson:

> That good shall fall
> At last—far off—at last to all
> And every Winter change to Spring.

Elisabeth Barret Browning.—A. D. 1809–1861.

The reader of the greatest English poetess finds the "divine event to which the whole creation moves" to be the keynote of her sublime strains.

Some years since Rev. Charles H. Leonard, of Tufts College, visited Mrs. Browning, and the following letter to the compiler of this volume describes the interview:

* * * I hardly know how it was that the conversation took such direction, and deepened at last to such themes, but one could hardly help speaking his best, and of the best in her presence. She said that she had thought a good deal on the problem of destiny, referring as she went on in our talk to many things that had come to her in highest moments. I was so led to speak of our own ideas of God and the absolute life of the soul. One thing I remember seemed to impress her. I said:—"With me, it is not so much a question of destination as of destiny, and that means inward life, a life of the soul in God, and of God in the soul." "What do you call these views?" said she. I said, "We are Universalists. Our religion is known as Universalism." I shall never forget the light that spread over her face as she repeated the word several times, "Universalism, Universalism!" After a little she said, "How full the word is, how strong, and how fine in literature!" She said this last as if she were recalling something which she had read. But I did not interrupt her. She then spoke again of the name Universalist, and seemed to like to hold it close to her thought, and often to take it upon her lips. "These ideas of religion are the highest," she said.

>   And who saith "I loved once?"
> Not God, called Love, his noble-crown name,—casting
>   A light too broad for blasting!
> The great God changing not from everlasting,
>   Saith never "I loved once."

>   I am strong—
> Knowing ye are not lost for aye among
> The hills, with last year's thrush. God keeps a niche

In heaven to hold our idols; and albeit
He brake them to our faces, and denied
That our close kisses should impair their white,
I know we shall behold them raised, complete,
The dust shook from their beauty,—glorified,
New Memnons singing in the great God-light.

We will trust God. The blank interstices
Men take for ruins, he will build into
  With pillared marbles rare, or knit across
With generous arches, till the fane's complete;
  This world has no perdition, if some loss.

Her "Drama of Exile," a glorious poem founded on the original lapse of man, sings the exalted strains of the great restitution. As the exiled pair slowly pass out of Eden, into the desert, a semi-chorus is heard, saying,—

> So in the universe's
> Consummate undoing,
> Our angels of white mercies
> Shall hover round the ruin!
> Their wings shall stream upon the flame,
> As if incorporate of the same,
>   In elemental fusion;
> And calm their faces shall burn out
> With a pale and mastering thought,
> And a steadfast looking of desire,
> From out between the clefts of fire,
> While they cry in the Holy's name!
>   To the final Restitution!
>   Listen to our loving!

She represents Christ as saying:

> For, at last,
> I, wrapping round me your humanity,

> Which, being sustained, shall neither break nor burn
> Beneath the fire of Godhead, will tread earth,
> And ransom you, and it, and set strong peace
> Betwixt you and its creatures. With my pangs
> I will confront your sins, and since your sins
> Have sunken to all nature's heart from yours,
> The tears of my clean soul shall follow them,
> And set a holy passion to work clear
> Absolute consecration. In my brow
> Of kingly whiteness, shall be crowned anew
> Your discrowned human nature. Look on me!
> As I shall be uplifted on a cross
> In darkness of eclipse; and anguish dread,
> So shall I lift up in my pierced hands
> Not into dark, but light—not unto death,
> But life, beyond the reach of guilt and grief,
> The whole creation.

Well does this sublime composition end by saying to our sinful race,—

> Hear us sing above you,
> Exiled but not lost!

Abraham Lincoln.—A. D. 1809–1865.

The martyr-president was known to be of liberal religious principles. On one occasion he listened to a discussion on human destiny, in which L. C. Marvin, author of "My Boy," was a participant. When asked his opinion on the question, he replied:

"It must be everybody or nobody."

Richard Moncton Milnes.—A. D. 1809.

O ye! who talk of Death, and mourn for Death,
Why do you raise a phantom of your weakness,
And then shriek loud to see what ye have made?
There is no Death, to those who know of Life—
No Time to those who see Eternity!

Professor J. S. Blackie.—A. D. 1809.

This author and scholar thus testifies:

The generations of uncounted men
Have hymned thy praises, Lord. Their stammering tongues
With strange, crude doctrines magnify the power
Of him whose vastness they were fain to grasp,
But could not. Even the folly of the fool
Shall praise thee, Lord. Thou hast a place for all.
The wicked and the weak are but the steps
Whereon the wise shall mount to see thy face,
And mighty churches, and high vaunted faiths,
Are but the schools, wherein thy centuries train
The infant peoples to the manly reach
Of pure devotion; and most wise are they
Who hear one hymn of varied truth through all
The harmonious discord of strange witnesses,
Prophets and martyrs, priests and meek-eyed saints,
And rapt diviners with imperfect tongue,
Babbling thy praises.

* * * * * *

A "Sabbath Meditation," in "Songs of Religion and Life":

* * * * *

There's my apology for the poor Hindoos,

Convert them if you can, but do not damn;
Curse not the beggar when you dole your doit;
Preach, like St. Paul, in gentlemanly wise,
And do not swear that brindled hides are black
To make yourself look whiter. I believe
There is much high and holy wisdom hid
In what you damn wholesale; but, if you find
No sheep outside the Presbyterian fold,
(All else being goats), and what I take for gold
You deem base brass, till stamped in thine own mint,
I would not strive with thee; God made thee so;
My thoughts would not lodge sweetly in thy skin.

Prof. Blackie, in his "Natural History of Atheism," p. 201, observes:

It does not require any very profound scholarship to know that the word *aiōnios*, which we translate everlasting, does not signify eternity, absolutely and metaphysically, but only popularly, as when we say that a man is an eternal fool, meaning by that, he is a very great fool.

John R. Beard, D. D.

The author of "Bible Dictionary," Manchester, Eng., thus writes:

For one moment let us dwell on that word—the word "everlasting," or "eternal." Now, in the first place, the readers of the English Bible have not to do with that word itself, but with a translation of it. Are the two identical in meaning? Do they each cover the same ground? Certainly not. Our conception of eternity is much more absolute than that of either the Greeks or the Hebrews, with whom the corresponding words denoted generally an indefinite and unknown period. Can we speak of eternities? They could. Yea, "eternities of eternities; "before the eternities," and "to the eternities of eternities," are forms of speech employed in the New Testament. What then? There are several eternities, and eternities are appended to eternities. Clearly, the Greek original signifies much less than its English representative; and if anything, less than endless; the word expresses time, and not what we call eternity. Then, the word is also used of subjects which in their nature are of limited duration. It is used of things. Is a thing imperishable or perishable? It is used of this world; but this world passeth away. It is used of times; times, however, can be nothing more than repeated years, days and hours. It is used of fire; but unquenchable fire is an impossibility, unless fire, which, consuming other things, consumes itself, shares God's deathlessness. It is used of punishment; but the punishment which does not end in reformation is vindictiveness, which cannot be ascribed to the Merciful Father, whose name and whose essence is love.

How, then, has it come to pass that the belief in eternal punishment took root in the Christian church?

By respect for the letter, and disregard for the spirit of the Gospel. The letter killeth; but the spirit giveth life.

Ancient doctors of the church, misled by theoretical conclusions, declared that sin was an infinite transgression, to be atoned for only by an infinite expiation. If sin is infinite, it is, of course, eternal. Eternal sin involves eternal punishment. Hence the doctrine. The doctrine is the child of human reasoning.

The eternal life, of which under God, Christ is the author and the source, is nothing less than the life of God himself, considered as evoked and developed in men by the quickening and fostering spirit of Christ. This life, which is a natural outcome under a divine training, grows constantly fuller, and becomes less incomplete in the true disciple as his days increase, and when at last, he throws off this mortal coil, it emerges, and unfolding into the proportions of Christ's own stature, becomes purely spiritual, and taking a glorified body after its kind, enters on a career of loving and blessed communion with God and beatified souls, which may rise forever, but can never end, since being of God it shares God's immortality.

> That one-half creation is to know
> Luxurious joys, and others only woe,
> And so go down into the common tomb
> With need to question their unequal doom—
> Shall we give credit to a thought so foul?
> Ah, no! the world beyond—the world beyond!
> There shall the desolate heart regain its own!
> There the oppressed shall stand before God's throne!
> There, when the tangled web is all explained,
> Wrong suffered, pain inflicted, grief disdained;
> Man's proud, mistaken judgment and false scorn
> Shall melt, like mists, before the uprising morn,
> And holy truth stand forth, serenely bright
> In the rich flood of God's eternal light!

Edward Clodd.

In seeking to show you by what slow steps man came to believe in one all-wise and all-good God, I wish to fix one great truth upon your young heart about him; for the nobler your view of him is, the nobler is your life likely to be.

Now, you would think your father very hard and cruel if he loaded you with all the good things he had, and sent your brothers and sisters, each yearning for his love and kisses, to some homeless spot to live uncared for and unloved, and to die unwept. And yet this is exactly what some people have said that God does. They have spoken of him, who has given life to every man, woman and child, without power on their part to take or refuse what is thus given, as being near only a few of his creatures, and leaving the rest, feeling a soul-hunger after him, to care for themselves and never find him.

Believe that he who is called our Father is better, more just, more loving, than the best fathers can be, and that he "is not far from any one of us."—*Childhood of the World.*

Mary Carpenter.

This distinguished English philanthropist said, among her latest utterances:

There are some things of which the most clear and unanswerable reasoning could not convince me. One of these is that a wise, all-powerful and loving Father can create an immortal spirit for eternal misery. Joguth's answer to such people is the best I ever heard! "If you are a child of the devil, good! But I am the child of God."

Frances Power Cobbe says in "Personal Recollections of Mary Carpenter," *Modern Review*, April, 1880:

Mary Carpenter's theology was, I believe, exactly that of her beloved father, Dr. Lant Carpenter. [See page 117 of this book.]

Theodore Parker.—A. D. 1810–1860.

The great radical cherished the hope of final good:

In darker days and nights of storm,
Men knew thee but to fear thy form;

And in the reddest lightning saw
Thine arm avenge insulted law.

In brighter days we read thy love
In flowers beneath, in stars above,
And in the track of every storm
Behold thy beauty's rainbow form.

And in the reddest lightning's path
We see no vestiges of wrath,
But always wisdom, perfect love,
From flowers beneath, to stars above.

See from on high sweet influence rains
On palace, cottage, mountains, plains;
No hour of wrath shall mortals fear,
For their Almighty Love is near.

Anonymous.

This sublime chant entitled "Lucifer Redux," is by an unknown author:

Prince of the fallen stars,
Thy front shall lose its scars!
The fires shall cease to burn,
Thy legions shall return!

The demon's crown of woe
No more shall gird thy brow;
The fires shall cease to burn,
Thy legions shall return!

In heaven thy starred domain
Shall greet its chief again;

The fires shall cease to burn,
Thy legions shall return!

Thine ancient halls of state,
So long left desolate,
Shall ring with joy once more,
Shall bloom with wreath and flower.

The constellations bright,
The torches of the night,
Around thy steps shall chant
A pæan jubilant.

The wheels that o'er thee drove,
The sword thy mail that clove,
Shall lead thy glad return,
Before thy march shall burn!

From "The Butterfly":

If with Deity 'tis just
That a worm goes back to dust;
Tell me, tell me, ye who can,
What supports the hope of man?
What have we received by birth,
More than crumbles back to earth?
O, I'd die to-day to know
That it is not even so.

Yet, if this be all we get,
We should make the most of it.
Let us love and laugh our fill;
Let the senses have their will:
And, to check the gushing tear,
Since we know that death is near,
Hope some other world of bliss
Will amend the wrongs of this.

> Hold!—the soul of Nature saith,
> There is no such thing as death;
> Every form is marked by Change,
> But to take a Higher Range.
> On the metamorphosis
> Of a folded chrysalis,
> Hope this truth may predicate:
> All that live doth heaven await.

Margaret Fuller Ossoli.—A. D. 1810–1850.

Margaret Fuller's name is one of the "immortal few." Her soul was full of the great faith that

> Whatever has been permitted by the law of being, must be for good, and only in time not good. Evil is obstruction; good is accomplishment.—*"Life," Vol. II, p. 89.*
>
> I do not myself see how a reflecting soul can endure the passage through life, except by confidence in a Power that must at last order all things right, and the resolution that it shall not be our fault if we are not happy,—that we will resolutely deserve to be happy. [See her "Life and Letters."]

J. S. Taylor.

J. S. Taylor, in "Clouds and Sunshine," expresses the prevailing sentiment of modern literature:

> I cannot believe that God has doomed any creatures of his, in any part of his dominions, to endless misery. That every sin must have its attendant sorrow; that the penalty of every transgression must be paid to the full; that no sophistry or

ingenuity can evade that payment; that guilt and wretchedness still abound on earth, and in other worlds, and that they will long continue to impair their beauty and happiness, all these things who will presume to question? But that this sad history is to remain so forever, or that any star in the universe is destined to be the theater of eternal suffering, or that any being exists in any part of it, so steeped in guilt and anguish (no, not Satan himself,) as to be beyond the redeeming love or healing power of the Creator, I no more believe it than I do that there is any intellect that can baffle God's wisdom, or any force that can resist his supremacy. Oh, no; on the contrary, I believe that in this mysterious, but divinely ordained conflict of good and evil, the powers of light, are, everywhere, slowly but surely gaining the ascendancy over the powers of darkness, and that it will continue to be so, even unto the perfect day; yes, that perfect day, wherein all these blessed victories over sin and ignorance shall have been consummated, these transformations completed, and no solitary stain of folly, guilt, or grief, be left to mar the luster of the universe.

George Moore.

Author of a singular and able work, "Body and Mind," Moore tells us among other things:

To believe in him who is the reconciler of all things to himself, is to believe in the ultimate vindication of all his attributes, and to feel that the stability of his throne is as sure as eternity. The love that originated all creatures has never allowed his own nature to be involved in the contradiction of their necessarily narrowed understandings, and when their round of error is completed according to their little wills, it shall still be found that his will triumphs, and the boundless universe must everlastingly declare in every color of three-fold light, and in the lines of darkness that divide its rays, in spite of sin, in spite of suffering, in spite of death, that God is love, the source of endless light.

"*Turpis universo non congruens,*" wisely says the strong-hearted Augustine, since every soul that is out of keeping with divine order must remain, in the license of a perverse will, forever vile, until restored to the dominion of truth by the attractiveness of light and the miseries of darkness.

Martin Farquhar Tupper.—A. D. 1810.

The author of "Proverbial Philosophy" thus exalts the omnipotent power that is destined to conquer the world:

Love is the weapon which Omnipotence reserved to conquer rebel man when all the rest had failed. Reason he parries; fear he answers blow to blow; future interests he meets with present pleasure; but love, that sun against whose melting beams Winter cannot stand—that soft, subduing slumber, which wrestles down the giant—there is not one human creature in a million, not a thousand men in all the earth's huge quintillion, whose clay heart is hardened against love.

Charles Sumner.—A. D. 1811–1874.

The eloquent reformer and senator thus speaks in his oration on "Progress":

Every victory over evil redounds to the benefit of all. Every discovery, every human thought, every truth when declared, is a conquest of which the whole human family are partakers. * * * * * *

>Thus does the "Law of Human Progress"
>   Assert eternal Providence,
>   And justify the ways of God to man,

by showing Evil no longer a gloomy mystery, binding the world in everlasting thrall, but as an accident, destined under the laws of God to be slowly subdued by the works of men, as they pass on to the promised goal of happiness.

It is true that there are various races of men, but there is but one great human family, in which Caucasian, Ethiopian, Chinese and Indian are all brothers, children of one Father, and heirs of one happiness.

Horace Greeley.—A. D. 1811–1872.

The ablest American journalist was a zealous Universalist. He was an active member of Rev. Dr. E. H. Chapin's parish in New York. Here is a sentence worthy of being engraved on a panel of gold. May it not contain the secret of his zeal?

Believing most firmly in the ultimate and perfect triumph of good over evil, I rejoice in the existence and diffusion of that liberty, which, while it intensifies the contest, accelerates the consummation.

In his "Recollections of a Busy Life" Mr. Greeley declares:

I had read the Bible through, much of it repeatedly, but when quite too infantile to form any coherent, definite synopsis of the doctrines I presumed to be taught therein. But soon after entering a printing office, I procured exchanges with several Universalist periodicals, and was thenceforth familiar with their methods of interpretation and of argument.

I am not, therefore, to be classed with those who claim to have been converted from one creed to another by studying the Bible alone. Certainly, upon re-reading that book in the light of my new convictions, I found therein abundant proof of their correctness in the averments of patriarchs (Gen. iii: 15; xii:3), prophets (Isa. xxv: 8; xlv: 22-25), apostles (Rom. v:12-21; viii:19-21; I. Cor. xv:42-54; Eph. i:8-10; Colos. i: 19-21; I. Tim. ii:3-6), and of the Messiah himself (Matt. xv: 13). But, not so much in particular passages, however pertinent, and decisive as in the spirit and general scope of the Gospel—so happily blending inexorable punishment for every offence with unfailing pity and ultimate forgiveness for the chastened transgressor—thus saving sinners from sin by leading them, through suffering, to loathe and forsake it; and in laying down its golden rule, which, if of universal application, must be utterly inconsistent with the infliction of infinite and unending torture as the penalty of transient, and often ignorant, offending, did I find ample warrant for my hope and trust that all suffering is disciplinary, and transitional, and shall ultimately result in universal holiness and consequent happiness

W. M. Thackeray.—A. D. 1811–1863.

We place this man of genius in our constellation of great names. In the absence of other evidence, the following is sufficient authority. Speaking of the genius of Charles Dickens, he says:

I recognize in it—I speak it with awe and reverence—a commission from that Divine Beneficence, whose blessed task we know it will one day be to wipe every tear from every eye.

J. H. Scholten.—A. D. 1811.

The Professor of Theology, Leyden, declares:

The restoration of all things to be inferred from the efficacy of the Spirit of Christ seems to be declared by Christ (Matt. xiii: 13; John xii: 32), and by Paul, (I. Cor. xv: 22-28; Rom. v: 18; xi: 32; Col. 1: 19, 20; Phil. ii: 10; I. Tim. ii: 4; iv: 10). It is a doctrine in accordance with the spiritual nature of man, and is demanded as well by the holiness as by the love of God, with which the thought of eternal evil is inconsistent. Passages in which everlasting misery or absolute destruction seem to be taught are to be explained either by the popular mode of expression or by the eschatological representation prevalent among the Jews (Matt. xxv: 46). Or, they are meant to indicate the wretched condition in which the world unsaved by Christ lies (Rom. ii: 8, 9; iii: 19); or, in fine, they describe the absolute misery of sin, the loss to the sinner of all spiritual life, certain to come unless he repent and God avert it (Matt. 19: 25, 26; xii: 31; Mark iii: 29). This is the biblical doctrine of the restitution—as by sin all are obnoxious to death, corruption, perdition, condemnation, the wrath of God, destruction, judgment, æonian punishment, so by Christ through the efficacy of the Holy Spirit, all shall sooner or later be restored to life, so that there shall be no place in the universe without the worship of the true God in the name of Jesus Christ (Phil. ii: 10).—*Dogmat. Christ. Initia 270.*

Harriet Beecher Stowe.—A. D. 1812.

Mrs. Stowe's writings abound in satire of the absurd vagaries of the Puritan theology. While we do not feel certain that she has anywhere avowed faith in the ultimate redemption of all souls, we are sure that the drift of her words is against the opposite error.

In "The Minister's Wooing" (p. 139) Candace utterly repudiates the teachings of Dr. Hopkins and the catechism, and declares:

"I didn't do dat ar' for one, I knows. I's got good mem'ry,—always knows what I does,—neber did eat dat ar' apple,—neber eat a bit ob him—don't tell me!"

She records, with evident satisfaction, that the facts of the Divine administration seemed horrible to Jonathan Edwards, and that the puritanic theories on many minds had the effect of "slow poison," resembling "the New Testament as the living embrace of a friend does his lifeless body, mapped out under the knife of the anatomical demonstrator." When James Marvyn was supposed to have died, his mother, in view of his probable damnation, declared God to be "hard, unjust, cruel;—to all eternity I will say so." And in contrast with Dr. Hopkins' outrageous theology, Mrs. Stowe brings out the simple truth from the lips of the poor negress, Candace:

"Why, de Lord a'n't like what ye tink—he loves ye, honey! Why, jes' feel how I love ye—poor, old, black Candace,—an' I a'n't better'n him as made me! Who was it wore de crown o' thorns, lamb? Who was it sweat great drops o' blood? Who was it said,—'Father, forgive them?' Say, honey, wasn't it de Lord dat made ye?"

These simple allusions to the boundless love of God accomplished what the theology of New England failed to accomplish, and we read with delight how the sorrowful experiences of Mary Scudder won her away from the heartless teachings of her minister, who was no other than the high priest of error, Dr. Hopkins, himself, till one day

> In a praying circle of the women of the church, all were startled by the clear silver tones of one who sat among them and spoke with the unconscious simplicity of an angel child, calling God her Father, and speaking of an ineffable union in Christ, binding all things together in one, and making all complete in him.

Her opinion of the old puritanic scheme is well expressed by Sam Lawson, who, when the parson had described the small number of the finally saved, said, —"Well, any on ye's welcome to my chance." And the reader of "The Minister's Wooing" cannot fail to sympathize with the model Yankee, Prissy, who said:

> I hope I may be accepted on account of the Lord's great goodness; for if we can't trust that, it's all over with us all.

Norman MacLeod, D. D.—A. D. 1812–1872.

This eminent Scottish divine and author, owned MacLeod Campbell and Erskine, of Linlathen, as his teachers. In his biography by his brother, Dr. Donald MacLeod, it is shown that the idea of universal restoration grew on him to the last, and his friend, Alex. Strahan, relates, (*Contemporary Review*, pp. 297–8, Vol. XX:)

When our common friend, Mr. George Macdonald, was about to write for *Good Words*, of which Dr. MacLeod was editor, Dr. MacLeod was anxious that no heterodox views should be introduced into it. For hours the two discussed the matter in the publishing office with the friendliest warmth. At length in tripped a little girl, and by her simple, wise prattle, not only put an end to the controversy, but actually became the model for the most interesting character of the story. Before his death Dr. McLeod had adopted Mr. Maurice's standpoint on this question, as he emphatically made manifest in the last sermon I heard him preach at Balmoral.

Charles Mackay.—A. D. 1812.

This cheerful singer indicates the true philosophy when he says:

> Once we thought that Power Eternal
>   Had decreed the woes of man;
> That the human heart was wicked
>   Since its pulses first began;
> That the earth was but a prison,
>   Dark and joyless at the best,
> And that men were born for evil,
>   And imbibed it from the breast;
> That 'twas vain to think of urging
>   Any earthly progress on.
> Old opinions! rags and tatters!
>   Get you gone! get you gone!
>
> Old opinions, rags and tatters;
>   Ye are worn;—ah, quite threadbare!
> We must cast you off forever;—
>   We are wiser than we were;

Never fitting, always cramping,
   Letting in the wind and sleet,
Chilling us with rheums and agues,
   Or inflaming us with heat.
We have found a mental raiment
   Purer, whiter to put on.
Old opinions! rags and tatters!
   Get you gone! get you gone!

A little child beneath a tree,
Sat and chanted cheerily
A little song, a pleasant song,
Which was—she sung it all day long—
"When the wind blows the blossoms fall;
But a good God reigns over all."

There passed a lady by the way,
Moaning in the face of day;
There were tears upon her cheek,
Grief in her heart too great to speak;
Her husband died but yestermorn,
And left her in the world forlorn.

She stopped and listened to the child,
That looked to heaven, and singing, smiled;
And saw not, for her own despair,
Another lady, young and fair,
Who also passing, stopped to hear
The infant-anthem ringing clear.

For she but a few sad days before
Had lost the little babe she bore;
And grief was heavy at her soul
As that sweet memory o'er her stole,
And showed how bright had been the Past,
The Present drear and overcast.

And as they stood beneath the tree,
Listening, soothed and placidly,
A youth came by, whose sunken eyes
Spake of a load of miseries;
And he, arrested like the twain,
Stopped to listen to the strain.

Death had bowed the youthful head
Of his bride beloved, his bride unwed;
Her marriage robes were fitted on,
Her fair young face with blushes shone,
When the destroyer smote her low,
And changed the lover's bliss to woe.

And these three listened to the song,
Silver-toned, and sweet, and strong,
Which that child, the live-long day,
Chanted to itself in play:
"When the wind blows the blossoms fall,
But a good God reigns over all."

The widow's lips impulsive moved;
The mother's grief, though unreproved,
Softened, as her trembling tongue
Repeated what the infant sung;
And the sad lover, with a start,
Conned it over to his heart.

And though the child—if child it were,
And not a seraph sitting there—
Was seen no more, the sorrowing three
Went on their way resignedly,
The song still ringing in their ears—
Was it the music of the spheres?

Who shall tell? They did not know.
But in the midst of deepest woe

The strain recurred when sorrow grew,
To warn them and console them, too:
"When the wind blows the blossoms fall,
But a good God reigns over all."

Charles Dickens.—A. D. 1812–1870.

The cheerful, sunny, genial spirit of Dickens' works is the soul of our faith. His books are pervaded by it, and saturated with it. Here is a favorable specimen:

Ye men of gloom and austerity, who paint the face of Infinite Benevolence with an eternal frown, read in the everlasting book, wide open to your view, the lesson it would teach. Its pictures are not in the black and sombre hues, but bright and glowing tints; its music, save when ye drown it, is not in sighs and groans, but in songs and cheerful sounds. Listen to the million of voices in the summer air, and find one dismal as your own. Remember, if you can, the sense of hope and pleasure which every grand return of day awakens in the breast of all your kind, and learn wisdom even from the witless, when their hearts are lifted up, by all the happiness it brings.

Robert Browning.—A. D. 1812.

Bishop Gilbert Haven, of the Methodist church, in the New York *Independent*, accuses Browning of being guilty of the heresy of modern poetry, of hoping that "good will be the final goal of ill," in these words:

My own hope as a sun will pierce
  The thickest cloud earth ever stretched,
That after Last returns the First,
  Though a wide compass round be fetched,
That what began best can't be worst,
  And what God blest once prove accurst.

Henry Ward Beecher.—A. D. 1813.

The great Brooklyn divine has often spoken in a way to indicate broader views than those of his church. The following is an example:

When I see what the old rocking continents are doing, and have been doing, from the creation, from the days of the flood, through all the treacheries and pitfalls wherein the human race has been reeling and staggering down to modern times; when I look at Asia and Africa, and Europe, and America, and both continents of it, and see what the actual condition of the neglected, the stripped, the peeled, the despoiled, the downtrodden races of men has been; if I thought that in addition to all this there was a God that was clothed in thunder, and whose business it was to stand at the door where men go out of life and crush them downward into eternal hell,—every instinct of charity, of sympathy and of love that is born in me by Christ, would stand crying, "Annihilate him! Annihilate him!" It would be the sorrow of the universe that would raise this cry.

His latest utterance (in 1880) is to the effect that while he rejects endless punishment, as unscriptural and unreasonable, the final outcome can only be inferred by analogy and reason.

J. Ross Browne.

This popular writer in "Yusef," p. 136, says:

> Is it for self-constituted judges to say that these people (the Turks) taught from infancy to regard their peculiar belief as the only true means of salvation, should be rewarded for their sincerity by everlasting torment? Oh, ye who are wrapt in the selfishness of a single idea! ye who bode destruction to others! look out upon the broad universe and learn that there are millions of human hearts as sincere and devoted as yours, and that there is a Divine power great and good and merciful enough to save all, even to the weakest and most benighted.

Sylvester Judd.—A. D. 1813–1852.

The author of "Philo," "Margaret," "Richard Edney," etc., says:

> I had as lief be damned, as see another damned.

Again:

> The stars are out, all out, heaven's telegraph
> By night. What the intelligence, dear Faith?
> 'Tis thine to spell the twinkling syllables.
> It is the same old word since time began,
> Repeated seven nights a week—God loveth."

Rev. C. A. Bartol.—A. D. 1813.

The idea that God changes, turns his face from the sinner who passes unreconciled, takes, beyond any profane swearing, his name in vain. No repentance or hope beyond the death-bed? As the tree falleth it must lie? The human soul is not a fallen tree! The best repentance for the worst transgressor or most precious saint is after earthly decease, and Watts' line is true of neither,—

> Fixed in an eternal state;

for it were a fine degradation of the future to annul there the law of progress which is the sole comfort here.

That a babe is born totally corrupt, that a favored few are chosen and the rest eternally doomed, that any child of God can be finally lost, that his innocent son could be punished, doctrines once unthinkingly proclaimed,—are now impossible propositions; not discarded from among the articles, but suffered to sleep, given the go-by, laid upon the table, because there is no chamber open to them in the human brain.

Sorely as we have offended, we can do nothing fatal. Sheer blasphemy and inhumanity in the old theology is the doctrine of a doom to perdition and eternal woe for our personal or our ancestral delinquency. The bottomless pit were a blot on Deity, though but one soul wallowed in it!

Rev. Fergus Ferguson.

Rev. Fergus Ferguson, of the United Presbyterian church, of Scotland, who is honored by being called a heretic, has recently lectured on "Modern Orthodoxy." The dilemma of self-styled orthodoxy, in the opinion, and in the language of Mr. Ferguson, is, in cherishing the doctrine of the eternity of evil,—

> A notion not only incompatible with every one of the fundamental propositions of pure orthodoxy, but logically destructive of every one of them.

Caroline M. Sawyer.—A. D. 1812.

A sheep is lost! A restless lamb astray,
Hath wandered from the fold! Send forth the cry,
"'Twill be devoured!" Fierce, ravening monsters lie
In wait to rend it! Rouse the shepherd! Nay!
Since the first dawning of the murky day,
He has been out among the desert hills
Where lurks the brood whose fang a drop distils,
Whose touch is death! He knows the wolf may slay
His helpless lamb; far down the precipice
That jagged rocks may crush its tender form,
And the Good Shepherd will search on, nor cease
Till in his arms he bear it safely home.
O Savior! Shepherd! 'mid the wastes of sin,
Still seek thy wandering sheep and bring the last one in!

Daniel Schenkel.—A. D. 1813.

Prof. Schenkel is eminent as a theologian, in Heidelberg:

In the common doctrine of the eternal damnation of those who persist in unbelief during this life, there lies the recognition of a truth—that the sin of this life will influence the life to come. But this recognition has been presented in a form quite self-contradictory, and essentially injurious to faith. The conception that a considerable portion of the human race, appointed by God to salvation, is sunk in the endless pain of damnation, has in every age brought heavy burdens of difficulty on the consciences of all believing Christians. These burdens reason has sought to remove, either by supposing the damnation only hypothetically everlasting, i. e., measured as to comparative lightness or severity by the degree of guilt to be punished. The notion of a conditionally, i. e., under certain circumstances, eternal punishment of finite sins is in itself contradictory and untenable (§§156, etc., 188, etc.). Another conception, therefore, has secured for itself acceptance under different forms—the obstinately unbelieving, it is thought, will in consequence of their unbelief be punished after death with annihilation, and this of course will put an end to their suffering. As sin, however, according to its nature, cannot have infinite but merely finite results, the conception of an endless punishment of sinners, whether it be regarded as unconditional or conditional, is to be at once rejected.

But other weighty reasons stand in the way of the doctrine of "eternal damnation." It surely stands particularly in contradiction to the absolute Divine Nature which is love, to suspend an absolute evil over those who are appointed to bring the Divine Nature to manifestation (§140). By an absolute evil inside the world, the harmony of the universe would unavoidably be disturbed, and the absolute might and glory of goodness be injured. Besides the "eternal" torment endured by a finite person, would at last of necessity come to an end, since it would destroy its victim.

Therefore, the doctrine of an eternal damnation of sinners is an imaginary instrument of terror intended for coarser nerves. The punishment of the unbeliever lies, as is testified in the fourth Gospel, in the unbelief itself, in the entire or partial destruction of the communion of the personal life with God. Personal life is not annihilated by the entire cessation of Divine fellowship, but is pressed down almost to the level of brutish stupidity, and to work up again from this requires heavy labor and long time. This is the "outer darkness," the spiritual death which Holy Scripture so startlingly pictures. But even into this night the ray of Divine grace can penetrate, for the nature of man may be injured by sin, but never can be destroyed. We believe not in death, we believe in eternal life, for God hath given us the victory through our Lord Jesus Christ. (Isa. lxvi: 24; Matt. xxv; Mark ix: 44; Matt. xxv: 30; Rom. xi: 32; Jno. iii: 18; I.Cor. xv: 54 and etc.)—*Die Grundlehren des Christenthums, Leipsic, 1877.* [Original translation.]

Franz Delitzsch.—A. D. 1813.

Ps. cl:6. The call to praise has thus far been addressed to persons not mentioned by name, but, as the names of instruments thus heaped up show, to Israel especially. It is now generalized to "the totality of breath," i. e., all the beings who are endowed by God with the breath of life (nishmath chayyim), i. e., to all mankind.

With this full-toned finale the psalter closes. Having risen as it were by five steps, in this closing psalm it hovers over the blissful summit of the end, where, as Gregory of Nyssa says, all creatures, after the disorder and disunion caused by sin have been removed, are harmoniously united for one choral dance (eis mian chorostasian), and the chorus of mankind concerting with the angel chorus are become one cymbal of divine praise, and the final song of victory shall salute God the triumphant conqueror (tōi Tropaiuchōi) with shouts of joy. There is no need for any special closing beracha (blessing). This whole closing Psalm is such. Nor is there any need even of an amen (cvi:48, comp. I. Chron. xvi:36). The "Hallelujah" includes it within itself and exceeds it.—*Commentary on the Psalms, by Franz Delitzsch, D. D., Professor of Old and New Testament Exegesis, Leipsic. Translation of Clark, Edinburgh, 1873.*

Delitzsch has the highest reputation for scholarship and orthodoxy.

This same writer, in the same commentary, says, Ps. lxxxiii:18, 19:

The aim of the wish is that they, in the midst of their downfall, may lay hold upon the mercy of Jahve as their only deliverance. First, they must come to nought, and only by giving Jahve the glory will they not be utterly destroyed. In view of v. 17, that they may know (as in lix:14), has not merely the sense of perceiving so far as the justice of the punishment is concerned; the knowledge which is not salvation, is not excluded. The end of the matter which the poet wishes to see brought about is this, that Jahve, that the God of revelation may become the all-exalted one in the consciousness of the nations. [Original translation.]

Rev. Alexander Schweizer.

Equally must be corrected the error of a coördinate dualism in the award of Blessedness and Damnation. Hence, also the representation of the punishment of hell as applied by a divine justice wholly severed from love, and hence a punishment embracing in it no more any element of reformation, as if the justice of God could ever at any time become destitute of love, and make reformation quite impossible. In fine, the idea must be corrected of punishments in hell which never end, because the infinite Being injured by sin must eternally punish. If one says with Lessing that sin once done can never be undone, and therefore can never cease to have consequences, inasmuch as he who reforms can never absolutely restore what he neglected; the answer may be given that sin repented of may contribute even to the hastening of the process of sanctification. At all events, the consequences of former sins in the case of the penitent and justified serve for chastisement, and therefore cease to be punishment. As in fine the peculiar evil of punishment is itself one with sin, namely, loss of fellowship with God and childlike trust in him, and as these are restored in the new birth, yea, even become closer out of gratitude for rescuing grace, penal judgment altogether ceases for him who becomes alive to the religion of redemption, and only where this religion ever remains absent must judgment ever abide. Life, however, in a religion of mere law is, but an initial and transitional condition, which God can never fix if he really appoints all to the religion of redemption.

It has been found so very difficult to hold simply by the eternity of punishment that the dogmatic theologians, thinking of all sorts of alleviation, sometimes speak of a merely hypothetical eternity of damnation. God alone, they say, is absolutely eternal, and we had beginning in time, and so of course the reference can only be to a never ending future—an inkling this that the conception of eternity is here unsuitable.

If the damned have become so by their unbelief, then never ending punishment is only tenable in the case of never ceasing unbelief, and this is only conceivable by God's absolute withdrawal of his gracious love, a thing incompatible with the idea of God. Just as incompatible is the eternal suffering of many brothers with the blesssedness of the rest, for what Zwingli objects against the prayers of the blessed for us pilgrims on earth must, apart from this application, certainly be regarded as valid "that if the blessed know our troubles they could not be blessed, since blessedness can only exist in the absence of sorrow and care." Schleiermacher carries out this thought as follows:—"The blessed could not but have sympathy for the condition of the damned; this however, would of necessity disturb their blessedness on account of the hopelessness of the condition; and its influence would be the more disturbing the more they looked at the condition in contrast with that allotted to themselves once as far astray." But apart from its incompatibility with the idea of God and with the brotherly love of the Blessed, eternal damnation is in itself an untenable conception. Christianity will in any case put away the religious dualism which in the form of Manichaëism endeavors to press into her.

Evil, moreover, as such, has no real being coördinate with God. It is not substance but only corrupt condition in a being which is of God. It is corruption of a finite being, privation of its integrity and reality, and can never exist otherwise than as perverted condition of an actual creature. Never can it appear without such a being and by itself, nor can it ever become by itself a substantial being. The subject of sin remains however a creature of God, were it ever so corrupted, and though God negatives the sin he yet sustains every substantial being; wills it, bears it and loves it. He never can hate, negative, destroy the corrrupted being as he does its sin—but ever seek to heal, rescue, restore, just as the Christian is to love even his most malicious enemy, and in this very thing be God's child formed in his likeness.

The (accidentally so-called) Apokatastasis of all, even of Satan, has therefore pressed itself on devout Christian teachers, and in spite of ecclesiastical rejection, seeks ever anew entrance into the creed. Even Zwingli remembers (Op. vii: 124) that "the substance of the evil angels is simple, and, as such, good, their morals only being godless, though not equally so in all; and that therefore Origen seems not unreasonable when he says that at the future judgment some of these angels would return to grace." The objection brought against the ultimate universalism of Origen which deduces the final deliverance of all from the boundless extent of the divine compassion does not well bear examination.

As regards acquittal and condemnation, and the resulting happiness or misery, the principle always holds good; whoever becomes alive to the religion of redemption is also justified, and has peace and restored fellowship with God; while he that persists in the religion of law is condemned and separated from God, has an *Ego* to which the law as an outward despotic commandment prescribes servile tasks, so that obeying he remains away from God, and transgressing he stands directly opposed to God. Here, however, we cannot set up the notion of eternal punishment in the sense of never ending, but must preserve the true sense of eternity; for it stands unalterably settled beyond all time that the religion of law necessarily issues in judgment. As this, however, is but the first form of the religious relationship to God, merely a state of transition pointing away beyond itself, and as the grace of God has appointed all to sonship and keeps intent on redeeming every one from legal servitude which works itself out into misery, and on bringing every one to sonship through Christ, it must be that at last the finite creature shall be freely won by infinite grace, and that a man still remaining condemned in the religion of law is to be viewed as one not yet arrived at his destination.—*Original translation, Vol. II, Christliche Glaubenslehre, Leipsic, 1877.* [Prof. Schweizer is Professor of Theology in Zurich.]

Rev. John Page Hopps.

It is impossible that God will punish eternally. He could not do it out of mere revenge, that it is utterly impossible to believe. He need not do it to vindicate his law, since that is better provided for in the happiness of those who do well than in the misery of those who do ill. He will not do it to deter the guiltless, since his perfect justice could never admit an eternal wrong, in the case of even the meanest of his creatures, to achieve even the greatest good, for the allotments of God, even to the guilty and castaway, are guided by infinite justice and eternal beneficence and love. I believe, then, that in our Father's house beyond, there are many mansions, places suited for every grade of spiritual and moral condition, that all little children go at once to God, "their angels" beholding his face forever; and that all sorrowing, struggling, ignorant, and careworn people, will find education, and light, and a helpful hand hereafter. To believe anything else than this would be to accuse God of cruelty, would be to make our life a curse, and make us all feel that it would have been better for us that we had never been born. I believe that this world is only one of the rooms in the great Father's house, that in the other world, as well as in this, God's "tender mercies are over all his works," and that whatever men and creeds may say, our God is love, and will be love to all men and in all worlds forever. (Leicester, Eng.)

Rev. G. Vance Smith, D. D., Ph. D.

Our Lord Jesus Christ, when he speaks of God as "our Father in heaven," and in many other expressions (e. g. Matt. v: 44-48; Luke vi: 36), appeals to the emotions and feelings of the human mind for language wherewith to convey to us his own conception of the moral nature of God. How is this plain fact in the Christian teachings to be reconciled with statements which would represent the Almighty Being as doing that from which our nature leads at once to shrink with aversion and horror? How is the clear and constant representation of God by Christ, as "our heavenly Father" to be reconciled with a doctrine which makes him do that which not merely no human father would do to his child, but no human being whatever, possessed of anything like a human heart, could do even to his bitterest enemy? What should we think of a man who should consign one who had injured him to torment for his life in a place of fire and brimstone, if such a thing were possible? And what must we think of a God who would consign his creatures who had offended him to torments, not of lifelong, but of everlasting duration? who should even keep them alive to no other end than that they might endure the fierceness of his wrath for ever and ever? We know that it is a property of fire to consume and destroy, and that if our present bodies were subjected to the power of even ordinary fire they would quickly perish. This would be a merciful alternative to those who are doomed to hell. But the common belief does not allow them to have it. It assumes that the body will be continually renewed and strengthened, or so changed that it shall not perish. The lost shall not be allowed to die, but shall be maintained in life able to feel and to endure for untold ages—ages which shall never be exhausted, never come to an end—able to feel and to endure the unspeakable anguish of the fire which is not quenched, and the worm which dieth not. And this destiny is reserved, or shall we say appointed, for inconceivable multitudes of men by him who is their "Father in heaven," a "God of mercy," and a "God of love," and the

Gospel in which it is said to be announced to us is often spoken of as a Gospel of "good tidings of great joy which shall be to all people."

If all this be true of God, surely man had better not be told to imitate him, and never can love him with any genuine, durable love. He may, indeed, fear or even hate the author of his existence, but how on this theory of an eternal hell, he can love him, we are at a loss to conceive.

* * A true faith in the living God will not forget that it may be even a suggestion of that inspiration which "giveth us understanding" which is impelling so large a number of devout and thoughtful men to rebel against and throw aside the old belief in an endless hell as something essentially heathenish, and out of harmony with any right feeling of reverence in us toward the God and Father of Jesus Christ. The ever-present Spirit, let us nothing doubt, can speak to us even now, as of old to patriarchs, prophets, and apostles, and if he should be leading us to see that much in their beliefs was wrong, the mere product of an age of ignorance, unworthy of him whose name is Love, and Mercy, and Holiness, surely it is our part, not to resist or despise, but gratefully to acquiesce in this advance toward a clearer, fuller apprehension of divine truth.

The Rev. G. Vance Smith, B. A., D. D. and Ph. D., London, Eng., was a member of the English Commission for the Revision of the Bible, and Principal of the Presbyterian College, Caermarthen.

Bishop Colenso.—A. D. 1814.

In the last seven years I have carefully studied it, with an earnest desire to know the truth of God upon the matter, and with an humble desire for the guidance and teaching of the Holy Spirit in the search for it. I now declare that I can no longer maintain or give utterance to the doctrine of future punishment—that I dare not dogmatize at all on the matter—that I can only lay my hand upon my mouth, and leave it in the hands of the merciful God.

Jules Francois Suisse Simon.—A. D. 1814.

This celebrated French statesman declares:

The guilty will be punished; this alone concerns us, since this alone concerns the justifying of Providence; the nature of the punishment is to us indifferent. We know that it will be proportioned to the guilt, for the Judge is infallible. We ought to hope that God will mingle mercy with justice and grant to the guilty the opportunity of winning amelioration by repentance.. Punishment serves a two-fold purpose,—expiation of the guilt and reformation of the guilty. We are asked whether punishment will endure eternally? It is a question which should not be introduced by itself into philosophy. The eternity of punishment destroys one of the two objects of punishment, purification, reformation; it exaggerates the other beyond possibility, for there is no sin committed in time which calls for an eternal punishment. There is no principle of reason which either leads to the doctrine of the eternity of punishment or even admits of it.—*La Religion Nationelle, p. 304 1857.*

George Dawson.

Take the question upon which modern thought is more troubled than any other. Take the doctrine in which most of you were brought up—that every man who is not saved theologically will go to hell, and that hell is a wonderful torment, a constant fire, whereunto a man, forever and forever, for the brief mistakes and sins of three score years and ten, must be condemned. I am told this is in the Scriptures. I can't find it; but if it were there I would not believe it. I can't say that I ever believed it. I was told that it was so, and I have no doubt I said it was so, but whether I had then ever examined the matter I hardly know. But now I disbelieve it. If this is backsliding I will backslide.

Well, how came we ever to doubt this tremendous doctrine? Not that any commentator with marvelous exegesis showed us that the text did not mean that;—for I am but little interested in the quibble that the fire burns forever, but that the thing put into the fire burns only so long as it is capable of burning. What has put hell fire out, is the better understanding of God, the glorious growth of science, an insight into the eternal principles of law, and a fuller comprehension of the divineness of God's love. The love of God has conquered the assertion of orthodoxy.—*Sermons on "Disputed Points," p. 65, London, 1878.*

Charles Reade.—A. D. 1814.

The great novelist declares:

Eternal punishment! if it is not a fable, who has earned better than I am earning if I go on. It is a fable, it must be so. Philosophers always said so, and now even divines have given it up. From "Put Yourself in his Place," chap. xxiii.

John Cooper Vail.—A. D. 1815.

As the burning bush on Sinai did the shepherd seer surprise,
All shall see the star of Mercy on the wings of prayer arise,
To guide the last-forgiven to the gates of paradise.

Philip James Bailey.—A. D. 1816.

The author of "Festus" causes the great truth of the final redemption of man to burn along the lines of his thought

>   ——They who read not in the blest belief,
> That all souls may be saved, read to no end;
> We were made to be saved.

Again:

>   Nought eternal is
> But that which is of God. All pain and woe
> Are therefore finite.

> I come to repay sin with holiness,
> And death with immortality; man's soul
> With God's Spirit; all evil with all good.
> All men have sinned; and as for all I died,
> All men are saved. Oh! not a single soul,
> Less than the countless all can satisfy
> The infinite triumph which to me belongs.

>   The hour is named
> When seraph, cherub, angel, saint, man, fiend,
> Made pure and unbelievably uplift
> Above their present state—drawn up to God,
> Like dew into the air—shall be all heaven;
> And all souls shall be in God.

Again:

> Thus heavenward all things tend, for all were once
> Perfect, and all must be at length restored,
> So God has greatly purposed; who would else,
> In his dishonored works himself endure
> Dishonor, and be wronged without redress.

Again:

> But human nature is not infinite,
> And, therefore, cannot suffer, endlessly

> Evil is
> Good in another way we are not skilled in.

> And though ye died,
> And fell, and fell again, and again died,
> There is a life to come, a rise for all,
> A life to come forever, and a rise
> Perpetual as the Spring is in the year.

Stay, Spirit! All created things unmade;
It suits not the eternal laws of good,
That evil be immortal. In all space
Is joy and glory, and the gladdened stars
Exultant in the sacrifice of sin,
And of all human matter in themselves,
Leap forth as though to welcome earth to heaven,
Leap forth and die. All nature disappears.
Shadows are passed away. Through all is light.
Man is as high above temptation now,—
And where by Grace he always shall remain,
As ever sun o'er sea; and sin is burned
In hell to ashes with the dust of death.
The worlds themselves are but as dreams within
Their souls who lived in them, and thou art null,
And thy vocation useless, gone with them.
Therefore shall heaven rejoice in thee again,
And the lost tribes of angels, who with thee
Wedded themselves to woe, and all who dwell
Around the dizzy centers of all worlds,
Again be blessed with the blessedest.
Lo! ye are all restored, rebought, rebrought
To heaven by him who cast ye forth, your God.
Receive ye tenfold of all gifts and powers.

And thou, who cam'st to heaven to claim one soul,
Remain possessed by all. The sons of bliss
Shall welcome thee again, and all thy host,
Whereof thou first in glory as in woe—
In brightness as in darkness erst—shalt shine.
Take, Lucifer, thy place. This day art thou
Redeemed to archangelic state. Bright child
Of morning, once again thou shinest fair
O'er all the starry ornaments of light.

LUCIFER.—The highest and the humblest I of all
  The beings thou hast made, eternal Lord!

ANGEL.—Behold, they come, the legions of the lost,
  Transformed already by the bare behest,
  Of God our Maker, to the purest form
  Of seraph brightness.

THE RESTORD ANGELS.—His be all the praise!
And ours submissive thanks. When Evil had done
Its worst, then God most blessed us and forgave.
Oh, he hath triumphed over all the world,
In mercy over death, and earth, and hell!

SON OF GOD.—All God hath made are saved. Heaven is complete!

My Lord, my God!
Thine is the Spirit which commands and smiles;
The soul which serves and suffers:—thine the stars
Tabled upon thy bosom like the stones
Oracular of light, on the priest's breast;
Thine the minutest mote the moonbeams shew!
Let but thy words come true, and all are blest;
Be but thine infinite intents fulfilled,—
And what shall foil the covenanted oath

Whereon the mounded earth is based?—and lo!
The whole at last redeemed and glorified.
—*Angel World.*

James Gaylord Clark.

Clark is one of the most popular of modern song-writers:

>We shall meet again in the By-and-by,
>Where the mountains gleam in the morning sky,
>We shall meet again in the land of love,
>>Our Father's home above.

Cho.:—We shall meet again, we shall meet again,
>In the beautiful Isles of the By-and-by,
>We shall meet again, we shall meet again,
>>In the Isles of the By-and-by.

>In the balmly Isles where the angels roam,
>By the crystal seas of our Father's home,
>There are forms of grace and of beauty rare
>>And the ones we have lost are there.

>We must part in tears when the twilight dies,
>On the far-off hills of our evening skies,
>We shall meet in joy where our loved dear stand,
>>In the gates of the morning land.

>We shall fall asleep where the Autumn grieves
>O'er the faded flowers and the falling leaves,
>We shall wake again where the angels sing,
>>In the bloom of eternal Spring.

John G. Saxe.—A. D. 1816.

There is a saying of the ancient sages,—
　No noble human thought,
However buried in the dust of ages,
　Can ever come to naught.
With kindred faith that knows no base dejection,
　Beyond the sage's scope
I see afar the final resurrection
　Of every glorious hope.

The Brontë Sisters.—A. D. 1816–1855.

The authoresses of "Jane Eyre," "Wuthering Heights," "Shirley," "Poems," etc., have repeatedly developed the doctrine we cherish. Witness the following from "Music on Christmas Morning," by Acton Bell:

With them I celebrate his birth—
　Glory to God, in highest heaven,
Good will to men, and peace on earth,
　To us a Savior-King is given;
Our God is come to claim his own,
And Satan's power is overthrown!

A sinless God for sinful men,
Descends to suffer and to bleed;
Hell must renounce its empire then;
The price is paid, the world is freed,
And Satan's self must now confess
That Christ has earned a right to bless.

Now holy peace may smile from heaven,
　And heavenly Truth from earth shall spring,

The captive's galling bonds are riven,
   For our Redeemer is our king;
And he that gave his blood for men
Will lead us home to God again!

You may rejoice to think yourselves secure;
   You may be grateful for the gift divine,—
That grace unsought which made your black hearts pure,
   And fits your earth-born souls in heaven to shine.

But is it sweet to look around, and view
   Thousands excluded from that happiness
Which they deserve at least as much as you—
   Their faults not greater, nor their virtues less?

And wherefore should you love your God the more
   Because to you alone his smiles are given,—
Because he chose to pass the many o'er
   And only bring the favored few to heaven.

And wherefore should your hearts more grateful prove
   Because for all the Savior did not die?
Is yours the God of Justice and of Love?
   And are your bosoms warm with charity?

Say, does your heart expand to all mankind?
   And would you ever to your neighbor do—
The weak, the strong, the enlightened, and the blind,—
   As you would have your neighbor do to you?

And when you, looking on your fellow-men,
   Behold them doomed to endless misery,
How can you talk of joy and rapture then?
   May God withhold such cruel joy from me!

That none deserve eternal bliss, I know;
   Unmerited the grace in mercy given;

But none shall sink to everlasting woe,
  That have not well deserved the wrath of heaven.

    And oh, there lives within my heart,
      A hope long nursed by me;
    And should its cheering ray depart,
      How dark my soul would be!

    That as in Adam all have died,
      In Christ shall all men live;
    And ever round his throne abide
      Eternal praise to give.

    That even the wicked shall at last
      Be fitted for the skies;
    And when their dreadful doom is past
      To life and light arise.

    I ask not how remote the day,
      Nor what the sinner's woe,
    Before their dross is purged away;
      Enough for me to know,

    That when the cup of wrath is drained,
      The metal purified,
    They'll cling to what they once disdained
      And live by him that died.

"And remember, Helen," continued she, solemnly, "'the wicked shall be turned into hell, and they that forget God.'" And suppose, even, that he should continue to love you, and you him, and that you should pass through life together with tolerable comfort, how will it be in the end, when you see yourselves parted forever; you perhaps taken into eternal bliss, and he cast into the lake that burneth with unquenchable fire —there forever to—"Not forever," I exclaimed, "'only till he has paid the uttermost farthing,' for, 'if any man's work abide not the fire he shall suffer loss, yet himself shall be saved,— but so as by fire,' and he that is able to subdue all things unto himself, will have all men to be saved, and will, 'in the fulness of time gather in one all things in Christ Jesus, who tasted death for every man, and in whom God will reconcile all things to himself, whether they be things in earth, or things in heaven.'"

"O Helen! where did you learn all this?"

"In the Bible, aunt. I have searched it through, and found nearly thirty passages, all tending to support the same theory."

"And is that the use you make of your Bible? And did you find no passages tending to prove the danger and falsity of such a belief?"

"No; I found, indeed, some passages that, taken by themselves, might seem to contradict that opinion; but they will all bear a different construction to that which is commonly given, and in most, the only difficulty is in the word we translate 'everlasting' or 'eternal.' I don't know the Greek, but I believe it strictly means for ages, and might signify either endless or long enduring. And as for the danger of the belief, I would not publish it abroad, if I thought any poor wretch would be likely to presume upon it to his own destruction, but it is a glorious thought to cherish in one's own heart, and I would not part with it for all the world can give."

Again:

"O Frederic, none can imagine the miseries, bodily and mental, of that death-bed. How could I endure to think that that poor, trembling soul was hurried away to everlasting torment? it would drive me mad! But thank God! I have hope —not only on a vague dependence on the possibility that penitence and pardon might have reached him at the last, but from the blessed confidence that, through whatever purging fires the erring spirit may be doomed to pass, whatever fate awaits it, still it is not lost, and God, who hateth nothing he hath made, will bless it in the end!"—*Tenant of Wildfell Hall.*

J. J. Van Oosterzee.—A. D. 1817.

The learned author of "Christian Dogmatics"—Professor of Theology in the University of Utrecht, concludes that the New Testament teaches "an everlasting Too Late," but he confesses—p. 807, "Watson's Translation," *Scribner:*

From Origen to not a few Christians of our age we see the doctrine of the Apokatastasis confessed with inner conviction and warmth, and within his own heart many a one hears a voice which pleads in favor of the eventual general blessedness of all. The idea of an absolutely endless perdition has about it for our natural feelings something indescribably harsh, and appears, indeed, absolutely irreconcilable with all which we believe of God's redeeming love.

He also thinks God willing and able to conquer sin; that the idea of God's kingdom is of a universe of blissful creatures, and that Paul and John "waken and cherish" a "silent expectation" of universal salvation, and says:

On all these grounds one would almost feel justified in expunging, from the door of woe, the terrible inscription:—"All hope abandon, ye who enter here"; and substituting for it the jubilant chorus of sensuous joy:—"Allen Sünden soll vergeben, und die Hölle nicht mehr sein"; all sinners shall be forgiven, and hell be no more."

J. A. Froude.—A. D. 1818.

One of the most vigorous of modern writers, J. A. Froude, M. A., in his "Nemesis of Faith," gives vent to the feeling which is now so general in churches of all communions, of horror and disgust in reference to eternal punishment. He says:

> I know but one man, of more than miserable intellect, who, in these modern times, has dared defend eternal punishment, on the score of justice, and that is Leibnitz;—a man, who, if I know him rightly, chose the subject from its difficulty, as an opportunity for the display of his genius, and cared so little for the truth, that his conclusions did not cost his heart a pang, or wring a single tear from him. No; if I am to be a minister of religion, I must teach the poor people that they have a Father in heaven, not a tyrant; one who loves them all beyond power of heart to conceive; who is sorry when they do wrong, not angry; whom they are to love and dread, not with caitiff coward fear, but with deepest awe and reverence, as the all-pure, all-good, all-holy. I could never fear a God, who kept a hell prison-house. No; not though he flung me there because I refused.

The young Episcopal clergyman, who is the hero of the book, finds the absurdity of endless punishment an impassable barrier between his profession and his duty.

Acton Warburton.

Acton Warburton, the eloquent author of the "Footsteps of the Normans," says:

He (the Norman) looks forward to the time when he shall complete that acquaintance, where they have preceded, and await him in

> The land of souls, beyond the sable shore,

and knowing that the Sun of Mercy shines beyond the clouds of ancestral error, he would fain hope that one day would unite them all,—

> No wanderer lost,
> A family in heaven.

James Russel Lowell.—A. D. 1819.

O chime of sweet Saint Charity
    Peal soon that Easter morn,
When Christ for all shall risen be,
    And in all hearts new born!

That Pentecost when utterance clear
    To all men shall be given,
When all shall say, My Brother, here,
    And hear My Son in heaven!
Though earth swing wide of God's intent,
    And though no man nor nation
Will move with one consent
    In heavenly gravitation,
Yet by one Sun is every orbit bent.

O wandering dim on the extremest edge
    Of God's bright providence, whose spirits sigh
Drearily in you, like the Winter sedge
    That shivering o'er the dead pool stiff and dry,
A thin, sad voice, when the bold wind roars by,

  From the clear North of Duty,—
Still by cracked arch and broken shaft I trace
That here was once a shrine and holy place
  Of the Supernal Beauty,—
A child's play-altar reared of stones and moss,
With wilted flowers for offering laid across,
  Mute recognition of the all-ruling Grace.

  One band ye cannot break,—the force that clips
And grasps your circles to the central light;
  Yours is the prodigal comet's long ellipse,
Self exiled to the farthest verge of night;
Yet strives with you no less that inward might;
  No sin hath e'er imbruted
The god in you the creed-dimmed eye eludes;
The law looks not to have its solitudes
  By bigot feet polluted;—
Yet they who watch your God-compelled return
May see your happy perihelion burn
  Where the calm sun his unfledged planets broods.

Anonymous.

She stood outside the gate of heaven and saw them entering in,
A world-long train of shining ones, all washed in blood from sin.
 *   *   *   *   *   *   *
And when into the glory the last of all did go,
"Thank God! There is a heaven," she cried, "though mine is endless woe."

The angel of the golden gate, said, "Where then dost thou dwell,

And who art thou that enterest not?" "A soul escaped from
    hell."
"Who knows to bless with prayer like thine, in hell can never
    be;
God's angel could not if he would bar up this door from thee."
She left her sin outside the gate, and meekly entered there,
Breathed free the blessed air of heaven, and knew her native
    air.

Dr. R. A. Lipsius.

Professor of Theology, Jena:

Along with the idea of an eternal death even of a definitive damnation of the godless to eternal pain, there is also found, especially in Paul, the opposite expectation of a future conversion and blessedness of all.—*Lehrbuch der Dogmatik, 846.*

John Ruskin.—A. D. 1819.

John Ruskin, the greatest of art critics, and the greatest living master of English, has so expressed himself as to be entitled to rank among our "Cloud of Witnessess." In his "The Lord's Prayer and the Church—Letters Addressed to the Clergy," he says:

And the first clause of it—the Lord's Prayer—of course rightly explained, gives as the ground of what is surely a mighty part of the Gospel—its first great commandment, namely, that we have a Father whom we can love, and are required to love, and to desire to be with him in heaven, wherever that may be. and to declare that we have such a loving Father, whose mercy is over all his works and whose will and law is so lovely and lovable that it is sweeter than honey, and more precious than gold, and to those who can taste and see that the Lord is good —this surely is a most pleasant and glorious good message and spell to bring to men—as distinguished from the evil message and accursed spell that Satan has brought to the nations of the world instead of it that they have no Father, but only a consuming fire ready to devour them unless they are delivered from its raging flame by some scheme of pardon for all, for which they are to be thankful, not to the Father but to the Son.

Arthur Hugh Clough.—A. D. 1819–1861.

Ah, yet, when all is thought and said,
The heart still overrules the head;
Still what we hope we must believe,
And what is given us receive;
Must still believe for still we hope
That in a world of larger scope,
What here is faithfully begun
Will be completed, not undone.

Walt Whitman.—A. D. 1819.

This original poet thus chants:

All, all for Immortality!
Love, like the light, silently wrapping all!
Nature's amelioration blessing all!

The blossoms, fruits of ages—orchards divine and certain;
Forms, objects, growths, humanities, to spiritual images ripening.
Give me, O God, to sing that thought!
Give me—give him or her I love this quenchless faith
In thy ensemble—whatever else withheld, withhold not from us
Belief in plan of thee enclosed in Time and Space,
Health, peace, salvation universal.
Is it a dream?
Nay, but the lack of it a dream,
And, failing it, life's lore and wealth a dream,
And all the world a dream!

Louis Figuier.—A. D. 1819.

In "The To-morrow of Death" this French scientist teaches that each soul undergoes many reincarnations in human bodies, growing purer, until at length, no longer residence in flesh is necessary, and they all find their final home in the sun. He very truly says, chap. iv:

The explanation that we give of the punishment of the wicked is certainly preferable to the hell of Christianity, which is at once atrocious and absurd, [meaning, of course, the "orthodox hell."] These reincarnations must be repeated until the faculties of the soul are sufficiently developed, or its instincts sufficiently improved, so that the man can raise himself above the common level of our species. Then, only, this soul, fittingly purified, freed from its imperfections, can quit the earth, and after the death of the body, soar into space, and enter that new organism which succeeds that of man in the hierarchy of Nature.

Referring to the miserable lot of many, he says:

God would be unjust and wicked if he imposed so miserable an existence upon beings who have done nothing to incur it, and who have not asked for it.

He reconciles such facts by supposing that

Our presence on such and such a part of earth is no longer the effect of a caprice of Fate, or the result of chance, it is merely a station in the long journey that we make through the world... Our sojourn on the earth is, then, only a kind of probation, imposed on us by Nature, and during which we have to refine our souls, to free them from earthly ties, and faults that weigh them down and keep them from rising, glorious, to the etherial spheres... Bad men, we think, are those who have lived before, are going through another year in the same rank. They will be thus delayed till their souls are fit to rise in the hierarchy of beings... Chemistry, since Lavoisier, has brought to light a grand truth,—that nothing of the elements of matter is lost; that bodies change their form, while the material element, the body pure and simple, is imperishable and indestructible, and will always be found in unimpaired integrity, in spite of its thousand transformations. If this be true that nothing is lost in the material world, it is equally certain that in the spiritual world there is no loss, only transformation. Thus nothing is lost in material or immaterial beings; and we may place this new principle of moral philosophy by the side of that principle of chemical philosophy established by the genius of Lavoisier.—*Chap. xvii.*

Why, among all men and all peoples, are the eyes turned to heaven in solemn moments, in bursts of passion, in the anguish of pain? Was any one ever known at such times to gaze with the same intensity upon the ground, or whatever stretches beneath the feet? It is always to heaven that our eyes and our hearts turn. The dying bend their failing sight heavenward; and toward the celestial realms we look longingly, when wrapped in one of those vague reveries that we have just described. We may believe that this universal tendency to look towards heaven is an intuition of what lies beyond our earthly life, a natural revelation of the domain that will be ours some day, and which stretches into the celestial realms, to the very bosom of ether.

Charles Kingsley.—A. D. 1819–1875.

Canon Farrar says:

Canon Kingsley's opinions may be found in "The Water of Life," p. 76, etc., and are repeatedly referred to in his "Biography." It has been asserted that he abandoned these opinions. So far is this from being the case, that, had he lived, he intended to preach them with greater distinctness.

"We do not deny that the wages of sin is death. We do not deny the necessity of punishment, the certainty of punishment. We see it working awfully enough around us in this life; we believe it may work in still more awful forms in the life to come. Only tell us not that it must be endless, and thereby destroy its whole purpose, and, as we think, its whole morality. We, too, believe in an eternal fire; but we believe its existence to be not a curse but a blessing, and a Gospel, seeing that that fire is God himself, who taketh away the sins of the world, and of whom it is therefore written, "Our God is a consuming fire."—*Sermon on the Shaking of Heaven and Earth.*

J. G. Holland.—A. D. 1819.

The sentiments of Dr. Holland on this subject are unknown to the compiler of this volume, but "Bittersweet" contains several passages that belong to these pages. In "A Song of Faith" we are told that

> Evil is only the slave of God.

Ruth says:

> If evil live
> Against God's will, evil is king of all,
> And they do well who worship Lucifer.

And David declares

> Evil is not a mystery, but a means
> Selected from the infinite resource
> To make the most of me.
>
> God never fails in an experiment,
> Nor tries experiment upon a race
> But to educe its highest style of life,
> And sublimate its issues.

Sarah C. Edgarton Mayo.—A. D. 1819.

Oh, yes! there is joy in sincerely believing,
   No heart that is faithless can dream of, or know;
There is strength in the thought that our souls are receiving
   Such wealth as a Father alone can bestow.
Then away with the dogma that sin is eternal!
   It dims the bright glow of Immanual's name;
For it was not to build up a kingdom infernal
   That Jesus, the friend of the sorrowful, came.

It was not to lay in the path of the blinded
   High walls over which they must stumble and fall
That he came, all sublime and serene, and high-minded,
   And laid down his life a redemption for all!

It was not to slaughter, in anger and blindness,
   The wandering lambs that were dying of cold,
That he lifted them up to his bosom of kindness,
   And brought them all home to their rest in the fold!

He is good, and the heart that serenely reposes,
   And lays down his burthens to rest in his love,
Will find that the door of salvation ne'er closes,
   So long as one sinner continues to love.
He loves the young lambs though afar they are straying,
   He seeks out the weary with tender concern;
Oh hear his soft voice in the wilderness praying,
   "To the arms of your Savior, poor lost ones, return!"

Professor E. H. Plumptre.—A. D. 1821.

This brilliant scholar and contributor to the *Contemporary Review* has written much on this theme. We have only room for these lines:

    Are there no souls behind the veil
      That need the help of guiding hand;
      Weak hearts that cannot understand
    Why earth's poor dreams of heaven must fail?

    Are there no prison doors to ope,
      No lambs to gather in the fold,
      No treasure-house of new and old,
    To meet each wish, and crown each hope?

    We know not; but if life be there
      The outcome and the crown of this,
      What else can make their perfect bliss
    Than in the Master's work to share?

> Resting, but not in slumberous ease,
> Working, but not in wild unrest,
> Still ever blessing, ever blest,
> They see us, as the Father sees.

William Howard Russell.—A. D. 1821.

William Russell, and his successor as editor of the *Scotsman*, Dr. Wallace, have set forth the great doctrine in that greatest of Scottish papers.

W. R. Greg.

The celebrated author of "Enigmas of Life," "Creed of Christendom," "Rocks Ahead," etc., in the first edition of "Enigmas" looked forward to an eternal separation between the righteous and the wicked. Frances Power Cobbe reviewed the work, demolishing his positions in her great essay "The Life After Death," whereupon Mr. Greg admitted the force of the strictures, and added a "Postscriptum" to the 7th edition of his "Enigmas," in the course of which he says:

> Given a hell of torment and despair for millions of our friends and fellowmen, can the good enjoy heaven, except by becoming bad, without becoming transformed? Miraculously changed, and changed deplorably for the worst? without, in a word, putting on, along with the white garments of the redeemed, a coldness and hardness of heart, a stony, supercilious egotism,

which on earth would have justly forfeited all claim to regard, endurance or esteem? * * Assuming the hell of theologians, those affections must be foregone or trampled down in heaven, or else heaven will itself become a hell. As a condition, or a consequence, of being admitted to the presence of God, we should have to preserve the little that is godlike in our composition. Do not these simple reflections suffice to disperse into thin air the current notions of a world of everlasting pain?

Anonymous.

This splendid production is from an unknown author. It appeared originally in the London *Leader*, an English publication, and deserves to be printed in letters of gold.

> The Seraph Uriel as the records tell
> That angels write, from his allegiance fell;
> And he who rules the world beyond the sun—
> He in whom love and wisdom are made one—
> Did hurl from him his royalty of light,
> To dwell amid the souls that wail in night.
> Then Uriel felt his beauty fade away,
> And a great grief lay on him day by day;
> But, as his splendor withered for his sin,
> Stronger and brighter grew the love within;
> And so in silence in his fiery jail,
> He stood, rejoiced that love could yet prevail.
>
> One day the ancient Gods that howl below
> Accosted Uriel:—"Uriel, this great woe
> Will never pass; the stars will seek the sun,
> The universe shall end as it begun;
> But through the endless circle of the years

That angels know, shall neither hopes nor fears
Visit the dwellers in this world of fire;
Therefore, when hate and anguish shall inspire,
Ease your full heart with curses deep as ours;
Your love will never win you Eden's bowers."

Then Uriel answered:—"He who made the night,
Crown'd it with stars and with the pure delight
Of the clear moon; he who made all things frail,
Decrees that sovereign beauty shall prevail.
There is no sorrow, friends, but it has still
Some soul of sweetness in it; there's no ill
But comes from him who made it, and is good
As fruit in season, leaf in budding wood.
But if in this drear world all hope were vain—
If penance were eternal—if such pain
He could inflict and I endure—my will
Would be to love, thro' all his cruel ill.

He ended; and the ancient Gods below
Ceased howling, when they saw the sweet, calm glow,
That wander'd over that good angel's face,
Making a moonlight round them, till the grace
That was in his brave bearing and mild speech
Melted the hatred from the hearts of each;
And they stood up, and through the streets of hell
The sound of countless voices rose and fell,
Praising the silent soul that dwells above,
Singing, "We love thee, Lord, for thou art love."

Then the dark dungeon burst its grates and bars,
And light came glowing in from suns and stars,
Lapsing down dreadful rifts; the shapes below
Saw fragments of blue sky above them glow,
Like windows through the rents; they felt the air
Cooling their branded foreheads; everywhere
They saw the faces of young angels shine,

And golden fingers point to thrones divine,
While a low whisper murmured like the breeze
That comes and goes on tops of mulberry trees;
And thus it said:—"Oh, loving angels, rise,
Borne by strong love through the unfolding skies,
There is no sin, no sorrow, and no hell,
But they must cease, where hearts love long and well,
Where lips praise God in anguish and confess
There's love in pain—that even wrong can bless."

The whisper ceased; and every soul, forgiven
By Love for Love's sweet sake, went up to heaven.
Each stood before his throne—fair, glad and calm;
And God sat in the midst, and heard the psalm
Which joyful angels raised in chorus bland;
And Uriel sat like God, at God's right hand.

Stopford A. Brooke.

This famous preacher, chaplain to the Queen, abounds with the sentiment of Universalism. It is difficult to select from Stopford A. Brooke on Universalism unless we copy all he says, for every sermon is inspired with the spirit of our doctrine. He says:

But since God has been united in Christ, not to a few, but to the whole of the human race—this Fatherhood is necessarily universal. All doctrines of favoritism are at once expelled by this; all despair of races is at once destroyed; all hopelessness for those who suffer and those who are evil, perishes; all contempt for our brother men is no more; for all men are divine in God since they have been in Christ. Thus follows the necessary immortality of all mankind. Men are not becoming immortal—they are immortal now. Death, annihilation, must touch God himself ere it can touch the meanest human soul, for all the race is hid in Christ, and Christ is hid in God.

So also the dreadful dream that any one can be forever exiled from God and buried in ever-enduring evil, passes away and ceases to sit as a nightmare on the bosom of religion. Do you think that God will come short of his own conception?

Do you think that he can for one moment endure the thought that any one man or woman should be left forever to the embrace of evil?

That men should contend with evil we can understand! That they should wander far from their Father's house and waste their immortal substance we can endure, for they are treated as free subjects who must develop by effort and through failure, but that all this should be done without an end—except a cruel end, that he should have descended to assume the nature of all men and made it divine in himself, only to cast away as refuse to be burned, the greater part of those made holy in himself, all this does so contradict and vilify his revelation that it is no wonder that the idea of everlasting damnation should have destroyed men's belief in the idea of the incarnation; he who believes the one cannot rationally (though he may do it blindly,) believe the other. No, the incarnation rightly understood, necessitates the final righteousness and godlikenesss of all. How long the making righteous may endure none can tell. But through sphere after sphere of just retribution—through the change of the miserable circumstances of earth into happy circumstances—for I often think that what many a poor criminal wants to make him right is not punishment so much as comfort,—step by step, age after age, in world after world, perhaps, all the past dead are moving on, all the future dead will move on, a mighty stream to mingle in the ocean of the righteousness of God on that far-off but certain day when the idea of the incarnation will be fully realized, that hour to which the Apostle, in a lofty flight of inspiration, looked forward when he said:—"And when all things shall be subdued unto him, then shall the Son also himself be subject to him that put all things under him that God may be all in all." It is sufficient to say now that its practical results are as important as they are many. It is the foundation of all efforts to civilize the barbarian peoples—it is the root and end of all noble legislation, of all just government, it is the inspiring impulse of the theory and practice of natural education, it is the mainspring of all charity, it is the foundation from which flows all redemptive measures for the outcast and criminal, it is the principle on which all relations between capital and labor should be based, it is the idea which overthrows all tyrannies, all oppression, all slavery, all class domination, it has been the war cry and watchword of all noble revelation. It will finally end in the destruction of all international trickery and in the establishment of a unity of mankind in which all shall be free, equal and fraternal, so that the unity of the human race, in some sort like the unity of God, will exist in the midst and because of our infinite manifoldness.—*Christ in Modern Life, pp. 84-86.*

A. C. Campbell.

I deem they greatly err, who hold
   That he who made the human soul,
   Will not its destinies control
For final good—but, wrathful, fold
It in the shrouds of hopeless woe,
   Of deathless gloom, of quenchless fire,
   The creatures of his vengeful ire,
Whence it can never ransom know.

    *   *   *   *

So, in the world to come, his love
   Shall freely unto all abound;
   Even prisoners in the depths profound
Shall see his kind face beam above

Their dreary cells, and hear his voice,
  Unheeded once, in mercy call,—
  "Turn, turn to me and live!" and all
Shall hear the summons and rejoice.

Lost men, lost angels, shall return,—
  Satan himself be purified;
  Death shall be conquered in his pride,
And hell's fierce fires shall cease to burn.
Then shall our God be all in all—
  His love bear universal sway;
  His love preserves all souls for aye,
Nor shall the weakest fear a fall.

Leopold Shceffer.

Be not impatient! All will come to be,
That yearns toward being in thy teeming breast,
And in men's hearts. All yet will ripen, all!
And unexpectedly, prepared by heaven,
As after a long Winter, it will lie
Before thee, as upon thy table lies
The flowering stalk, or full-grown ear of grain
Which Nature with enormous energies
Drew from the bosom of the universe.

Matthew Arnold,—A. D. 1822.

"He saves the sheep, the goats he doth not save!"
So rang Tertullian's sentence, on the side
Of that unpitying Phrygian sect which cried,—
"Him can no fount of fresh forgiveness lave

Who sins, once washed by the baptismal wave!"
So spake the fierce Tertullian. But she sighed,
The infant Church, of love she felt the tide
Stream on her from her Lord's yet recent grave,
And then she smiled, and in the Catacombs,
With eye suffused but heart inspired true,
On those walls subterranean, where she hid
Her head in ignominy, death and tombs,
She her Good Shepherd's hasty image drew,
And on his shoulders, not a lamb, a kid.

Frances Power Cobbe.—A. D. 1822.

One of the greatest of English women, in "Doomed to be Saved," says:

I challenge those who forbid us to believe in the infinite mercy of God to say which of these three ways of viewing sin is most godlike, most probably nearest to the way in which God must view it. Will he feel pleasure in it? Assuredly not. Will he feel mere anger and wrathful indignation? I think it was very natural that the old Hebrews, who had just reached that stage themselves, should suppose he did so; and I also think it is monstrous for a race who have for two thousand years taken Christ's blessed parable of the Prodigal Son as the very word of God to do anything of the kind. I think, if we were not caught in the meshes of that wretched Augustinian scheme of theology which makes the atonement necessary to appease God's wrath, and postulates eternal hell to compel us to accept it,—I think, I say, if it were not for this theology, all Christendom must have long ago come to see, that, at the very least, God feels towards a sinner as a father or a saint would do, and not as a man less good or wise or merciful,—the great Policeman of the universe. And remember, when we are presuming to speak of the awful character of God, it is not our business to inquire what it is just possible he may be or do without injustice or cruelty, but what is the very highest, the noblest, the kindest, the most royal and fatherlike thing we can possibly lift our minds to conceive. When we have found that, we may be assured it is the nearest we can yet approach to the truth. By and by, when we are loftier, nobler, and kinder, too, we shall get nearer to it still. Of all impossible things, the most impossible must surely be, that a man should dream something of the good and the noble, and that it should prove, at last, that his Creator was less good and less noble than he had dreamed. We theists, then, I conceive, are justified (even in this dim world of imperfect and uncertain vision), in holding clearly and boldly, as the very core of our faith, that God loves eternally and unalterably every creature he has made; and that our sin, while it draws a thick veil over our eyes, and makes it impossible to give us the joy of communion with him, never blackens that Sun of love in the heavens, nor is it only by argument and analogy that we come to this conclusion. The Lord of conscience who bids us forgive till seventy times seven, the Lord of life, the Father of spirits, who reveals himself to us in the supreme hour of heartfelt prayer; that God whose voice has so often called us back from our wanderings, and put it into our hearts to pray, and then has blessed and restored us again and yet again,—that God, we know, is never to be alienated. We do not think man's evil can, in the long-run of the infinite ages, outspeed finally God's ever-pursuing mercy. He must overtake us sooner or later. We may doom ourselves to groan beneath the burden of sin, and writhe beneath the scourge of just and most merciful retribution again and yet again, no one knows how long. We may choose evil rather than good, and vileness instead of nobleness, and be ungrateful and sinful almost as he is long-suffering and infinitely holy; but it is almost, not quite. God will get the better of us at last.

A. J. H. Duganne.—A. D. 1823.

Heimgang! So the German people
   Whisper when they hear the bell
Tolling from some gray old steeple
   Death's familiar tale to tell;
When they hear the organ dirges
   Swelling out from chapel dome,
And the singers chanting surges,
   "*Heimgang!*" He is going home.

Heimgang! Quaint and tender saying
   In the grand old German tongue
That hath shaped Melanchthon's praying,
   And the hymns that Luther sung;
Blessèd is our loving Maker,
   That where'er our feet shall roam,
Still we journey toward "God's Acre"—
   "*Heimgang!*" Always going home!

*   *   *   *   *

Heimgang! We are all so weary,
   And the willows, as they wave,

Softly sighing, sweetly, dreary,
   Woo us to the tranquil grave.
When the golden pitcher's broken,
   With its dregs and with its foam,
And the tender words are spoken,
   "*Heimgang!*" We are going home.

T. W. Higginson.—A. D. 1823.

The Past is dark with sin and shame,
   The Future dim with doubt and fear;

But Father, yet we praise thy name,
  Whose guardian love is always near.

'Tis dark around, 'tis dark above,
  But through the shadow streams the sun;
We cannot doubt thy certain love,
  And man's great aim shall yet be won.

Thomas L. Harris.—A. D. 1823.

Death is the fading of a cloud,
  The breaking of a chain;
The rending of a mortal shroud
  We ne'er shall see again.

Death is the close of Life's alarms,—
  The watch-light on the shore,—
The clasping in immortal arms
  Of loved ones gone before.

Death is the gaining of a crown
  Where men and angels meet;
The laying of our burden down
  At the Deliverer's feet.

George Rust.

George Rust, bishop of Dromore, an Episcopal Ecclesiastic in Ireland, in a work on Origen, says:

To think they (the damned) are not beyond the power of redress and recovery, and that that great punishment they shall undergo, in this world, may contribute thereunto, and yet to imagine they shall, for all this their disposition, be kept in it forever and ever, is to fix so harsh a note upon the mercy and equity of the righteous Judge of all the world, that the same temper in a man we should execrate and abominate. . . .

Whithersoever we look, whether to the gracious Providence of God, or the necessity of the nature of things, we find some probable hope that the punishment of the damned, as it implies the sense of pain, shall not be eternal, in the highest sense of the word.

The Encyclopedia Americana.

The Encyclopedia Americana speaks of an eminent German theologian who voices an instinct honorable and general to human nature. He says:

I cannot see how a virtuous soul can be happy in heaven, while conscious that there is even one soul condemned to suffering in hell.

It is, no doubt, this generous feeling that has caused the doctrine to be almost universally abhorred in cultivated and educated Germany.

Rev. John Wallace.

Of a volume of sermons by this gentleman, recently published, the *Spectator*, London, said by Charles Sumner to be the ablest weekly journal in the English language, writes:

One admirable sermon on "Eternal Punishment" is especially to be commended to the notice of readers. Expounding the words "These shall go away into everlasting punishment," Mr. Wallace insists that their meaning is, that the fire is eternal, the punishment eternal, but not the suffering of the individual human child. Where there is a moral government, punishment must be eternal in possibility, if not in actuality. This interpretation of a passage, which to many is a difficult one, is very forcibly drawn out by the writer, and seems to us to be the true one.

Bishop Ewing.

This "brightest and ablest of the Scotch prelates," according to Canon Farrar,—Bishop of Argyll and the Isles—says:

Unless this be held as a matter of faith and not as a speculative dogma, it is practically valueless. With me this final victory is not a matter of speculation at all, but of positive faith; and to disbelieve it would be for me to cease altogether either to trust or to worship God.

The *Spectator*, speaking of his biography by Alexander Ross, B. D., says:

He fought for truth, not for dogmas; he cared little for theological definitions, and much for everything that brought God nearer to the human soul and gave a fuller meaning to life. His own cry was for more light, and it was not the painful cry of doubt or of despair, but of a man who held with undoubting faith the fatherhood of God, and believed that all things were working together for good, not for a few elect souls, but for the whole world which Christ had died to redeem. Alexander Ewing acknowledged Erskine as his spiritual father, and there can be no doubt that he was also greatly influenced by the teaching of Maurice, McLeod Campbell, and Robertson, of Brighton. God as a father can never destroy one of the children whom he has created and redeemed; all mankind are God's children, and therefore by some means all will be brought under the influence of divine love. This was his belief, and instead of making him apathetic, it stimulated his energy, so assured was he that the recollection that man is God's creature, however far he may have wandered from God's house, is on the lines of the highest theolgy.

Mrs. A. D. T. Whitney.—A. D. 1824.

Mrs. Whitney is one of the best American writers. Her productions are full of the broadest Christian faith.

> God does not send us strange flowers every year.
> When the Spring winds blow o'er the pleasant places,
> The same dear things lift up the same fair faces.
>   The violet is here.
>
> It all comes back, the odor, grace and hue;
> Each sweet relation of its life repeated,
> No blank is left,—no looking-for is cheated.
>   It is the thing we knew.
>
> So after the death-Winter it must be,
> God will not put strange signs in the heavenly places;
> The old love shall look out from the old faces.
>   I shall have thee.

Mrs. Whitney's "Maiden of Four Years Old," disgusted with a caterpillar, said to her mother, "while about it, I wish they had finished the butterfly." The poet moralizes:

> They were words to the thought of the soul that turns
>   From the coarser forms of a partial growth,
> Reproaching the infinite patience that yearns
>   With an unknown glory to crown them both.
>
> Ah, look then, largely, with lenient eyes,
>   On whatso beside thee may creep and cling,
> For the possible glory that underlies
>   The passing phase of the meanest thing.
>
> What if God's great angels, whose waiting love
>   Beholdeth our pitiful life below,
> From the holy height of their heaven above,
>   Couldn't bear with the worm till the wings should grow?

S. Baring Gould.

The key to the transformation is the growing belief that the relation of God to the world is less fairly set forth by the relation of a king to his subjects, than by that of a father to his household, in which in the worst case, he has to do, not with enemies, but with prodigals, the objects of his profound compassion, and in spite of their recklessness, as the parable teaches us, of his yearning love. The key to the theology which has ruled in the church thus far, has been the monarchic principle of government, with which especially in its most absolute, despotic forms, man has been through all too sadly familiar. The key to the theology which is winning its way, and which will rule in the church of the future, is the Father's authority in and government of a household—that household of God being not an elect company, but the wide human world. The problem of the future is the reconciliation of all the dark and difficult passages of the Divine government as we gather our knowledge of it from Scripture on the one hand, and from the lust of this sad world on the other, with the fatherly heart and fatherly reign of God.

Lucy Larcom.—A. D. 1824.

This woman of genius has given utterance to the great hope of man's ultimate deliverance. In "Weaving" she sings:

> So at the loom of life we weave
> Our separate shreds, that varying fall,
> Some stained, some fair; and passing, leave
> To God the gathering up of all,
> In that full pattern, wherein man
> Works blindly out the eternal plan.

The cheerful optimism that distinguishes most of the great modern poets, pervades her sweet and healthful lines.

Thomas Griffith.

The celebrated Prebendary of St. Paul's, in his "Fundamentals or Bases of Belief," (London, 1871,) observes:

We do get good out of evil. Our gracious Educator does evolve for us out of corruption, temptation and sin, new purposes, new skill, new triumphs. If evil is present only as a thing to be removed, permitted only to be cast out, then what is called the development of humanity assumes the freer, nobler form of deliverance, redemption, restoration. Beyond this overruling of intermediate evil into subserviency to a higher good, we are entitled to assume ourselves that what has been superinduced as a transition state of things is therefore necessarily only for a time. It will pass away with the functions which it is made to fulfill. It will at last be superseded by the highest good for the world, and for God's offspring, man. This has ever been the dream and hope of every lover of truth and beauty and goodnesss. It has formed the theme of poets and sages and righteous men in every age.

George Macdonald.—A. D. 1824.

One of the most unique of modern writers is this celebrated novelist and preacher. He says:

Nothing is inexorable but love. For Love loves unto purity. Love has ever in view the absolute loveliness of that which it beholds. Therefore all that is not beautiful in the beloved, all that comes between and is not of love's kind must be destroyed. And "our God is a consuming fire." It is the nature of God so terribly pure that it destroys all that is not pure as fire. He will have purity. It is not that the fire will burn us if we do not worship God, but that the fire will burn us until we worship thus, yea, that will go on within us after all that is foreign to us has yielded to its force, no longer with pain and consuming, but as the highest consciousness of life, the presence of God. In the outer darkness, where the worst sinners dwell, God hath withdrawn himself but not lost his hold. His face is turned away, but his hand is laid upon him still. His heart has ceased to beat into the man's heart, but he keeps him alive by his fire. And that fire will go searching and burning on in him, as in the highest saint who is not yet pure as he is pure. But at length, O God, wilt thou not cast death and hell into the lake of fire even into thine own consuming self? Death shall then die everlastingly,

And hell itself will pass away,
And leave her dolorous mansions to the peering day.

Then indeed wilt thou be all in all. For then our poor brothers and sisters, every one,—O God, we trust in thee, the consuming fire, shall have been burnt clean and brought home. For if their moans, myriads of ages away, would turn heaven for us into hell, shall a man be more merciful than God? Shall, of all his glories, his mercy alone not be infinite? Shall a brother love a brother more than the father loves a son? more than the brother Christ loves his brother? Would he not die yet again to save one brother more?

Of the lowest of women he makes Falconer say:

They are in God's hands. He hasn't done with them yet. Shall it take less time to make a woman than to make a world? Is not the woman the greater? She may have her ages of chaos, her centuries of crawling slime, yet rise a woman at last. It always comes back upon me, as if I had never known it before, that women like some of those were of the first to understand our Lord. * * *

Upon the text "Thou shalt love thy neighbor as thyself," he says that

St. Paul would be wretched before the throne of God, if he thought there was one man beyond the pale of his mercy, and that as much for God's glory as for man's sake, and what shall we say of the man Christ Jesus? Who, that loves his brother, would not, upheld by the love of Christ, and with a dim hope that in the far off time there might be some help for him, arise from the company of the blessed, and rush down into the dismal regions of despair, to sit with the lost, the only

unredeemed, the Judas of his race, and be himself more blessed in the pains of hell, than in the glories of heaven! Who, in the midst of the golden harps and the white wings, knowing that one of his kind, one miserable brother in the old-world time when men were taught to love their neighbor as themselves, was howling unheeded far below in the vaults of the creation, who, I say, would not feel that he must arise, that he had no choice, that, awful as it was, he must gird his loins, and go down into the smoke and the darkness and the fire, traveling the weary and fearful road into the far country to find his brother?
—*Unspoken Sermons.*

The following is commended to the consideration of those who are troubled at the thought of dying unprepared for the immortal life:

"What a thing it must be, Mr. Sutherland, for a man to break out of the choke-damp of typhus-fever into the clear air of the life beyond!"

"Yes," said Hugh; adding, after a slight hesitation, "if he be at all prepared for the change."

"Where a change belongs to the natural order of things," said Falconer, "and arrives inevitably at some time, there must always be more or less preparedness for it. Besides, I think a man is generally prepared for a breath of fresh air."

"We are, perhaps, too much in the habit of thinking of death as the culmination of disease, which, regarded only in itself, is an evil and a terrible evil. But I think rather of death as the first pulse of the new strength, shaking itself free from the old mouldy remnants of earth garments, that it may begin in freedom the new life that grows out of the old. The caterpillar dies into the butterfly. Who knows but disease may be the coming, the keener life, breaking into this, and beginning to destroy, like fire, the inferior modes or garments of the present? And then disease would be but the sign of the salvation of fire; of the agony of the greater life to lift us to itself, out of that wherein we are failing and sinning. And so we praise the consuming fire of life. (p. 354.)

>My child is lying on my knees;
>   The signs of heaven she reads;
>My face is all the heaven she sees,
>   Is all the heaven she needs.
>
>*   *   *   *
>
>I also am a child, and I
>   Am ignorant and weak;
>I gaze upon the starry sky,
>   And then I must not speak.
>
>For all behind the starry sky,
>   Behind the world so broad,
>Behind men and men's souls doth lie
>   The Infinite of God.
>
>Lo! Lord, I sit in thy wide space,
>   My child upon my knee;
>She looketh up into my face,
>   And I look up to thee!

Adelaide A. Procter.—A. D. 1825–1864.

The poems of this sweet singer, daughter of Barry Cornwall, are frequent with the beauty of the universal hope. In "Our Dead" she sings:

>Nothing is our own, we hold our pleasures
>   Just a little while ere they are fled;
>One by one life robs us of our treasures,
>   Nothing is our own except our dead.

Justice pales; truth fades; stars fall from heaven;
    Human are the great whom we revere;
No true crown of honor can be given,
    Till we place it on a funeral bier.

Death more tender-hearted, leaves to sorrow
    Still the radiant shadow, fond regret;
We shall find, in some far, bright to-morrow,
    Joy that he has taken, living yet.

The "Triumph of Time" thus closes:

> More bitter far than all
> It was to know that love could change and die!
> Hush for the ages call,
> "The love of God lives through eternity,
> And conquers all!"

Still our place is kept, and it will wait,
Ready for us to fill it, soon or late,
No star is ever lost we once have seen,
We always may be what we might have been,
Since Good, though only thought, has life and breath,
God's life can always be redeemed from death,
And evil in its nature is decay,
And any hour can blot it all away.

If, in my heart, I now could fear
    That, risen again, we should not know
What was our Life of Life when here,—
    The hearts we loved so much below,—
I would arise this very day
And cast so poor a thing away.

But Love is no such soulless clod—
    Living, perfected it shall rise

> Transfigured in the light of God,
>   And giving glory to the skies,
> And that which makes this life so sweet,
> Shall render heaven's joy complete.

Bayard Taylor.—A. D. 1825–1878.

Bayard Taylor, in his last great work, "Prince Deukalion," sings:

> For Life, whose source not here began,
> Must fill the utmost sphere of man;
> And, so expanding, lifted be
> Along the line of God's decree,
> To find in endless growth all good—
> In endless toil, beatitude.
> Seek not to know him, yet aspire
> As atoms forward to the central fire!
> Not lord of race is he, afar,—
> Of men, or earth, or any star,
> But of the inconceivable All;
> Whence nothing that there is can fall
> Beyond him—but may nearer rise,
> Slow-circling through eternal skies.

Dinah Mulock Craik.—A. D. 1826.

The author of "John Halifax" and other popular novels, breathes the spirit of our faith throughout her beautiful stories. We give a passage from "Mistress and Maid." After Ascott Leaf has committed his crime, the author says:

Whose fault is it? Aye, whose? The eternal, unsolvable problem rose up before Hilary's imagination. The ghastly spectre of that everlasting doubt, which haunts even the firmest faith sometimes, and which all the nonsense written about that mystery which

> Binding nature fast in fate,
> Leaves free the human will,

only makes darker than before—oppressed her for the time being with an inexpressible dread

Aye, why was it that the boy was what he was?

From his inherited nature, his temperament, or his circumstances? What, or, more awful question still, who was to blame? But as Hilary's thoughts went deeper down the question answered itself—at least as far as it ever can be answered in this narrow, finite stage of being. Whose will—we dare not say whose blame—is it that evil must inevitably generate evil? that the smallest wrong-doing in any human being rouses a chain of results which may fatally involve other human beings in an almost incalculable circle of misery. The wages of sin is death. Were it not so, sin would cease to be sin, and holiness, holiness. If he, the all-holy, who for some inscrutable purpose saw fit to allow the existence of evil, allowed any other law than this, in either the spiritual or material world, would he not be denying himself, counteracting the necessities of his own righteous essence, to which evil is so antagonistic that we cannot doubt it must be in the end cast into total annihilation—into the allegorical lake of fire and brimstone, which is the "second death"?

Nay, do they not in reality deny him and his holiness almost as much as atheists do, who preach that the one great salvation which he has sent into the world is a salvation from punishment—a keeping out of hell and getting into heaven—instead of a salvation from sin, from the power and love of sin, through the love of God in Christ?

In "John Halifax" she says:

What are we that we should place limits to the infinite mercy of the Lord and Giver of life, unto whom all life returns?

There is no such word as "too late" in the wide world—nay, not in the universe. What! shall we, whose atom of time is but a fragment out of an ever-present eternity—shall we, so long as we live, or even at our life's ending, dare to cry out to the Eternal One, "It is too late!"

These lines express her faith:

> Take thou then
> Our bitterness of loss, aspirings vain,
> And anguishes of unfulfilled desire,
> Our joys imperfect, our sublimed despairs,
> Our hopes, our dreams, our wills, our loves, our all,
> And cast them into the great crucible
> In which the whole earth, slowly purified,
> Runs molten, and shall run, the will of God.

In "Woman's Kingdom":

Lost—how sad a word it is—how sad and yet how common! And who are the lost? Not the dead—God keeps them, safe and sure; though how and where we know not, until we go the way they all have gone. But the living lost—the sinners who have been over-tempted and have fallen—the sinned against, who have been hunted and tortured into crime—the weak ones, half good, half bad, with whom it seems the chance of a straw whether they shall take the right way or the wrong —who shall find them? He will one day, we trust; he who in his whole universe loses, finally, nothing.

From the "Lost Silver:"

> Holy Lord Jesus, thou wilt search till thou find
> This lost piece of silver,—this treasure enshrined
> In casket or bosom, once of such store,
> Now lying under the dust of thy floor.

* * * * *

Loving Lord Jesus, thou wilt come thro' the dark,
When men are all sleeping and no eye can mark,
Thou "clean forgotten like a dead man out of mind,"
This lost piece of silver thou wilt search for and find.

Elisabeth Arundel Charles.

The author of the "Schonberg Cotta Family," in the *Sunday Magazine*, describes the deathless and triumphant love of Christ.

> Great Shepherd of the sheep!
>   The sheep are thine, not mine!
> Thou thy great flock wilt surely keep,
>   And each one lamb of thine,
>
> Ever, the wide waste o'er,
>   A lamb upon thy breast!
> Thy lost thou seekest evermore,
>   I seek, with thee, and rest.

Henry James.

This distinguished author writes:

I mean simply to indicate the spiritual significance of the Christ. I mean to say that the birth, life, death, and glorification of Christ, spiritually imply that infinite love and wisdom constitute the inmost and inseparable life of man, and will ultimately vindicate their creative presence and power by bringing the most degraded and contemned forms of humanity into rapturous, conscious conjunction with thee.

Wilde.

Whilst far and wide thy scattered sheep,
   Great Shepherd, in the desert stray,
Thy love, by some, is thought to sleep,
   Unmindful of the wanderer's way.

But truth declares they shall be found,
   Wherever now they darkling roam;
Thy voice shall through the desert sound
   And summon every wanderer home.

Upon the darkened paths of sin,
   Instead of terror's sword of flame,
Shall love descend, for love can win
   Far more than terror can reclaim.

And they shall turn their wand'ring feet,
   By grace redeemed, by love controlled,
Till all at last in Eden meet,
   One happy, universal fold!

Anonymous.

There's good in everything we view,
   The truth we none can hide,
In every heart there's goodness, too,
   We've all our angel side.
Though from our senses it is hid,
'Twill show itself when it is bid,
   For still 'tis true
We've all our angel side.

There never yet was found a heart,
   Where goodness all had died,

'Twas hidden in some unseen part,
  We've all our angel side,
Thy fallen brother hath a soul,
God's mercy yet will make him whole,
  For still 'tis true
We've all our angel side.

S. A. Tipple.

The author of "Echoes of Spoken Words" observes:

When Christ says, Better life with self-mortification than self-indulgence with Gehenna, Gehenna on his tongue must needs stand for corruption, since corruption is the antithesis of life, and the literal Gehenna, as we have seen, was emphatically the place of corruption. For what were the fires of Gehenna lighted? To inflict pain and anguish? No; but to get rid of the city's impurity. All its various filth was there, and for what purpose? That by the action of fire it might be licked up and purged away. The flame of the valley of Hinnom cannot be made to represent the awful suffering in store for sin; it can only fitly represent the certain consumption of sin, to be effected through the sharpness of fire.

"I pray thee, Father, send him to my father's house, for I have five brethren, that he may testify to them that they come not to this place of torment." Why, what a transformation was here! Who could have anticipated that the selfish sensualist described in the 9th and 10th verses of the chapter would be seen ere long pouring himself out in concern for others; seized and possessed amid his anguish with anxiety for the good of others—moved by the pains he was enduring not to rave or complain, not to curse or growl, but to make efforts to save others. Better, by far, already, you will notice, than those redeemed saints of whom we have heard, whose happiness is to be intensified by witnessing and watching the torments of the damned; he is burdened in his damnation with yearnings for the deliverance of such as appear to him in danger of becoming damned.

But surely, my friends, if according to Jesus Christ a man in hell may come to be inspired with the missionary spirit, and to pray and intercede that his brethren on earth may not be lost,—surely souls in heaven will long to be able to rescue the lost, and will be constrained to attempt it. Can there possibly be less bowels of compassion there? And, then, what of God himself, the all-merciful, and his infinite love?—*Echoes of Spoken Words, London, Sampson Low, 1877.*

Rev. Charles Short, M. A.

Rev. C. Short is minister of Ward Chapel, Independent, Dundee, Scotland, the largest independent congregation in Dundee.

But still you say that suffering and remorse are not redemption, even though prolonged through centuries of suffering. Granted. But may they not be the preparation for redemption, just as the operation of the divine law is a preparation for the exercise of divine grace? If men in this life were too busy and too pre-occupied to think of God and their duty, would they refuse to listen to him when worn out yonder with self-torture and the wrath of God? If they rejected Christ here because they were too full of sinful desire to see any beauty in him would they refuse there his call to rest and forgiveness, when heavy laden with the burden of their remembered sins? And if Jesus Christ is the same yesterday, to-day, and forever, would not he who went and preached to the spirits in prison, who had sinned in the days of Noah, go still and preach to other spirits in prison now, breaking in upon their despair and darkness with the glad tidings of God to the lost? Did he not say that he had come to seek and to save them that were lost, and that the Good Shepherd goes after the lost sheep until he find it? And are we at liberty to suppose that he will abandon his search after the lost ones when they have strayed beyond the bounds of this world; that his love is local and temporal, confined to sinners in this life only? Or that his love for men turns into anger after they die, and will remain anger to all eternity? I know no blasphemy against the divine goodness so great as that.

But it will be asked, Is not this a dangerous doctrine to preach? Is it not dangerous to hold that God will be satisfied with less than a whole eternity of suffering for the sins committed in this life? Do you know what you are saying? Have you any idea what a whole eternity of suffering means? Can you conceive of suffering for a thousand or ten thousand years? Can you realize the thought of a creature enduring agony of mind or body for ten hundred thousand years, a million years? If you can, you are only on the threshold of that creature's sufferings; for what are a hundred millions of years to an eternity? And then try to think of the unnumbered millions of human beings that have gone into eternity and are still going, out of all lands, who have either never heard of Christ or have lived unrighteous lives and have died impenitent, and who, according to your theory, must have gone to suffer for ever and ever the consequences of their sins here. Upon your theory hell must be by hundreds of millions a larger and more populous place than heaven. And that great universe of miserable, suffering souls must continue miserable and suffering through all eternity, the smoke of their torment ascending up to blacken the heaven of light for ever and ever. And you think it safe to preach such a doctrine as that? I should say it was the most dangerous doctrine that was ever conceived, the most dreadful ever uttered by human lips; for it has already done and is doing his religion infinite harm. No wonder, if Christ is made responsible for this doctrine, that men should turn away from his Gospel, and try to throw all manner of doubt and discredit upon it. And this is what thousands in this country at this day are doing—drifting farther and farther away from Christ, because some of his followers say that he taught that future punishment was to last forever. But, according to my view, it is the very spirit and teaching of Christ imbuing the modern mind, which are causing a wide revolt against this cruel creed. It is because men are receiving the truth that God is the Father of the human race, that Christ is the Good Shepherd—that they find it impossible to believe that hell will burn forever. The spirit of Christ is in men without their knowing it, without their tracing its source, humanizing their beliefs, lifting up their theology and compelling them to think "that God is good, and that his tender mercies are over all his works." The teaching and character of Christ operating silently and imperceptibly on the modern mind have taught us to hold "that love is the ground of all creation. The word 'God is love' has of late so filled our minds and hearts and souls, we are so divinely haunted by it, so possessed by it, it so rules us from the surface to the center of our being, that we are sure that Love is the Alpha and Omega, the beginning and the end of all."—*Duration of Future Punishment, and Other Sermons.*

John Brown, M. D.

John Brown, of Edinburgh, author of "Spare Hours," son of John Brown, D. D., the eminent Presbyterian minister, was not a Universalist, it is presumed, but he has recorded the following:

A poor woman of great worth and excellent understanding, in whose conversation my father took much pleasure, was on her death-bed. Wishing to try her faith he said to her,

"Janet, what would you say if after all he has done for you, God should let you drop into hell?" "E'en as he likes; he'll lose more than I do."

The Spectator.

The Spectator, a liberal, broad church organ of English opinion, London, says:

It is a remarkable fact that the discussion which has more than once been raised in our columns as to the Christian doctrine of retribution and its continuance, has now been revived by Canon Farrar's striking sermons in the pages of the *Guardian*, and that not a few clergymen maintain in that journal that the doctrine of the endlessness of moral evil, and of the pain which is involved in evil, is nowhere taught in the New Testament, while there is much teaching of St. Paul's which distinctly points in the opposite direction. It is evident, moreover, that this view is taken, not by the lax and latitudinarian party in our church, so much as by the earnest and enthusiastic party who lay the most stress on the conquest over indifference and frigidity of soul. Mr. Brooke Lambert, for instance, in this week's *Guardian* insists that if salvation comes through "hope," as the apostle says, the more you teach men to hope for their moral regeneration, and the more you represent God as intending and providing for it, the more chance you have of practical success. Certainly, very little success has come of the assumption that we are saved by fear.

This journal says in another place:

The best tendencies of our time are enlisted in the search for and salvation of the lost. They will all recoil from a creed which puts a limit to this aim in a Being whose power to pursue it is unlimited.

Mrs. Bloomfield.

In her novel, "On Dangerous Ground, or Agatha's Friendship," a romance of American society, (H. Moore, 1876,) expresses these thoughts:

"I cannot see God's will in any rash acts of our own; if I could, I would soon learn a lesson of submission. A man's life seems to me to be made up of a series of perpetual blunders, and just as he arrives at an age to profit by his experiences and become wiser, his mental and bodily powers fail him, or else the end comes, and he dies like the worm that he is."

"Do not say that! There is no end; we are immortal."

"I do not dispute that. I wish that I could, if there is to be for any of God's creatures an immortality of suffering."

"But you do not believe any such dogma, you cannot be so unjust to our Creator, you must know that although we are punished for our sins, punishment is of a reformatory and not of a vindictive character. If it were eternal, what end could be gained?"

"I was not touching upon that question, too monstrous to entertain—that of everlasting punishment. I could not conceive a God so merciless, so wanting in all the attributes of a father; but believing as I do that when the end comes to us here it is but the beginning of an advanced stage of our being, a stage of progress," etc.

Eliza Scudder.

Thou Grace Divine, encircling all,
  A soundless, shoreless sea!
Wherein at last our souls must fall,
  O Love of God most free!

When over dizzy heights we go,
   One soft hand blinds our eyes,
The other leads us, safe and slow,
   O Love of God most wise!

And though we turn us from thy face,
   And wander wide and long,
Thou holdst us still in thine embrace,
   O Love of God most strong!

Charles C. Ames.—A. D. 1862.

He is eyes for all who is eyes for the mole,
All motion goes to the rightful goal,—
O God! I can trust for the human soul.

Joseph John Murphy.

In his "Scientific Basis of Faith" Murphy inclines to the idea of the annihilation of the sinner, but is free to make some observations which indicate the "larger hope." He remarks:

Painful as the process must be whereby sin is to be destroyed, we have yet the blessing of knowing that it is destructive and consequently will come to an end with that which it is to destroy. The worm will never die until it has eaten all that there is for it to eat; the fire will never be quenched, but it will cease to burn when there is nothing left for it to consume. Either the sin and the sinner shall be destroyed together, or the sin shall be destroyed so that the sinner shall arise out of the fire, purified. In no case are we to think of any creature of God without hope. There are, however, sayings of Christ and Paul which appear to point to the ultimate salvation of all, without the destruction of any (John xii : 32; Rom. xi : 32).

James Hinton,

In his "The Mystery of Pain," remarks:

Accustomed as we have been to be in darkness, and to bear sorrow unassuaged (debarred by loss and lapse from our privilege as Christian men), have we not almost forgotten that the Spirit is the Comforter; that the Gospel claims, as one of its chief ends, that we might have great consolation; that God has undertaken himself to wipe away all tears from his children's eyes; and that Christ, foretelling tribulation, has bidden us to be of good cheer?

Mrs. E. H. J. Cleaveland.

The author of "No Sects in Heaven," teaches, in that popular satire, that all those little resorts and expedients on which so many rely to secure heaven, will be in vain. The Churchman, the Quaker, Dr. Watts with his psalms, Wesley, old school and new school, and Baptist, all struggled across the river, each imagining his the only way to heaven. But the author, after describing their useless struggles, says:

I watched them long in my curious dream,
Till they stood by the border of the stream,
Then, just as I thought! The two ways met,
But all the brethren were talking yet,
And would talk on, till the heaving tide,
Carried them over, side by side;
Side by side, for the way was one,
The toilsome journey of life was done,
And priest, and quaker, and all who died,
Came out alike on the other side.
No forms or crosses or books had they,
No gowns of silk or suits of gray,
No creeds to guide them, or MSS.,
For all had put on "Christ's righteousness."

Gerald Massey.—A. D. 1828.

I cannot believe in endless hell
And heaven side by side. How could I dwell
Among the saved, for thinking of the lost?
With such a lot the best would suffer most.

Sitting at feast all in a Golden Home,
That towered over dungeon-gates of Doom,
My heart would ache for all the lost that go
To wail and weep in everlasting woe;
Through all the music I must hear the moan,
Too sharp for all the harps of heaven to drown.

Heaven will not shut for evermore,
Without a knocker left upon the door,
Lest some belated wanderer should come
.Heart-broken, asking just to die at home;
So that the Father will at last forgive,

And, looking on his face, that soul shall live.
There will be watchmen through the night,
Lest any far-off turn them to the light;
For he who loved us into life must be
A Father, infinitely fatherly,
And groping for him there, shall find their way
From outer dark, through twilight into day.

———

That all divergent lines at last will meet,
To make the clasping round of Love complete.
The rift 'twixt Sense and Spirit will be healed,
Ere the Redeemer's work be crowned and sealed.
Evil shall die like dung about the root
Of good, or climb converted into fruit.

———

Love must be
The missionary of Eternity!
Must still find work in worlds beyond the grave,
So long as there's a single soul to save—
Must from the highest heaven yearn to tell
God's message—be the Christ to some dark hell.

———

Theodore Winthrop.—A. D. 1828–1861.

This brilliant but early called writer says in "John Brent":

A clergyman who starts with believing in hells, devils, original sin, and such crudities, can never be anything in the nineteenth century but a tyrant or a nuisance, if he have any logic, as, fortunately, few of such misbelievers have.

Alexander Smith.—A. D. 1830–1867.

This poet says:

> God is a worker. He has thickly strewn
> Infinity with grandeur. God is love.
> He yet shall wipe away creation's tears,
> And all the worlds shall summer in his smile.

Anonymous.

The author of "Complete Triumph of Moral Good Over Evil," (London, 1870,) thus discourses:

We are allowed to cherish the consolatory idea that all the kindly bonds of friendship and affection formed on earth will be finally and eternally renewed, although an incalculable duration of gloomy darkness and misery may separate the sons of light from many who were dearly loved. We are cheered by the prospect, that, although the dispensation of sorrow must endure so long as moral evil exists, and must penetrate into the most elevated regions of holiness and love, yet, that a time will come, when "God shall wipe away all tears from the eyes of men," and "there shall be no more death; neither sorrow, nor crying; neither shall there be any more pain;" when the whole creation shall exult in the conviction that "the former things are passed away." They (the redeemed) will be permitted to co-operate in the great measures for the extinction of evil; and their perception of its intensity and virulence will constantly acquire additional force, as new proofs are afforded that it can only be vanquished by divine energy. They may even, as the angels, find again and again that their utmost efforts are unavailing to soften malignity and to dissipate darkness. But their disappointments will not be embittered by despondency, nor be followed by the languor of inertion. Such disappointments will be the means of salutary discipline, expanding the noble thoughts and feelings of which they acquired the rudiments on earth, and tending to elevate them to ever-growing conformity with the divine characteristics of patient, untiring benevolence. Although celestial sorrow must endure so long as any part of the creation groans and travails in pain, it will be so softened and mitigated by firm confidence in a God, and the cheering prospect of universal happiness, that it will have none of the bitterness which is associated with sorrow in our present experience. It will also be counterbalanced by a succession of stirring events, which will agitate the realms of light. The principle of self-sacrifice will develop heroism, of an order which we can but dimly conceive from earthly analogies and Scriptural intimations. Daring inroads will be made into the kingdom of darkness, and conquests will be effected by the display of that glorious banner, which is the symbol of divine love. That wondrous love, so touchingly manifested, and operating with such patient, unwearied persistence, will gradually penetrate the deepest recesses of malignity and corruption, and will vanquish the enmity of the most obdurate and rebellious, "until all things shall be subdued unto God, by Christ, that God may be all in all."

Albert Laighton.—A. D. 1829.

This world is bright and fair, we know;
　The skies are arched in glory;
The stars shine on, the sweet flowers blow
　And tell their blessed story.

But softer than the Summer's breath,
　And fairer than its roses,
Will be the clime afar, when Death
　The pearly gate uncloses;

The land where broken ties shall twine,
  And fond hearts will not sever,
Where Love's pure light shall brighter shine,
  Forever and forever!

Jean Ingelow.—A. D. 1830.

He waits for us, while, houseless things,
We beat about with bruiséd wings
On the dark floods and water springs,
  The ruined world, the desolate sea;
With open windows from the prime,
All night, all day, he waits sublime,
Until the fulness of the time
  Decreed from his eternity.

Edwin Arnold.

The author of the "Light of Asia" thus sings:

He who died at Azan sends
This to comfort all his friends.

Faithful friends! *It* lies, I know,
Pale and white and cold as snow;
And ye say, "Abdallah's dead!"
Weeping at the feet and head.
I can see your falling tears,
I can hear your sighs and prayers;
Yet I smile, and whisper this—
"I am not the thing you kiss;

Cease your tears and let it lie;
It was mine, it is not 'I.'"

Sweet friends! what the women lave
For its last bed of the grave
Is a hut which I am quitting,
Is a garment no more fitting,
Is a cage, from which at last,
Like a hawk, my soul hath passed;
Love the inmate, not the room;
The wearer, not the garb; the plume
Of the falcon, not the bars
Which kept him from the splendid stars!

Loving friends! be wise, and dry
Straightway every weeping eye
What ye lift upon the bier
Is not worth a wistful tear.
'Tis an empty sea-shell—one
Out of which the pearl has gone;
The shell is broken—it lies there;
The pearl, the all, the soul, is here.
'Tis an earthen jar whose lid
Allah sealed, the while it hid
That treasure of his treasury,
A mind that loved him; let it lie
Let the shard be earth's once more,
Since the gold shines in his store!

Allah glorious! Allah good!
Now thy world is understood;
Now the long, long wonder ends!
Yet ye weep, my erring friends,
While the man whom ye call dead,
In unspoken bliss, instead,
Lives and loves you; lost, 'tis true,
By such light as shines for you;

But in light ye cannot see
Of unfilled felicity—
In enlarging paradise—
Lives a life that never dies.

Farewell, friends! Yet not farewell;
Where I am ye too shall dwell.
I am gone before your face
A moment's time, a little space;
When ye come where I have stepped
Ye will wonder why ye wept;
Ye will know, by wise love taught,
That here is all, and there is naught.
Weep awhile, if ye are fain—
Sunshine still must follow rain—
Only not at death; for death,
Now I know, is that first breath
Which our souls draw when we enter
Life, which is of all life center.

Be ye certain all seems love
Viewed from Allah's throne above;
Be ye stout of heart, and come
Bravely onward to your home!
La Allah illa Allah! yea!
Thou Love divine! Thou Love alway!

He that died at Azan gave
This to those who made his grave.

Canon H. W. Harray.—A. D. 1831.

Thou, O Father, wilt not be angry with thy child because he thought—and tried to bid others to think just and noble things of thee; thou, O Savior, wilt not frown at him because he trusted in the infinitude of thy compassion; and thou, O Holy Spirit, whose image is the soft stealing of the dew and the golden hovering of the dove, wilt know that if he erred it was because he fixed his eyes, not on the glaring and baleful meteors of anathematizing orthodoxy, but on the star of Bethlehem and the clouds that began to shine above the coming of the Lord; and that—if perchance he erred—the light which led astray was light from heaven. * * * But if there be one thing which he must loathe whose name is Love, it is the hallelujahs of exultant anathema, and the thinly disguised hate which rages and protests with so fierce an ignorance against a trust in Mercy founded only on these two great doctrines (which they say they own)—the doctrine of Christ's infinite redemption; the doctrine of God's boundless love.

I am alluding, not to humble and holy Christians who hold such opinion, but to men like the preacher, described by Dr. Guthrie, who declared that he had a bad opinion of the condition of those who did not rejoice that God's enemies were destroyed without remedy. I thought I saw the man stamping with his foot, and putting out the smoking flax. It was a horrible caricature of the Gospel.

Shall nature fill the hollows of her coarse rough flints with purple amethyst; shall she out of the grimy coal, over which the shivering beggar warms himself, form the diamond that trembles on the forehead of a queen; shall even man take the cast-off slag and worthless rubble of the furnace and educe from it his most glowing and lustrous dyes—and shall not God be able to make anything of his ruined souls? * * * We made them not; they are not people of our pasture, or sheep of our hands; yet if we can feel for sinners a yearning love, a trembling pity, and if that love and pity spring from all that is holiest and most Christlike in our souls,—and if it would be wholly impossible for any wretch among us to be so remorseless as to doom his deadliest enemy to an endless vengeance—are we to believe this of God?—to believe that he who planted mercy in us is merciless, and that he will "hold us up with one hand and torment us with the other," who knoweth our frame, and remembereth that we are but dust? Or shall we not rather believe as the wise woman of Tekoah said to David three thousand years ago, "We must needs die, and are as water spilt on the ground, and God does not take away life, but devises devices that the wanderer may not forever be expelled from him" (2 Sam. xiv : 14).

Robert Bulwer Lytton.—A. D. 1831.

"Owen Meredith" utters the spirit and language of our faith in these lines; they are found in "Lucile":

> The dial
> Receives many shades, and points to the sun,—
> The shadows are many, the sunlight is one.
> Life's sorrows still fluctuate; God's love does not,
> And his love is unchanged, when it changes our lot.

> "And is it too late?"
> No! for time is a fiction, and limits not fate,—
> Thought alone is eternal, time thralls it in vain.
> For the thought that springs upward and yearns to regain
> The pure source of spirit, there is no too late.

> There is purpose in pain,
> Otherwise it were devilish. I trust in my soul
> That the great master-hand which sweeps over the whole
> Of this deep harp of life, if at moments it stretch
> To shrill tension, some one wailing nerve, means to fetch
> Its response the truest, most stringent, and smart;

Its pathos the purest from out the wrung heart,
Whose faculties, placid it may be, if less
Sharply strung, sharply writhen, had failed to express
Just the one note the great final harmony needs.

There is no death! The stars go down
  To rise upon some fairer shore;
And bright in heaven's jeweled crown
  They shine on high forevermore.

There is no death! the dust we tread
  Shall change beneath the Summer showers
To golden grain or mellow fruit,
  Or smile in rainbow-tinted flowers.

There is no death! An angel form
  Walks o'er the earth with silent tread;
He bears our best loved things away,
  And then we think that they are dead.

He leaves our hearts all desolate—
  He plucks our sweetest, fairest flowers;
Transplanted into bliss, they now
  Adorn in heaven immortal bowers.

William Morris.—A. D. 1834.

In a remarkable poem republished from the English, by Roberts Brothers, in 1879, entitled "The Epic of Hades," Hades is represented under its pagan aspects, and the author describes the *dramatis personæ* of the old mythology,—Tantalus, Sisyphus, Helen,

Artemis, Psyche, Medusa, Phædra, Clytemnestra—each of whom tells his or her sad story. Even the very worst of these lost souls—the tyrant Tantalus, the murderer Phædra, Medusa, the snake-crowned—all are to be healed and saved. The punishment of Hades will one day

> Grow to healing, when the concrete stain
> Of life and act were purged, and the cleansed soul,
> Renewed by the slow wear and work of time,
> Soared after æons of days.

Rev. John Orr,

Professor of Biblical Criticism, Queen's College, Belfast, Ireland.

If the inflictions visited on men by human law are intended to be a merciful chastisement; if the inflictions occasioned by natural law also acknowledge a benignant aim, what ground have we for supposing that the punishments of eternity are exclusively retributive, intended to vindicate the majesty of an outraged law, and having nothing to do in the way of improving the offender himself? Does not the mercy apparent in all natural castigation, authorize the expectation that a benignant purpose toward the sufferer will characterize the punishment of eternity? Over the porch of the hell described by Dante was written the dreary inscription:—"Hope cannot enter here"; but such a prison-house of unending torments is not the hell of him who punishes us for our good; who, in all the length and breadth of this creation has not admitted a single contrivance intended to inflict pain—and only to inflict pain. And in the case of human legislation, increasing mercy to the offender has come, as it ever will come, with our increasing civilization. The better man is, the stronger his recoil against the mere punishment of vengeance; therefore, against the capital penalty of human law, as well as against the capital penalty of supposed Divine law, that is, everlasting punishment. Would not the conscience of the community rise up in indignant reprobation if the law of man condemned to the severest of penalties, him who for the first time stood in the category of the "drunken and disorderly"? And is the disproportion between offence and punishment greater in this case than in the case of one condemned to misery unending, never to cease or be mitigated forever, on account of a few years in time? While all enlightened communities, therefore, are shaping their penal codes, it cannot be improper or unreasonable for us to ask of popular orthodoxy to relax the penal code, and to obliterate from its statute books barbarous laws, and laws, too, that to their barbarism add injustice, making no distinction between the major and the minor in offence.

J. B. Munroe.

"All ye are brethren!" Down the aisle of ages,
The Master's word comes ringing from afar,
And the sad Past's tear-blotted, sin-stained pages,
Are lit with brightness from the Bethlehem star.

The sightless stranger by the wayside crying,
The lonely widow of her son bereft,
The helpless cripple at Bethesda lying,
The leper by his nearest kindred left,
These were his brethren; to one certain haven
We voyage on across the same deep sea,
And upon every brow alike is graven
The common seal of our humanity.

H. G. Wilkins, M. A., L. L. M.

Mr. Wilkins is chaplain to the English residents of Hanover.

A Being capable of deliberately punishing with everlasting torment any one of his creatures, whatever that creature has done or left undone, cannot be trusted by any one of his creatures, whatever that creature does or leaves undone. All creatures are in peril of everlasting torment, if one creature is in that peril. The word, the solemn promise of a Being capable of inflicting, under any circumstances, such a punishment, is entirely worthless.

Bret Harte.—A. D. 1839.

Just now I missed from hall and stair
  A joyful treble, that had grown
  As dear to me as that grave tone
That tells the world my older care.

And little footsteps on the floor
  Were stayed. I laid aside my pen,
  Forgot my theme, and listened—then
Stole softly to the library door.

No sight! no sound!—a moment's freak
  Of fancy thrilled my pulses through;
  "If—no"—and yet that fancy drew
A father's blood from heart and cheek.

And then—I found him! There he lay,
  Surprised by sleep, caught in the act,

The rosy Vandal who had sacked
His little town, and thought it play.

The shattered vase, the broken jar,
   A match still smouldering on the floor,
   The inkstand's purple pool of gore,
The chessmen scattered near and far,

Strewn leaves of albums lightly pressed,—
   This wicked "Baby of the Woods,"—
   In fact, of all the household goods,
This son and heir was seized, possessed.

Yet all in vain; for sleep had caught
   The hand that reached, the feet that strayed,
   And, fallen in that ambuscade,
The victor was himself o'erwrought.

What though torn leaves and tattered book
   Still testified his deep disgrace!
   I stooped and kissed the inky face,
With its demure and calm outlook.

Then back I stole, and half beguiled
   My guilt in trust that when my sleep
   Should come, there might be One who'd keep
An equal mercy for his child.

Rev. William Archer Butler, M. A.

Rev. William Archer Butler, M. A., Professor of Moral Philosophy, University of Dublin, writes:

   Were it possible for man's imagination to conceive the horrors of such a doom as this (endless punishment), all reasoning about it were at an end; it would scorch and wither all the powers of human thought. Human life were at a stand could these things be really felt as they deserve, even for him who can humbly trust himself, comparatively secure in faith and obedience, were the thin veil of this shadowy life suddenly withdrawn, and these immortal agonies, that never dying death, made known in the way of direct perception,—and those, it may be, with the keen sympathies and characteristics that the Christian loves and values, seen to be at last among the victims of that irreparable doom,—can we doubt that he would come forth with intellect blanched and idealess from a sight too terrible for any whose faculties are not in the scale of eternity itself? It is God's mercy that we can believe what adequately to conceive were death.

Elisabeth C. Clephane.

This popular lyric is a perfect statement of the parable of the lost sheep, and of universal salvation. All the lost are saved.

> There were ninety-and-nine that safely lay
>   In the shelter of the fold,
> But one was out on the hills away,
>   Far off from the gates of gold—
> Away on the mountains wild and bare,
> Away from the gentle shepherd's care.
>
> Lord, thou hast here thy ninety-and-nine;
>   Are they not enough for thee?
> And the Shepherd made answer, "This of mine
>   Has wandered away from me;
> And, although the road be rough and steep,
> I go to the desert to find my sheep."
>
>   *   *   *   *   *

But none of the ransomed ever knew
    How deep were the waters crossed,
Nor how dark was the night that the Lord passed thro',
    Ere he found his sheep that was lost.
Out in the desert he heard its cry—
Sick and helpless and ready to die.

Lord, whence are those blood drops all the way,
    That mark the mountain's track?"
"They were shed for one who had gone astray
    Ere the Shepherd could bring him back."
"Lord, whence are thy hands so rent and torn?"
"They are pierced to-night by many a thorn."

And all thro' the mountains, thunder riven,
    And up from the rocky steep,
There rose a cry to the gates of heaven,
    "Rejoice, I have found my sheep!"
And the angels echoed around the throne,
"Rejoice! for the Lord brings back his own!"

John MacLeod Campbell.

John MacLeod Campbell is a Scotch clergyman remarkable for his abilily, erudition, insight, and the sweetness of his life. He is the spiritual father of some of the choice spirits of Scotland; Erskine, MacLeod, and others—all Universalists. We have, unfortunately, not obtained passages from his pen. But he is one of the chief apostles of the rising faith.

Rev. Albert Reville, D. D.

If we cease to fear the flames of hell, we ought only the more to dread the torments of conscience. Religion itself becomes more spiritual when its hopes have become so. The magnificent idea of universal salvation, that sacred affirmation, forms part, tacit or avowed, of the confession of faith of the *élite* of the church, and rests on the essential ethical character of the future life.

The Rev. Albert Reville, D. D., is minister of the French Reformed church, Rotterdam.

Dr. S. Fillmore Bennett.—A. D. 1836.

Dr. Bennett, Universalist, sings his faith in these sweet words:

> There's a land that is fairer than day,
>   And by faith we can see it afar,
> For the Father waits over the way,
>   To prepare us a dwelling place there.
> In the sweet By-and-by,
>   We shall meet on that beautiful shore.
>
> We shall sing on that beautiful shore
>   The melodious songs of the blest,
> And our spirits shall sorrow no more,
>   Not a sigh for the blessing of rest.
> In the sweet By-and-by,
>   We shall meet on that beautiful shore.
>
> To our bountiful Father above
>   We will offer the tribute of praise,

For the glorious gift of his love,
  And the blessing that hallows our days.
In the sweet By-and-by
  We shall meet on that beautiful shore.

In a note to the compiler of this volume Dr. Bennett writes:

Please remember that there are only three stanzas. The Methodists have added two stanzas, which I utterly repudiate as doing violence to the spirit, intent and teaching of the hymn.

Robert J. Ingersoll.—A. D. 1838.

Even the most noted "skeptic" of the present day obtains a glimpse of the grandest of truths:

Life is a narrow vale between the cold and barren peaks of two eternities. We strive in vain to look beyond the heights. We cry aloud, and the only answer is the echo of our wailing cry. From the voiceless lips of the unreplying dead there comes no word; but in the night of death hope sees a star, and listening love can hear the rustle of a wing. He who sleeps here, when dying, mistaking the approach of death for the return of health, whispered with his latest breath:—"I am better now." Let us believe, in spite of doubts and dogmas, and tears and fears, that these dear words are true of all the countless dead.

Rev. R. H. Pullman, of Baltimore, says:—I recall an incident in my acquaintance with Mr. Ingersoll. We were conversing one day on some topic that I have forgotten, when we were met by a mutual friend, a leading member of a Presbyterian church, who in a somewhat facetious way sought to cast a reflection upon me for my friendly relations with the celebrated infidel. Mr. Ingersoll on the instant replied:

> I don't know how Mr. Pullman feels about it, but for myself I can say, that if there is a God, and he is such a being as Mr. Pullman describes, I can bow before him, and give him all my heart. He says God is Love, made the world in love, and in perfect wisdom, and well adapted to serve the divine purpose. He then made a family, all of them have sinned, and some of them have fallen very low, but God is determined, according to Mr. Pullman, to stand by his family, every one of them, let come what will come, until he makes them all respectable. This standing by his family, as every true father ought to do, is what I like in Mr. Pullman's idea of God. But if there is a God, and he has created a family, and will at last turn against most of them, and in burning wrath cast them into hell forever, as you describe, I should hate him—he is not as good as I am, for I propose to stand by my family and every member of it as long as I live. It is an insult to ask me to love and worship a God who is guilty of doing what we would detest in an earthly father.

Author of "The Death of Death."

Evil shall not triumph over God in any case, but he shall triumph in every case over it; and there will come a glorious day when angels, and archangels, and men, and all creatures in heaven and on earth, and in the sea, and all things that are therein, shall unite in jubilant and exultant shouts and songs of praise and thanksgiving at the overthrow of all sin, and sorrow, and separation, in the universe of God, and the restoration of that universe to the favor of its Creator.

William L. Wallace.

"Cain's Prayer" by this author, opens the door, which once open, could never be closed. Cain is represented—during our civil war—"an awful shade, with blood-red hands, crying to God":

> Six thousand years! Six thousand years!
>   Must I still wander on this penal sod,
> That first I gave to penal tears,
>   O thou avenging God?"

At the end of the prayer the poet says:

> The wailing blood-worn spirit ceased—the sky
> By one great levin-bolt was riven,
> And thro' the parted clouds a lustrous eye
> Looked down while voices softly murmured by,
> And rainbows melted into melody,
> "Released, forgiven!"

Anonymous.

On Trinity Sunday the Athanasian Creed, a heathen document, is read in some Christian churches. The practice is well satirized in this brief strain:

> When fretted almost past endurance
> By bold and impudent assurance,
> Or angered by some bare-faced sham,
> A man lets out a hasty "damn,"
> The orthodox predict his bane,
> And stigmatize him as "profane;"
> But if within the church's bound,

> Where holiest emblems gird him round,
> He damns at least one-half mankind,
> Dooms them to Satan sealed and signed,
> And does this free from passion's bias,
> Lo! then they call him "good and pious!"

John Hay.—A. D. 1840.

In "Little Breeches" John Hay expresses a growing conviction among all Christian people, that a selfish seeking of one's own "salvation" is poor business, and that in the future life, self-sacrifice will be the brightest possible virtue, as here it is the noblest disposition. "Getting religion" is cheap, compared with serving and helping those that need, and increasing numbers will say with him:

> I think that saving a little child,
>   And bringing him back to his own,
> Is a durned sight better business
>   Than loafing around the throne.

In "Jim Bludsoe," he sets forth the truth that the germ of goodness is in all souls, and that even the worst posssess that which is worth saving. The engineer of the "Prairie Belle" "weren't no saint," but he'd resolved "if ever the Prairie Belle tuck fire

> He'd hold her nozzle agin the bank
> Till the last soul got ashore."

He was as good as his word, and all but himself

reached shore in safety. He "passed in his checks," and the poet voices the general verdict when he says:

> At the jedgment,
> I'd run my chance with Jim,
> 'Longside of some pious gentleman
> That wouldn't shook hands with him.
>
> He seen his duty, a dead sure thing,
> And went for it, thar and then;
> And Christ ain't agoin' to be too hard
> On a man that died for men.

The spirit of these and of hundreds of the most popular of modern poems is irreconcilably hostile to the doctrines of the partialist church.

Helen L. Bostwick.

A beautiful thought gains continual credence among Christians, that heaven's gates are always open, as saith the Revelator, "They shall not be shut day nor night." One of the sweetest of modern sacred lyrics tells this thought well:

> 'Twas whispered one morning in heaven,
> How the little white angel May
> Sat ever beside the portal,
> Sorrowing all the day,

Because of her mother, on earth, sorrowing over her departure. And she prayed that the gates of heaven might be placed ajar that a glimmer of light might

fall on the weeping mother. The stately warden
refused.

> Then up rose Mary, the blessed,
>   Sweet Mary, the mother of Christ,
> Her hand on the hand of the angel
>   She laid, and the touch sufficed.
>
> Then turned was the key in the portal,
>   Fell ringing the golden bar,
> And lo! in the little child's fingers,
>   Stood the beautiful gates ajar!
>
> "And this key for no further using,
>   To my blessed Son shall be given,"
> Said Mary, the mother of Jesus,
>   Tenderest heart in heaven.
>
> Now, never a sad-eyed mother
>   But may catch the glory afar,
> Since safe in the Lord Christ's bosom,
>   Are the keys of the gates ajar,
> Safe hid in the dear Christ's bosom,
>   And the gates forever ajar.

Robert Buchanan.—A. D. 1841.

In "The Vision of the Man Accurst" Buchanan represents judgment as over, and all the world redeemed save one man, an incarnation of depravity, who mocked God and holy things, and who so compelled the disgust of the blessed angels that they besought God to annihilate him. But God replied, "What I have made, a living soul, cannot be unmade, but endures forever." The "Man Accurst" only asked one thing, that one being might share his exile. Two seraphs volunteered to leave heaven and attend the monster.

>   Then said the Lord,
> "Will they go forth with him?" A voice replied,—
> "He grew within my womb—my milk was white
> Upon his lips. I will go forth with him!"
> And a voice cried, "I will go forth with him;
> I have kist his lips, I have lain upon his breast,
> I bare him children, and I closed his eyes;
> I will go forth with him!" Still hushedly
> Showered down the Thought Divine, the Waters of Life
> Flowed softly, sadly; for an alien sound,
> A piteous human cry, a sob forlorn,
> Thrill'd to the heart of heaven. The man wept;
> And in a voice of most exceeding peace
> The Lord said (while against the Breast Divine
> The Waters of Life leapt, gleaming, gladdening),—
> "The man is saved; let the man enter in!"

A spirited poem in the same volume entitled "Doom," is very suggestive:

> Master if there be doom,
>   All men are bereaven!
> If in the universe,
> One spirit receive the curse,
>   Alas for heaven!
> If there be doom for one,
> Thou, Master, art undone.
>
> Were I a soul in heaven,
>   Afar from pain,
> Yea, on thy breast of snow,

> At the scream of one below,
> I should scream again.
> Art thou less piteous than
> The conception of a man?

Buchanan's "Book of Orm," and notably "The Vision of the Man Accurst" utters throughout the spirit of the lines quoted above.

Hattie Tyng Griswold.—A. D. 1842.

A resident of Columbus, Wis., Mrs. Griswold is one of the sweet singers of the Universalist faith. "The Missing Ship" is one of her characteristic songs.

> From out a sheltered, sunny bay,
>   With white sails rustling in the breeze,
> The proud ship like a sea gull swept
>   Across the distant purple seas.
>
> But somewhere on the foaming deep,
>   The ship for angry waves was sport,
> And all we know is, that she ne'er
>   Dropped anchor in the wished-for port.
>
> And many an anxious, troubled heart,
>   Cries, "Where is she," with trembling lip.
> God only knows, for shades surround
>   That dreamy thing, a missing ship.
>
> In the broad sea, humanity,
>   A gallant bark with us set sail,
> But drifting on, our courses changed
>   With the first rising of the gale.

And we have spoken many a sail,
   And waited answer with white lip,
In hopes to hear from one who is
   To us, through life, a missing ship.

But never sounds the welcome name,
   When trumpets answer o'er the sea;
Yet "sail ahoy," still starts the thought
   That this the missing craft may be.

Is she afloat a shattered wreck,
   Or lies she deep in coral caves,
Or is she where those floating bergs
   Wedge them within their icy graves?

We cannot know, until we gain
   The port for which we all are bound—
But there we know all sails will meet,
   And every missing ship be found.

As this volume was ready to be issued from the press, the following additional testimonies were discovered:

From an oriental poem, translated by Rev. W. R. Alger:

And in His home though pæans swept the halls,
   And glory domed the universal height,
If over one poor soul hell spread its palls
   There would be night, and wailing in the night.

Euripides.—B. C. 480.

Goodness and being in the gods are one,
He who imputes ill to them makes them none.

Sharon Turner.—A. D. 1768.

All human nature will finally be led to the image of God. Obedience is essential to the immortality of humanity.

Seba Smith.—A. D. 1792–1868.

The famous author of "Jack Downing's Letters" thus declares:

In looking back upon a laborious literary life, extending through more than half a century, in which the drudgery of editorial duties greatly preponderates, and summing up the little it has apparently brought me in return, I should despair of human effort but for one comforting consideration. Thousands of men before me have lived and labored and died in the same path that fate hath led me in. I but follow in their footsteps. They lived not for themselves, but for the good of mankind—perhaps, some unconsciously—and, probably, some to little purpose; and yet, they were all in their way silent workers in solving the great problem of life—soldiers fighting in the great battle of good against evil—intelligence against ignorance. If every one of all the thousands only combatted a single error, or evolved a single truth, or threw a ray of light where erst was darkness, he surely had not lived in vain. And so I, taking heart of grace by these reflections, and the remembrance of their lives, would humbly add my life's testimony to theirs.

I know that sooner or later "God's kingdom will come, and his will will be done on earth as it is in heaven." It will come when good shall have triumphed over evil—when mankind shall understand and appreciate the beauty of holiness. I do not believe so much in human creeds as I do in the Sermon on the Mount. I have sought to understand that, and believe that I do. At all events, in looking back upon all my literary efforts, I cannot recall anything I have ever written, however humble its merits, which I should now blush to own, or which was not actuated by some motive which I believed to have been high and sincere. Believing that those who wield the power of the press had grave moral responsibilities—feeling that it ought to be the great humanizer, the mighty engine to combat sin and error, and bring to virtue and goodness the great and eternal victory, I have not been what the world would call a successful editor; but I have the satisfaction of believing if I have not done all the good with my pen that I have sought and hoped, it has never done any harm. And now I lay it aside—it may be forever—only praying if any of mine ever take it up that they will use it as I have sought to do,—and when their time shall come in turn to resign it, that the world's progress toward universal goodness may have had some stronger help from their hands than mine.

From "Waifs of Half a Century," soon to be published, communicated to us by his son Appleton Oak-Smith.

Julia H. (Kinney) Scott.—A. D. 1809-1842.

This woman of genius, early called away, answers the question "What is Universalism?" in these lines:

It is what dost thou ask? 'Tis the sunbeam that dries
The night-gathered tears from the violet's eyes—
That warms the cold earth round the valueless thorn,
And flings through the darkness a beautiful morn.

What is it? The perfume which steals from sweet flowers,
When the sick heart is pining for Summer's loved showers;
The rain-drop that falls on the desolate leaf;
The oil that composes the billows of grief.

What is it?   The young breeze, whose pinions unfurled,
Stay not till their choice gifts have circled the world;
A harp-tone at midnight, when nature is still,
Or the voice of a dove by a pine-shaded rill.

What is it?   A star on the wild heaving sea,
Prostrating the proud on a prayer-bended knee;
A fire that refineth the metal within;
The canker which gnaws at the vitals of sin.

What is it?   'Tis mercy, 'tis justice, 'tis truth—
The staff of the aged, the glory of youth;
The rainbow of promise, to brighten our tears;
A lamp in death's valley dispersing our fears.

What is it?   Thou askest—thy answer is there
In thy own swelling heart, with its beautiful prayer;
It breathes through all nature—it centers above—
'Tis our own spirit's essence—'tis infinite love.

Florence Nightingale.—A. D. 1820.

This immortal philanthropist found the incentive to her divine life in the doctrine of a universal deliverance from sin.   She says:

> God must be accomplishing a design invariable and without the shadow of turning, the design to save every one of us everlastingly.

Joaquin Miller.—A. D. 1841.

The poet of the Sierras voices the indignant feeling that possesss all genuine souls, when reflecting on "hell" and "heaven" as they must be if the common theories—and the only possible theories on which they can be maintained—are true.

> Take hell and heaven undenied,
> Yet were the two placed side by side,
> Placed full before me for my choice,
> As they are pictured, best and worst,
> As they are peopled, tame and bold,
> The canonized, and the accursed
> Who dared to think, and thinking speak,
> And speaking act, bold cheek to cheek,
> I would in transports choose the first,
> And enter hell with lifted voice.

Principal Caird.

Principal Caird, one of the most eminent of Scotch divines, speaks thus clearly in a sermon contained in a volume of "Scotch Sermons" published by the "Broad Church" Party of the Church of Scotland. His topic is "The Union of God."

The perfection of man is not the perfection of the Jew, nor of the Greek, nor of the Roman; but there is a richer, fuller, more complex life, into which the Hebrew consciousness of holiness and sin, the ideal of beauty of the Greek, the sense, law and order which Rome left as her legacy to mankind, flow together and are blended in the unity of Christian civilization of the modern world. And that, too, in its turn, is still far short of that ideal perfection which our Christian faith reveals, and for the realization of what it calls us to live and labor.

Eighteen centuries ago a vision of human perfection, a revelation of the hidden possibilities of our nature broke upon the world in the person and life of Jesus Christ, and, as we contrast with this the highest attainments which the best of men or communities have yet reached, it seems an ideal toward which as a yet far distant goal, with slow and stumbling steps, humanity is tending. . . . . . . For no ideal of a perfect state; no dream of a golden age or paradise restored which has ever visited the imagination of genius, or risen before the rapt gaze of inspired seer or prophet, can surpass the future of universal light and love which Christianity encourages us to hope for as the destiny of our race,—that time when human society shall be permeated through and through with the spirit of Jesus Christ, and the whole race and every individual member of it shall rise to the point of moral and spiritual elevation which that life represents when "we shall all come into the unity of the faith, and knowledge of the Son of God, unto a perfect man, unto the measure of the stature of the fullness of Christ."

The Cary Sisters.

The Cary sisters, Alice (1820–1871) and Phœbe (1824–1871), were born about eight miles north of Cincinnati, O., and began their literary career by writing for *The Star in the West*, a Universalist paper, Cincinnati, O. They were reared in the Universalist faith, and adhered to it until death, and died sustained by it. They have left many evidences of the power of their cheerful religion to inspire genuine poetry.

Of Phœbe, Mrs. M. C. Ames, in her "Memorial," says:—"Through the teachings of her parents, and the promptings of her own soul, Phœbe Cary believed in the final restoration, from sin to happiness, of the entire human race, through the love of the Father and the atonement of Jesus Christ." Of her father Phœbe says:—"He was a tender, loving father, who sang his children to sleep with holy hymns, and habitually went about his work repeating the grand old Hebrew poets and the sweet and precious promises of the New Testament of our Lord."

Writes Mrs. Clemmer Ames:—"Why should her 'Dying Hymn' be less the hymn of a dying saint, if she did believe that the mercy of her Heavenly Father and the atonement of Jesus Christ, would, in the fullness of eternity, redeem from sin, and gather into everlasting peace the whole family of man? Without this faith, at times human life would have been to her intolerable. It was her soul's consolation to say:

> Nay, but 'tis not the end:
> God were not God if such a thing could be,—
> If not in time, then in eternity
> There must be room for penitence to mend
> Life's broken chance,—else noise of wars
> Would unmake heaven.

Phœbe says of Alice:—"Though singularly liberal and unsectarian in her views, she always preserved a strong attachment to the church of her parents, and, in the main, accepted its doctrines. She most firmly believed in a God whose loving kindness is so deep and so unchangeable, that there can never come a time to even the vilest sinner, in all the ages of eternity, when, if he arise and go to him, his Father will not see him afar off and have compassion on him. In this faith, which she has so often sang, she lived, and wrought, and hoped; and in this faith, which grew stronger, deeper, and more assured with years of sorrow, and trial, and sickness, she passed from death unto life." It was this faith which caused her to sing:

> Free will cannot go
> Outside of mercy

And to say:

> Great God, we know not what we know,
> Or what we are, or are to be!
> We only trust we cannot go
> Through sin's disgrace outside of Thee;
> And trust that tho' we're driven in
> And forced upon thy name to call,
> At last, by very strength of sin,
> Thou wilt have mercy on us all!

Phœbe expresses the great thought in "Waiting for the Change":

> Though some, whose presence once
> Sweet comfort round me shed,
> Here in the body walk no more
> The way that I must tread,

Not they, but what they were,
    Went to the house of fear;
They were the incorruptible—
    They left corruption here.

The veil of flesh that hid
    Is softly drawn aside;
More clearly I behold them now
    Than those who never died.

Who died! What means that word,
    Of men so much abhored?
Caught up in clouds of heaven to be
    Forever with the Lord!

    *   *   *   *   *   *

Thank God for all my loved,
    That out of pain and care
Have safely reached the heavenly heights
    And stay to meet me there!

Her immortal hymn, "Nearer Home," is the consummate flower of our holy religion, in song:

One sweetly solemn thought
    Comes to me o'er and o'er;
I'm nearer home to-day
    Than I ever have been before.

Nearer my Father's home
    Where the many mansions be;
Nearer the great white throne,
    Nearer the crystal sea;

Nearer the bound of life,
    Where we lay our burdens down;
Nearer leaving the cross,
    Nearer gaining the crown.

But lying darkly between,
    Winding down through the night,
Is the silent, unknown stream
    That leads at last to the light.

Closer and closer my steps
    Come to the dread abysm;
Closer Death to my lips
    Presses the awful chrism.

Oh, if my mortal feet
    Have almost gained the brink,
If it be I am nearer home
    Even to-day than I think;

Father perfect my trust;
    Let my spirit feel in death
That her feet are firmly set
    On the rock of a living faith!

Anonymous.

The philosophy of Universalism imparts this optimistic spirit to the genuine believer:

    With patient heart thy course of duty run;
    God nothing does, nor suffers to be done,
    But thou woulds't do thyself, if thou coulds't see
    The end of all he does as well as He.

The compiler acknowledges his indebtedness to the following persons, who have aided him by referring him to authors, or by sending him extracts pertaining to the subject treated :—Revs. J. S. Cantwell, D. D., E. L. Rexford, D. D., N. S. Hill, J. Lyon, G. W. Whitney, Varnum Lincoln, Richard Eddy, C. W. Tomlinson, S. R. Ward, G. W. Lawrence, G. Collins, Geo. Hill, O. F. Safford, J. A. Hoyt, and J. F. Simmons, and Hon. Israel Washburne, Charles Doan, J. C. Cox, H.H. Watson, Dr. C. Woodhouse, and Mary A. Parker. Besides these, a large number of correspondents have expressed an interest in the work, and referred us to passages already in our possession.

We regret that we have been compelled to omit much that we had gathered, of the material for this volume. It so accumulated on our hands that we were forced to abridge our extracts, and even reject authors, to prevent the book from attaining inordinate proportions.

Four Valuable Sermons.

FORTY BIBLE REASONS.

THIS ABLE SUMMARY OF THE BIBLE ARGUment in behalf of Universal Salvation, is by Dr. Dolphus Skinner. It is a capital document for distribution.

THE RICH MAN AND LAZARUS.

THE EXPOSITION OF THE PARABLE OF DIVES and Lazarus is by the Editor of THE NEW COVENANT. It is a good tract for general circulation. It exhaustively treats that parable.

THE RESURRECTION OF DAMNATION.

IS BY THE EDITOR OF THE NEW COVENANT, and is a full exposition of that important subject.

THE MISTAKES OF INGERSOLL.

IS THE BEST REVIEW OF INGERSOLL, and the strongest reply to his attacks on the Bible that has yet appeared. By Rev. Dr. Ryder.

*₊*Any one of the above will be sent to any address for 5 cents, or *all* four for 15c. Six for 25c., or thirty for $1 of *any one of the series* will be sent.

The Bible Pro and Con.

OUR TWO VOLUMES "*BIBLE PROOFS*" AND "*BIBLE Threatenings Explained,*" present a bird's-eye view of the doctrines of the Bible on the great subject of the Final Destiny of Mankind. "*Bible Proofs*" begins with Genesis and traces the great doctrine of the final holiness and happiness of all mankind, to the end of Revelations, giving the prominent passages, and just enough of comment to weld the whole together in an unbroken chain. It is A MOST EFFICIENT MISSIONARY giving the Scriptural Proofs of the great doctrine of A WORLD'S SALVATION in a manner so convincing as to be unanswerable.

"It is the best Missionary Document we have," says Rev. J. P. McLean.

"*Bible Threatenings Explained*" takes up every so-called "orthodox" text and proves that all the passages that are ever employed as missiles against Universal Salvation are perfectly in accordance with the promises of the Bible.

With *Bible Proofs* in one hand, and *Bible Threatenings* in the other, any Universalist will be armed *cap-a-pie,* and thus armed "one can chase a thousand, and two put ten thousand to flight." It is the most valuable of documen s for distribution among those who think the law contradicts the promises. It shows conclusively that there is not a text in the Bible that sustains the doctrine of Endless Torment.

☞Either book will be sent by mail, postpaid, for 50 cents, or both for 90 cents.

Hanson-Lozier Debate.

THIS DISCUSSION OCCUPIED FOUR EVENINGS of two hours each, in West Side, Ia., in March, 1879. DR. HANSON defended UNIVERSAL SALVATION during the first two evenings, and MR. LOZIER replied. MR. LOZIER led in support of ENDLESS MISERY the two following evenings, and DR. HANSON replied. The struggle was *short, sharp,* and, any unprejudiced mind will say, *decisive.* It much resembles a jug, the handle on one side, and, very certainly in "our man's" hand. *Read it, and loan it.* AS A MISSIONARY WORK it will do much good. Send to THE NEW COVENANT Office, Chicago, for it. *Price, 30 cents.*

The Bible Hell.

THIS SMALL BUT COMPACT BOOK TRACES THE WORD HELL through the Bible, giving every passage in which it occurs, with a full exposition of each passage. The four words rendered Hell in the Bible are SHEOL, HADEES, TARTARUS, and GEHENNA. They are all explained, and it is shown that THE BIBLE HELL IS IN THIS WORLD, and that it is LIMITED IN DURATION. The book is only 50 cents. Address, J. W. HANSON, D. D., Chicago.

MANNA

IS A BOOK OF DAILY WORSHIP, containing a selection of Scripture, and a Prayer for Every Day in the Year, for Individual and Family Use.

A few weeks after its publication the first edition was exhausted. It elicits the highest praise from our people, and deserves a place in every family.

Here is what the critics say:

"The collection is of almost infinite variety, and adapted to a wide range of conditions and requirements."—*Alliance, Prof. Swing.*

"The book, we feel sure, will meet the wants of households and individuals of every creed and denomination."—*Inter-Ocean.*

"Helpful and comforting."—*Zion's Herald, Methodist.*

"The best book of its class now before the public."—*Star in the West.*

"We know of no book in the wide range of religious literature, which, for the purposes for which it is intended, surpasses 'Manna.'"—*Leader.*

Price in cloth, $1.25; in leather, $2.

CHRISTIAN CHORALS,

A HYMN AND TUNE BOOK for the Congregation and the Home. Containing 330 Hymns and 100 Tunes, the very best of the Hymnology and Music for the Church and the Home. 50c. each; $5 a dozen; $40 for 100. This is the cheapest, neatest and best Hymn and Tune Book published by our church. An Edition containing Responsive Services at 60¢ each; $6.00 a dozen; $50.00 a hundred.

A RESPONSIVE SERVICE.

THIS MANUAL IS FOR RESPONSIVE SERVICES in church. It contains Twelve Services, one for the Sundays of each month, consisting of appropriate Scripture Sentences and a brief prayer. They are printed in large, clear type, on pages uniform with *Christian Chorals*, and can be had separate or bound with the *Chorals*. Single copies of *Responsive Service*, by mail, post paid, 15 cents. By the dozen, $1.50, by mail, post paid. Ten dollars a hundred, by express, at expense of purchaser. When bound with the *Chorals* the book will cost 60 cents a copy, $6 a dozen, $50 a hundred. Nothing is needed to relieve the bareness of the Protestant church worship, so much as a simple responsive service, and congregational singing. "*Christian Chorals*," and the "*Responsive Service*," are just the books our people need. Send for a specimen.

UNIVERSALIST CATECHISM

IS THE NAME OF A MOST EXCELLENT LITTLE book of thirty-two pages, by REV. R. SLADE, issued from this office. A more valuable instrumentality in the Sunday School, Family and Church has not recently been published. It goes thoroughly over the wide field indicated in the title, and in a style satisfactory to the adult mind, as well as adapted to the young. The little Puritan girl, disgusted with the hard terms of the "Shorter Catechism," wanted to know why somebody did not make a *kitty*-chism, so that little girls could understand it. We have one here that all can understand, old and young. We will send it to any address as follows:—Single copies, 10c; 4 for 25c; 10 for 50c; $4.00 a hundred.

A CLOUD OF WITNESSES

IS A COLLECTION OF TESTIMONIES FROM MEN and women of genius, in behalf of the final triumph of good over evil. It embraces a large number of authors, and is a work of rare interest. By J. W. Hanson, D. D. Price, $1.00.

THE NEW COVENANT,

A FAMILY RELIGIOUS WEEKLY. Organ of the Universalist Church in the Northwest. J. W. HANSON, D. D., Editor and Business Manager, Chicago, Ill.

Subscription price, $2.00 per annum, postage prepaid. Six months, $1.25. For less than six months, 20 cents per month. If paid at the end of three months, $2.25 per annum. If paid at the end of six months, $2.50 per annum. Single copies, 5 cents. Fifty numbers in a year.

⁎ Any Universalist book or periodical, or any other work or journal published, sent by mail, postpaid, on receipt of retail price.

www.ingramcontent.com/pod-product-compliance
Lightning Source LLC
Chambersburg PA
CBHW030011240426
43672CB00007B/904